The Ministry of the Word

The Ministry of the Word

D. W. CLEVERLEY FORD

WILLIAM B. EERDMANS PUBLISHING COMPANY

Library of Congress Cataloging in Publication Data:

Ford, Douglas William Cleverley.
  The ministry of the Word.

Bibliography: p. 237
Includes indexes.
1. Preaching.   I. Title.

BV4211.2.F66 1979   251   79-13172
ISBN 0-8028-3524-4

To Olga,

my wife,

constructive critic of my preaching

for forty years

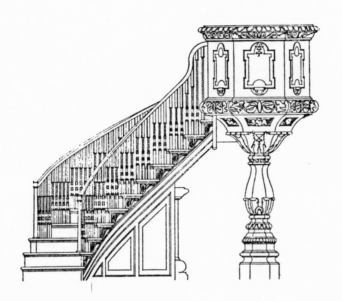

Acknowledgments

I am indebted to Donald Coggan, Archbishop of Canterbury, for encouraging me in the first place to write this book; to Edward England of Messrs Hodder and Stoughton, the publishers, for providing the final incentive by offering me a contract; to David Edwards, Dean of Norwich, for reading the finished typescript and making valuable suggestions; to the publisher's reader for providing the same service, and to Mrs J. Hodgson for typing my manuscript, preparing the indexes and reading the proofs, a painstaking worker. None of these, however, must be held to account for anything I have written, for this I must bear the entire responsibility.

LAMBETH PALACE   D. W. CLEVERLEY FORD

1978

Contents

Introduction

IN THE PRESENT CLIMATE OF OPINION PREACHING FACES FORMIDABLE obstacles. The fact had better be acknowledged, certainly in a book such as this which attempts to handle this precise situation. Not that I am so short-sighted as to imagine that preaching in Church is the only form of preaching. Indeed, if preaching is confined to Church worship, it will largely have failed in its purpose. The preacher is to preach to the Church in order that the Church may preach to the world. Regretfully, too few sermons recognise this. My point is that if preaching does not *start* in the Church the risk is that the Church may never get round to preaching to the world, not least by ways other than by verbal proclamation. Apparently John Donne, Dean of St Paul's Cathedral London (1621–31) had even greater fears. He wrote, 'If there be a discontinuing or slackening of preaching, there is the danger of losing Christ.'[1]

What are these formidable obstacles that the modern preacher has to face? They can be summed up in a phrase which became a catch-phrase in and after the 1960s. 'The day of preaching is over.' The implication is that it is our changed times that have rendered preaching ineffective. Preaching has served well in the past. Who with a knowledge of history can deny it? But then is modern man interested in past history? Is he not rather concerned with making history? The contention is that preaching does not belong to the modern world. It is out of place, and if the attempt be made to force it into a place, boredom, or even resentment to the Christian gospel, will result.

First and foremost, preaching suggests authority. It suggests that the preacher 'knows the answers'. It suggests a subtle form of patronage. And suppose the preacher happens to be a Professor of Divinity from one of the Universities, does he really know more about life than that woman with four children, whose husband deserted her, yet who,

[1] Quoted by F. D. Coggan, *On Preaching*, S.P.C.K., 1978, p. 13.

with inadequate financial resources, is struggling to keep a home going for the benefit of her family? And if the question could be asked of the Professor, how much more pointedly of the new curate straight from his theological college? Is it any wonder he is reluctant to preach? Indeed, the very word 'preach' suggests a kind of moral superiority which is worse. We hate being 'preached at'. Who then wants to be a preacher? Not that there is anything new in this feeling of inadequacy, what is new is the present extreme sensitivity to any form of superiority of any one person, class or religion above any other. Egalitarianism, however difficult to justify, is in the air, and the problem is how preaching is possible, even if desirable, in this climate.

And then there is the modern educational method. Little use is made of the monologue. Small reliance is placed on lectures nowadays. Modern man learns by way of the group discussion. He goes on a voyage of discovery with others. Child of the scientific method, he learns by way of experimentation. Indoctrination is 'a dirty word'. At first sight then, the pulpit stands out as a museum piece. And this is true for the young theological student. Not since the 1920s has theology been thought of as a body of knowledge able to be mastered in three years at some place of learning. Deduction, description and definition are out. Instead, there is involvement, and modern theology proceeds by way of hints and suggestions. It is true that Bishop Charles Gore (1853–1932), pointed the way to this view but even he assumed that all that was required was a new language to represent the old, solid structure. Perhaps Charles Raven, as seen through his book *The Creator Spirit* (1927) was the one exception. The theological student since the 1950s, however, has received his training in a world in which even Ecumenism has slowed down. We do not see only one form of Christian discipleship. Instead, we have theological pluralism, and our only possessions are models which show us what God's purposes may be. All certainties are dead certainties. Is it any wonder that the theological student of today shies off becoming a preacher? Is it surprising that he tends to think of communicating the gospel some other way than from a pulpit? Or if tradition seems to require him to fill a 'preaching slot' in the forms of public worship provided, that he does so perfunctorily and in consequence is boring, contributing yet further to a decline of preaching. But does this matter?

This may be the point at which to refer to the alleged gap between the man in the pulpit and the academic theologian, because the young clergyman is likely to sense it sharply on quitting his training for the ministry and actually embarking on his sermons. Every week, or nearly every week, he will be expected to produce 'a message', positive, assured and directly relevant to particular people, their needs and their questions. In the academic world he has just left, however, his aim was to proceed by way of doubt, even to employ it as his methodology, in so far as he was a theologian at all, seeking to arrive at the truth however disturbing. Is it possible for these two disciplines to be reconciled? And if not, can the theologian be a preacher? And then if he does nevertheless preach because the tradition requires it, is he not guilty of dishonesty? And does not the official Church contribute to that dishonesty by requiring preaching?

Let us leave the educational world. Let us enter the world where people actually live, not the supposedly artificial world of the Church congregation. What use is made there of the monologue? There is of course the party political broadcast, but to conceive of any form of address more suspect today would be difficult. And even this is being changed. In place of the monologue ideas are being *suggested* (that is the word), on the broadcasting media, by means of pictures covering action, events and situations, and by drama. Another form of communication is the interview, and yet another the discussion group with subtle questions asked and sharp minds answering them, or even with yet more subtle techniques, dodging them. What is happening in these new forms of communication is an avoidance of any vestige of authoritative indoctrination. No one is told what to believe, instead, various answers are given by different people in the light of which the viewers and listeners are invited to make up their own minds without feeling patronised. All this is in tune with the mood of the times.

And still we have not reached the end of the line with these new methods, there is now the 'phone-in'. The listeners can telephone the broadcasting station with their own questions and opinions. So even the broadcasting gap has been bridged. The need to sit still as a passive viewer or listener has gone. Participation is possible meeting the objection addressed even to an authority – 'Why cannot my views be placed alongside yours?' The answer is, they can be! So the spirit of modern egalitarianism is propitiated and the idea of élitism crushed. Moreover, these new communication methods, supplying as they do a change of speaker instead of forcing the hearers to listen to one voice or fix their gaze on one face, which may not be attractive, for more than a few minutes, has assisted – or so it is alleged – the ordinary non-scholarly member of the audience, and such constitute the majority, to absorb what is offered. Perhaps Bishop John Robinson neatly collected these new communication methods, and set the pulpit over against them when he coined the oft-repeated phrase about the preacher as 'six feet above contradiction'.

And now the pressing question of time. It was all very well for those giants in the past to produce their polished utterances, but the modern minister of the gospel does not live in this kind of world. The pace is ten times faster, the number of people to assist him ten times fewer. Servants do not exist. Ours is a world of 'do-it-yourself', praiseworthy, no doubt, but it takes time, and something has to go in the process. And all the while news from every quarter of the globe comes pouring in through the television box and the sound radio in the corner of the room, about which the clergyman is suppose to be *au fait*, unless he is willing to be dubbed 'completely out of touch'. How then can the pastor be expected to find the time for sermon construction? How can he be expected to find it when he knows from bitter experience that people will only listen to him if he has spent time on his sermon to make it worthwhile their giving him their attention? How can he be blamed if he decides that there are better ways of occupying his time, better because more effective in the way of pastoral care, as he is able to give it, than by struggling to compose orations for which he has no particular gift? And is it not true anyway, that oratory is out of fashion in the modern world? Clement Attlee, with his clipped, matter-of-fact style, mirrored our technological age more effectively than Sir Winston Churchill in the office of Prime Minister with his grand and flowing phrases. Today speech follows a flat conversational style. No one wants oratory. That the question should be raised about the propriety of spending—some would say wasting—time on sermon preparation is not therefore surprising in the world as we we know it.

Speed and the consequent lack of time is not the only characteristic of the modern world which appears to mitigate against preaching, there is also the widespread employment of a team to engage in an undertaking. Very infrequently today does one person carry through a task from start to finish alone. There is a researcher, a surveyor, a designer and an engineer; and behind the whole enterprise a committee with subsidiary boards of finance, public relations—to name only two. How out of keeping with all this is the preacher working solo in his study! And if there are parallels, are they not exceptional? And do they not belong to the man with unusual personal gifts, such as the poet? But can this be expected of the average minister of the gospel? There would be many in the pews quick to cast a doubt.

And then the rise of the visual image as the means *par excellence* of effective communication — television, the strip-cartoon, the exhibition, even the caption, the headline and the banner—how can the extended spoken utterance compare with this in a world which has been conditioned to the expectation of quick answers? Patience is in short supply today, and many have lost the capacity to follow an argument, if indeed they ever possessed it, if indeed it is able to be developed in 'the snap world' of modern communication.

These are some of the formidable obstacles preaching has to face in the modern world, and we have not taken up the somewhat hack complaints that we have been drenched with words, and that 'actions speak louder than words'. Nothing is to be gained by dodging these obstacles which is why this book does not begin with the practical section on preaching. There is a prior question to be faced before considering how preaching may more effectively be carried out, it is why should we preach at all? And what is preaching? What is this word to be ministered?

Let us turn back for a moment and survey these obstacles to preaching rather more closely. We may conclude that they cannot each be demolished at short range with one shot each, but are they quite so formidable as was supposed? Even so, I shall contend that preaching cannot be justified merely by the demolition of obstacles. It can be accomplished only by the steady building up of a theology of preaching establishing it as a form of discourse which is *sui generis*, that is, it stands in a class by itself. Of course there are similarities with every other form of discourse. The same vocal cords are employed as in an after-dinner speech, the same principles of communication apply, even to some extent the same devices for gaining the attention of the audience. And the material is the same—words. Furthermore, in comparison with the teacher in the classroom there is, or should be—a teaching content, and a personal authority however muted does operate. Nevertheless, preaching in the context of a congregation of people of faith worshipping God as known in Christ as Lord in the presence of Divine Spirit stands in a class by itself.

Take the parallel case of the Eucharist. There is an obvious similarity between the Eucharist and any and every other occasion of receiving bodily sustenance. The same organs of digestion operate, the same materials constitute the meal and the same hands receive it. What is more, those other occasions are far more effective and enjoyable for relieving hunger and assuaging thirst, but do they thereby disqualify the Eucharist for serious consideration in the modern world? Is not the Eucharist an activity *sui generis*? Does it not stand in a class by itself whatever use it may make of actions and materials common to other

2

actions? Has it not a special function to perform? So with preaching. Writing in the American College of Preachers *News Letter* in the spring of 1978, the Editor, the Reverend H. Barry Evans, gave as the title to his leading article *The Uniqueness of Preaching*. In it he drew attention to how different the Church is from other institutions in society, even the buildings are unusual, and what goes on in them is unusual—the group singing, the gestures, the costumes worn by the ministers. Why has the Church chosen to be different? 'It's more than archaism; the differences are intentional.' This leads him on to assert that preaching itself is a very different kind of discourse. 'Yet preaching is more than intellectual discourse and it is more than the recitation of history and theology. It also utilizes a unique methodology of communication and education.' Then he confesses that he was helped to understand this by the anthropologist Anthony F. C. Wallace in his book *Religion: An Anthropological View* (Random House, 1966), where the ritual learning process of many religions is described and explained. This applies to some extent to preaching. Ritual learning is based on what Wallace calls 'the law of dissociation'. Normal methods of learning operate with the transfer of information and memorisation. Not so ritual learning. Instead it operates on the assumption that what it has to communicate is different from other information, even competitive with it. And so its method is designed to exclude temporarily what would hinder its message being received. Even more when someone enters a church and hears a sermon in that context he is challenged to think of the world in an entirely different way. The sermon therefore has to be *sui generis*, has to stand in a class by itself, has to be unique in its style as well as its function if it is to achieve its purpose with power. Part of the aim of this book therefore is to enquire into the nature of the uniqueness of the sermon *in its context*. Only in this way is preaching defensible in the modern world.

But what about those formidable obstacles already listed? Does preaching suggest an authoritative approach to people? Is it a subtle form of patronage? There is no doubt it can be, and has been presented in this form. Suppose, however, that the preacher sees himself as the servant of the Word, suppose he consistently makes it obvious in the pulpit that he himself stands under the judgment of the word he is exposing no less than the hearers, is he then setting himself up as someone who 'knows all the answers'? Is he not rather placing himself on an equal footing with every member of his congregation? What then becomes of the complaint of élitism?

And now the complaint that the monologue sermon is contrary to the whole tenor of educational method, including that which operates in the sphere of theological learning. Does preaching have to imagine that the revelation which it seeks to expose was given in the form of theological propositions? Must it of necessity behave as if the preacher were some kind of shopkeeper reaching for packages of doctrine to be handed over the counter called the pulpit because the Church alone stocks the supplies? Is this how Jesus preached? What then was he doing with parables? And what about the guidance of the Spirit? To these points we shall address ourselves in this book.

Then the gap, the alleged gap, between the man in the pew and the academic theologian. Let us admit its existence. But is it a complete gap? Does the fissure[2] which appears on the surface extend without any coming together right down through the ground? Undoubtedly at surface level the academic theologian appears to be searching for truth by a purely intellectual process, but is intellect the sole operating factor? Is not the theologian attempting to provide an intellectual explanation of experience which does not only consist of cerebral activity but also of action, prayer and faith? And the preacher on his side, will he arrive safely at the truth if he only concerns himself with action, prayer and faith, neglecting rational considerations? The obstacle may not, therefore, be as formidable as it appears.

We come now to those pictures of actions, events and situations on television replacing the party political speeches, and with them the captions, the cartoons and the banners. But is the visual *capable* of communicating in depth? And if the subject to be communicated is the Unseen, as in preaching, is it to be preferred to all other methods? Could it even be that sound radio is more effective for stimulating the imagination? And as for the group discussion, whether broadcast or not, are we quite sure that more information is taken away than would be the case with one competent speaker? Whatever the value of the discussion group and the interview method, and they have real value, is the case for the monologue teacher lost?

We should have to concede that the case against preaching is strong if preaching were the only form of instruction which the Church employed. This however is by no means the case. There are lectures, study groups, pastoral counselling and the confessional. In all these participation by members of congregations is possible, indeed, is an essential part of them. They do not, however, outlaw the sermon, they complement it.

[2] I am indebted to the Reverend R. D. Harries, Vicar of All Saints, Fulham, London, at a College of Preachers (U.K.) discussion group for this simile.

Admittedly the problem of time required for sermon preparation is a real one, especially in the early years of a pastor's ministry. As the years go by, however, he learns the art of preaching, and can work with greater speed and with greater effectiveness, for he increases his knowledge of people, their needs and their reactions. And if he will only be patient and master his craft, he will be surprised at what he has accomplished. I can only speak from experience. There are rich rewards in spiritual results for the faithful preacher, and often from unexpected quarters. But hard work will be involved because he will need to be *au fait* with the world as well as with the things of the Spirit if he is to communicate. Moreover, to be a 'do-it-yourself' man is no bad thing when the majority of people are forced to do likewise. No doubt all this will operate against producing literary sermons, but this will be no loss in the 1970s and 1980s. A form of preaching tending towards a conversational style will be more easily heard.

The effectiveness of the sermon does, under God, depend on the labour the preacher is willing to put into it. This fact cannot be denied. Yet it does not only depend on the preacher. The congregation has some responsibility for the quality of the preaching it hears as those who persevere with this book will see. The story is told of a Bishop who spent hours seeking to provide a 'locum' for a certain vacant benefice. (This is an Anglican story.) The Churchwardens, however, were desperately difficult to please. Candidate after candidate was sent for a trial Sunday, but every Monday morning the Churchwardens telephoned complaining bitterly. Not surprisingly the barrel of the Clerical Registry was almost scraped clean, but there was one more priest. The Bishop, however, hesitated to send him, he was so ineffective, but no alternative lay open. So with trepidation at the possible explosion on the telephone the following Monday morning, he despatched this candidate. Monday morning came. It also went. No telephone. Another Monday morning. No telephone. More Mondays, the same. At the end of three months the Bishop could contain no longer. He telephoned the Churchwardens himself. To his astonishment he discovered that the parish was delighted with the clergyman he had sent. Pressing for more information he received this explanation— 'In this Church we have never wanted any preaching, and the man you have kindly sent comes closer to that ideal than we ever thought possible, he is almost wholly inarticulate.'

Yes, the congregation does have a part to play in the preaching it receives.

But why should *I* write about preaching? I am no giant of the pulpit. Neither do I possess what the French call 'la langue bien pendue'. I am not a ready talker. I am neither Welsh nor Irish. I was born and bred in Norfolk, and partake of the East Anglian temperament—reserved, cautious, even suspicious. If you ask a stranger in a Norfolk lane the way, as likely as not he will reply, 'What do you want to know for?' This makes me a kind of Exhibit A. 'If I have learned to be articulate in public any fool can.' Nevertheless since Paul boasted a little, may I follow him for a yard or two? and with the same intention—to supply some credentials. Twice a Sunday over thirty-five years I occupied a pulpit, not as a peripatetic preacher able to use the same material over and over again, but as (what is called in Anglican circles) a parish priest—in Bridlington (Yorks) for three years; in Hampstead (London) for twelve years; and in South Kensington (London) for twenty years. I know what it means to have to face the same congregation week in week out, and for them to have to face me. Apart from Bridlington where I was an assistant, I also know what it means to begin in a church with the tiniest of congregations. No doubt the West End of London, where I preached the longest, was sophisticated, but I learned my first lessons in Bridlington, where I was given partial charge of a church in a hamlet consisting of farming folk, the total population of the place not exceeding forty souls. (One of them still writes to me every Christmas.) This taught me how to preach to tiny congregations. And then there were the huge army parade services in Bridlington Priory, for it was wartime. How to capture the attention of hundreds of reluctant troops at compulsory church made me learn some other lessons.

Then in 1960 I became Honorary Director of the newly formed College of Preachers. The present Director is the Reverend John James. As leader of that organisation, which at the present moment has one thousand seven hundred and fifty annual subscription-paying members, every one of whom has passed through a residential course of training in preaching, I heard and counselled hundreds and hundreds of preachers, by no means all Anglican and many from parts of the world other than the United Kingdom. And this I can truthfully say, that although I discovered few 'star' preachers—perhaps they did not need any training—I found very few indeed who did not possess some capacity for preaching, able to be greatly improved to the benefit of their congregations, as some openly acknowledged. I also chaired over the years more than fifty discussion groups on the motion 'Is the day of preaching over?' and am bound to put on record that not one of those groups, fiercely as the matter might be argued, came up with any substitute for the sermon as part of the regular programme of worship in Church. Then there were the lectures on preaching given in various parts of Britain, and some overseas, bringing the total of those encountered in the task of encouraging preaching to some thousands. Yes, I am boasting and I must be careful, pride can be the besetting sin of preachers, but what I am really doing is modestly offering my credentials for what I have written, I am no arm-chair commentator on preaching. I have talked to hundreds and hundreds of preachers about their preaching and heard them at it. Moreover, I have preached myself, and still do occasionally when I am asked. But enough of this autobiography, after all, I did indulge a little in my book *Have you anything to declare?*[3] Suffice it to add that I have myself heard some of the famous preachers listed towards the end of Chapter 4 of this book. To that extent I have had personal acquaintances, at least with some of the masters of the pulpit.

What then is the plan of this book? First of all to enquire into the origin of preaching and to see what part it has played in the history of Israel and of the Church, both in New Testament times and subsequently down to our own day. Secondly to examine those theological fundamentals in the light of present-day understanding which must form the basis of preaching if it is to continue into the future. And thirdly, to offer some advice for preachers concerning the practical accomplishment of this ministry. I say 'offer' because I am not so conceited as to reckon that there are only two ways of preaching— my way and the wrong way.

[3] Mowbrays, 1973.

I
Biblical and Historical

1 The word in the Old Testament

2 The word in the ministry of Jesus

3 The word in the New Testament

4 The word in the history of the Church

An outline of the history of the ministry of the word both in the Biblical narratives and in the subsequent history of the Church pointing out the vicissitudes through which it has passed.

1

The word in the Old Testament

Is PREACHING NECESSARY? Is IT NOT POSSIBLE FOR A NATION, A FAMILY, or even an individual to be nurtured spiritually and morally without being subjected to verbal proclamation? Is preaching an essential requirement in the life of the Church or even a desirable extra? Does the ministry of the word in the form of preaching belong to the *esse* of the Church, or only to its *bene esse*? The probability is that these basic and related questions will be answered instinctively according to upbringing, ecclesiastical tradition or prejudice. The intention of this first chapter is to survey the Old Testament in the hope of discovering what part the ministry of the word played in Israel, and in doing so, to lay a foundation for a critical examination of the claims that are made for preaching.

The point at issue is the relation of preaching to the cultus, and it is this which will occupy a large part of the attention of this chapter. This is not a matter of mere antiquarian, academic or even Old Testament interest, it impinges on the life of the Christian Church whose first duty, like that of Israel, is to offer worship to the true God. This means a cultus, a liturgy, even a 'Christian Year' with its Feast Days and its Fast Days. The Church is inconceivable without these patterns, and prominent among them, indeed underlying them, and fundamental to them, is the sacramental system. What then is the relation of preaching to the Sacraments? What guidance can the Old Testament provide with which to answer this question? And as for preaching, is there anything in the prophetic preaching of the Old Testament which suggests that its omission by the Church could cripple its vitality?

Whatever were the origins of the religion of Israel, and we cannot be certain, preaching was not among them. No straight line can be drawn from an initial saving act of God, followed by the preaching or the proclamation of the same, followed by the formation of a community composed of those who responded to such a word of God. Israel not only came into being as the people of God without preaching, but for centuries were sustained in their faith without it. Preaching was a late-comer in the history of Israel. It cannot, therefore, in the light of history, be claimed as essential for the life of a Church in the sense that it cannot exist without it.

What then was the content of this 'proclamation-less', this non-preaching, religion, by which ancient Israel lived? Prior to the Settlement of the tribes in Canaan, and the occasion when Joshua at Shechem[1] imposed the recognition of Yahweh as the God of Israel upon all the tribes, we cannot be sure. This is because the Pentateuch, as we have it, has been constructed out of various complexes of tradition, not with the aim of setting out the story of the growth of Israel's faith, but rather to provide a source of reference and a legitimisation of the various practices of the cultus as they were actually followed in the religious life of the nation in the years and centuries following the Settlement.

This is not to deny that undoubted historical events lay behind the narrative as the Bible presents it. The experiences connected with the crossing of the Red Sea and the encounter at Mount Sinai were too epoch-making to have been invented. What exactly was the nature of the religion, however, we do not know. There was, of course, the Passover, and a clear awareness of deliverance and of the will of the Deliverer. And incorporated into this 'Mosaic religion' was older material dating from Israel's nomadic ancestors—circumcision, perhaps the Sabbath, and some kind of 'holy tent'.

The Settlement, however, was a turning point. Thereafter, the worship of Yahweh became the bond of unity for the tribes, and this was strengthened by the regular pilgrimages to a central sanctuary, first at Bethel,[2] then Shiloh,[3] then Gilgal.[4] So a definite cult emerged with the Ark as its central feature. There were, however, other sanctuaries in existence in Canaan where fertility cults were practised. To assimilate to these gods of the land seemed the course of wisdom, and the opportunity so to do, a gift from Yahweh himself, making for survival in a new and strange environment. So Yahweh was worshipped along with, and sometimes under the new forms, though stopping short of the divinisation of sex.[5] In one form or another, the cultus dominated the

---

[1] Joshua 24:1ff. See G. von Rad, *Old Testament Theology*, Vol. I, pp. 15ff (Edinburgh, Oliver & Boyd, 1962).

[2] Judges 20:26f.

[3] 1 Sam. 1:3ff; Jer. 7:12ff.

[4] 1 Sam. 10:8; 11:14ff; 13:4,7; 15:12, 21,33.

[5] 1 Kings 15:12; 2 Kings 23:7; Deut. 23:18.

whole life of the people, and everything that happened was interpreted in the light of it. Society was wholly sacral.

From this enclosed, sheltered, patriarchal society, Israel began to emerge with the setting up of the Monarchy. The old sacral society had in fact begun to wear out. Of this the sorry picture of the conditions at Shiloh at the end of the period of the Judges bears witness.[6] A new era of intellectual and spiritual vitality was coming into being. The poetry and literary compositions of the period bear witness. What is more, the old traditions were being interpreted differently, in short, a kind of secularisation was slowly ousting the sacral.

Into this changed climate of thought, David brought his own brilliant leadership and the power he acquired was something he himself built up as a result of his own military genius and political acumen. David was not a priest, but he saw the value of the cultus for the stabilisation of the kingdom he had established, so he connected with the old religion by bringing up the Ark into his new capital, Jerusalem. Solomon took care to house it in his temple built on crown land, and so the Jerusalem Temple became the place of worship for all Israel. At the same time Solomon's reign became an age of enlightenment. Interest arose in the origins of the nation, and in place of mere episodes in the past, a sense of history developed, indeed, both history and nature began to be released from the old sacral order which hemmed them in. And man himself became the centre of interest which showed itself in the narratives about his exploits. Speeches, too, were introduced into the stories, oratory was copied from Egypt, foreign trade encouraged, and a concentration on building.[7] Solomon's reign saw the growth of humanism and secularism alongside the old sacral apparatus still kept in working order.

Protests were made at these departures from traditional Yahwism. There was Jotham's fable directed against the monarchy[8] and Nathan's restraint on David replacing a tent for the Ark by a house.[9] There was the opposition by the Nazirites to the assimilation to the cults of Canaan, and there was the Rechabites' struggle for purity. But there was no power in any of these conservative movements to stem the degeneration of Israel's faith. They were backward-looking. They had no message, nothing to lead people beyond the decayed sacral approach and its secular successor, nothing to balance the growing power of

[6] I Sam. 2:12ff.
[7] I Kings 5:1ff; 7:51.
[8] Judges 9:6ff.
[9] 2 Sam. 7:4–8.

the state to regulate men's lives, the break-up of the old pattern of tribal existence, and the threat of foreign enemies across the frontiers.

Then something utterly new, something dynamic, arose within Israel, the like of which only Israel in the ancient world experienced, namely, *the preaching of the prophets*.[10] This preaching did not aim at producing a new spirituality, and certainly not one divorced from the cultus, nor was it a proclamation of universal truths. Nor were the men primarily preachers of social righteousness. They were preservers of the true Israel, and this meant not only the religious life of the nation, but also its political and social life. The prophets were the bearers of *the* word of Yahweh about the way the people were reacting to the particular situation of their own day. It was a word of judgment in the face of apostasy, brought about through religious syncretism, but it was a conditional word of judgment. That is to say, there was a promise of restoration if there was a recognition of the true Lord who had freely elected Israel to be his special people. But the return of the Lord was to be made, not by way of the cultus, but by the zealous application of God's righteousness to existing conditions of social injustice. So these preachers ceased to look to the past. The saving acts on which the nations had been built—the Exodus, Sinai, and the establishment of Zion—were no longer effective. Yahweh would act in a new way for his people. All this was preached into the vacuum brought about by the secularisation and humanism in and following the reign of King Solomon.

So Israel heard preaching late in her history. She encountered it on the lips of the prophets who did not make an appearance until the ninth century B.C., a time when the nation's faith and worship had grown and developed.

What exactly was the origin of prophecy is uncertain. Claims have been made for its rise from religious ecstasy, for it appears that an ecstatic movement of this kind developed outside Israel in the eleventh century, and Israel may have come into contact with it by way of Canaanite religion. Neither of these points, however, is certain. Nor can I Samuel 9:9 (N.E.B.), 'For what is nowadays called a prophet used to be called a seer'—be made to yield information about the early development of prophecy, for the word 'prophet' in the Old Testament covers different types of prophets. All we can say is that prophecy appeared as a new phenomenon in Israel about the ninth century B.C. and became one of the nation's most distinctive features.

[10] See G. von Rad, *Old Testament Theology*, Vol. II, Pts. 1 & 2.

The first notable prophet, the first notable preacher, was Elijah. It was he who ushered in a new age of prophecy. Similarly, in the New Testament[11] it was John the Baptist whose life-style reminded of Elijah, who heralded the Messianic age with his preaching. Nathan[12] and Ahijah of Shiloh[13] were prophets before Elijah, but they are shadowy figures, of whom little can be said. It is also true that Abraham,[14] Moses,[15] Aaron,[16] and Miriam[17] are all styled 'prophets', but the title in these cases must be counted as evidence for the way in which these people were regarded by a later age; in short, these titles are anachronisms. Deuteronomy, for example, was trying to explain every event in history as the result of the nation's attitude to the prophetic word.[18]

Elijah strides dramatically into the Biblical narratives[19] as a kind of superman, even so, his significance does not attach to him as a *persona dramatis*, but as an instrument Yahweh took up at a time when Israel's faith was in peril through syncretism and apostasy.

Elisha, who succeeded Elijah, refused to begin his work unless the charisma possessed by Elijah passed to him.[20] He was famous, not only for the charisma which enabled him to be a legendary miracle-worker, but because of his leadership of assemblies of prophets.[21] These assemblies probably represented pure and undefiled Yahwism to its members, outcasts living on the fringes of the current syncretistic religions, something which they, at a price, rejected. Perhaps the Essenes described in the Dead Sea Scrolls illustrate the kind of witness these protesting groups provided in Elisha's time. In any case, it was protest against apostasy which formed the essential element in all Israelite prophecy.

Since the prophets' preaching was a new phenomenon in Israel, an enquiry must be raised concerning the relation of the prophet to the cultus. It used to be taken for granted that the prophets as a body stood over against the priests, for they each represented two different,

[11] Mark 1:2-4.
[12] 2 Sam. 7:2.
[13] 1 Kings 11:29.
[14] Gen. 20:7.
[15] Deut. 18:15.
[16] Exodus 7:1.
[17] Exodus 15:20.
[18] See W. Eichrodt, *Theology of the Old Testament* (S.C.M. Press, 1961) Vol. II.
[19] 1 Kings 17:1.
[20] 2 Kings 2:9.
[21] 2 Kings 2:3.

even opposing, types of religion. Subsequently, the pendulum of opinion swung to the opposite extreme, and prophets were understood as cultic persons attached to a local sanctuary. More recently, however, this view has been recognised as extreme. The probability is that there did exist official prophets, and there probably were cultic duties for these official prophets to perform, especially in war, but there are a number of reasons why the classical prophets of the Old Testament must be seen as standing apart from them. They stood so far apart that they felt a necessity to describe their individual call to prophesy in order to establish what might otherwise on the surface appear to be illegitimate ministry. In this they were like the Apostle Paul.

In passing from the ninth-century to the eighth-century prophets, a change is apparent in the Biblical presentation. In the case of the ninth-century prophets information is provided about what manner of men they were, and what they did. Of the eighth-century prophets, how-ever, we have scant information about these aspects, and what little we have is derived from the content of their preaching, which in the form of *logia* is provided in the books that bear their names. The fact of this double presentation serves to stress an important aspect of preaching. What is significant is not only, or perhaps not even primarily what is said, but who the preacher is, and what he does. The priorities in order are being, doing, speaking.

The prophets were essentially bearers of the word of Yahweh. This concept of their ministry overrides even that of Spirit-filled men, and this is surprising. We read of the Spirit's indwelling in the case of the ninth-century prophets, but not of the eighth and subsequent cen-turies. It was in order to be communicators of a message from Yahweh that the prophets existed. Their characteristic form of speech was, 'Thus says the Lord,' or 'This is what the Lord says.' It is a 'message formula'. The prophets did not speak their own word, but Yahweh's word. It was, however, most frequently introduced by the prophets' own words indicating either a promise or a judgment thus interpreting what was to follow. So 'the prophetic oracle' was built up. Not that the message formula was the only form of speech adopted, there was a variety of methods, but the aim was always the same, to compel attention to what Yahweh had to say to his wayward people. And in order to achieve their purpose these preachers were ready to shock their hearers, not stopping short of turning some of the most sacred wording of the cultus upside down and even parodying it. It is not surprising, therefore, that they should frequently earn the title 'out-rageous'. We see them, therefore, under constraint as regards the content of their message, but free to develop its form as they thought best in communication.

Part of their problem in communication was the fact that the old cultic forms were insufficiently elastic to allow of their use as they stood, to convey the new message they had to give. So they over-spilled them, even at times overturning them, and going outside them and using secular categories. In doing so they blurred the distinction between sacred and secular, indicating a significant change of thought. Always, however, they kept sight of the cultus, even if they adapted it.[22] They did not reckon that they could operate without its frame-work, and their ultimate aim was never to destroy the old covenant on which the life of the nation was based, but to renew it, in short, to provide a new covenant. But the nation had to face drastic upheaval and change prior to the new covenant being established. This was the preaching Israel had to be made to hear.

It was, of course, radical preaching. The prophets were radicals. They have to be thus described because they declared that the acts of God in Israel's salvation history were inadequate to save the nation. New events had to come to pass,[23] and the people had to *hear* them before they came to pass. All this was profoundly disturbing to the traditionalists, for not only did the form of preaching sound out-rageous, but so also did the content. Israel did not, therefore, suddenly hear radical or a new kind of preaching in her history, she never heard any preaching at all except what was radical and new.

The 'word of Yahweh' which the prophets preached was some-thing transmitted to them. It was not the product of their own theo-logical reflection, nor did they theologise about the concept of 'the Word'. The word of Yahweh was not a proposition to be isolated and studied, it was Yahweh speaking. Neither was it a general word about certain kinds of situations which might occur. The prophets did not announce *a* word of Yahweh, but always *the* word of Yahweh, that is to say, the word of Yahweh to a particular person in a particular situation, calling for obedience. Furthermore, 'word' in itself did not convey to the prophet's mind an intellectual meaning as to a modern Westerner, but almost the opposite. These men were not accustomed to draw a sharp line of distinction between the material and the spiritual, they did not differentiate between word and object, nor between idea and actuality. Words in their understanding produced

[22] It was the weakness of Duhm's epoch-making book, *Israel's Profeten* (1922) that it made the prophetic preaching completely separate from the cultus.

[23] Isa. 42:9; 48:6. This is generally true of Jeremiah, Ezekiel and Deutero-Isaiah.

material expression. By means of language objects were given form, and the application of names to them differentiated them from each other. With this understanding of language the recitation of 'a myth' was not simply a primitive way of describing the world, but the means of bringing that world into existence. Given this dynamic use of language, words became creative instruments. They actually fulfil a purpose by being spoken, whether there is a partner in conversation or not. And if this is true of the words of man, how much more of the word of Yahweh. Psalm 33:6 is not therefore surprising, 'By the word or the Lord were the heavens made.'

There is a content common to the preaching of the prophets which can be found in what they each had to say, a prophetic message, a *kerygma*. They were all concerned about national apostasy. They were all faithful to the same foundations, of their national life, and to the cultus as the means of being incorporated into it. They all pleaded for a return to Yahweh who had called them into being, and for this return to be demonstrated by the application of his righteousness. And they all looked for a new act of Yahweh on behalf of his people. At the same time all these preachers were individuals each with a distinct style and message of his own. So individualistic indeed was the call to prophesy experienced by each one of them that they never urged or expected anyone to experience a similar call. Each prophet's call was his and his alone. The determining factors in this individualism were the prophet's temperament, personal experience and the distinctive circumstances in which he was called to proclaim the word of Yahweh. No two prophets therefore were alike. They were not alike in themselves and their ministries increased their unlikeness from each other. This basic dissimilarity is emphasised at the very outset of the rise of the prophetic movement in Israel by the startling differences between Elijah and Elisha, who nevertheless were both prophets. And the fact that the Spirit is mentioned in references to these two implies that wherever the Spirit operates there is bound to be differentiation and not uniformity. We should therefore be unwise at any time to look for, or encourage, moulds for preachers.

We glance now at some of the differences displayed by these prophetic preachers. First, Amos. Here we encounter the preacher who forces a hearing because of the daring with which he tears down the screens which hide the corruption of his contemporary society. He tells us more about men than he does about God, and in this he is astonishingly well informed, even the details of outrages committed beyond the borders of his own country are not only known to him but assessed by him.[24] Amos is the preacher impelled by moral indignation all the more compelling because the case he presents is thoroughly documented. Yet God is present in all his utterances, even if only as a roaring sound.[25] And if he as a preacher is fierce and fearless, he is not without tenderness for the little nation to which he belongs,[26] nor neglectful of a word of restoration as well as of judgment.[27] As for his preaching style, it is devastating, rich with sarcasm and biting metaphor,[28] forcing the reluctant to hear by means of the stunning starkness of his accusing statements,[29] and the insistent probing of his hurting questions.[30] This is the preacher on account of whom the religious as well as the irreligious wish to stop their ears but cannot, and no small part of his strength lies in his linguistic skill in presenting his message.

Hosea is almost, if not altogether, the counterpart of Amos. They differ from each other as greatly as Elisha compared with Elijah. Hosea does not initially hear God roaring over the far-flung cities of Damascus, Gaza and Tyre, but (as G. A. Smith expressed it) in the clinic of his own broken home. Hosea is the intimate preacher, the man who makes the hearer's heart beat because his own is beating with tenderness; who gets 'under the hearer's skin', who inclines him to do what he, the preacher, intends because to hurt him further with refusal is intolerable. Hosea speaks straight but not with devastating logic. If the form of his book is anything to go by in this respect, his message was confused. Order was not his strong point, but rather emotion-creating patterns of speech of rare beauty scattered across the floor of his auditorium with loving abandon. Hosea was the first preacher to lay bare the heart of God,[31] and even more arresting, indeed, daring, to allude to conflict in the heart of God.[32] Here is the preacher who introduces his hearers not simply to the knowledge of God but to the suffering love of God. This is rare preaching calling for a rare quality of preacher. Such was Hosea, the man who moves people because he has been, and still is, moved himself.

[24] Amos 1:3–2:3.
[25] 1:2; 3:4,8.
[26] 7:1–6.
[27] 9:9–15.
[28] 4:4,5.
[29] 2:6–12.
[30] 3:2–8.
[31] Hos. 11:1.
[32] 6:4.

3

Isaiah is supreme among all the Old Testament preachers. No one reached his stature though Jeremiah approached him in linguistic style. His intellectual vigour was immense, and his ideas broad and far-reaching. He possessed theological insight more penetrating and subtle than any other Old Testament speaker or writer. Isaiah was the aristo-crat of the pulpit, the preacher for the great occasion, the man at home with the leaders of national life in the capital city, the master of poetic expression and of prose, yet emotionally restrained as became a man of culture. So he retained his dignity in face of bitter disappoint-ment[33] at Israel's hardness of heart,[34] and of her inability to rise to the spiritual opportunities afforded her, for in spite of his astonishing skill in fashioning his basic themes to suit various occasions, his hearers did not receive his message, which was that Zion,[35] because it was God's chosen place, was unconquerable and that Yahweh would send his Anointed One for the people's deliverance. But no one believed this. So they were a faithless people. Yet such was the greatness of this man that he continued to hold to his conviction that God had a purpose for his people. Of Isaiah it could never be said that his God was too small. Never did he lose his hold on the sovereignty of God, man's refuge and strength, if only man knew. Herein lay the secret of this majestic preacher— an undying vision of the majesty of God, the God for whom he had cleansed and dedicated his lips[36] in order that he might proclaim him.

Jeremiah succeeded Nahum, Habakkuk and Zephaniah, three men who preached at the time of the epoch-making fall of Assyria (612 B.C.), a stern message of judgment. In the case of Habakkuk a completely new note of impatient questioning of Yahweh sounded.[37] Altogether a marked change was coming over preaching. It came to a head in Jeremiah, the spiritual child of Hosea (also of the Northern Kingdom of Israel), who was almost as different from Amos and Isaiah as a man could be. Like all the prophets, however, he spoke the word of Yahweh to his people, but not in the old prophetic forms of diatribe and threat, and rarely with the tense, clear-cut thrust of the 'message-formula'. With Jeremiah the old patterns were breaking up and their place was taken by Yahweh's long, agonised complaints about his people's way-wardness. He preached as a lyric poet drawing his materials out of his

[33] Isa. 22:4.
[34] 6:9–10.
[35] 28:16.
[36] Isa. 6:1–8.
[37] Hab. 1:2,3, 12–17.

inner personal experience, much of it despairing.[38] Less attention was given to the outside political scene, though like all these preachers he prophesied destruction for his own nation as well as for a number of foreign powers. Jeremiah is not everyman's preacher. Hearers do not grow enthusiastic about a man who gets no joy out of preaching, indeed who even hates it, and would rather do almost anything than have to engage in it.[39] And when a preacher lays bare his soul in this manner the result is embarrassing. It is no wonder Jeremiah became a laughing-stock.[40] They hated the taunting charge of apostasy and stupidity he flung at them, but to which they could not help but listen, so striking was his mode of expression, all of which made them hate him the more. So Jeremiah came to be the martyr-prophet, the preacher whose personal suffering was as distinctive as his message, marking him out as the lonely but faithful servant of Yahweh, an individual with a word of God for individuals, breaking away painfully from the solidarity and community of persons so characteristic of his nation.

Ezekiel, again, was different. He was a highly cultured, cool and detached theological teacher in the pulpit, given to reflective thought. He could also describe stylish literary visions.[41] Most significant of all, he was a priest in the pulpit. Preaching for him could not possibly be conceived of as a professional activity apart from the priestly office. Priestly work and prophesying work were one, coming as he did from a priestly background.[42] Although he held no priestly office himself, he nevertheless thought as a priest, he understood sin as a priest (sins were transgressions of sacral ordinances), and he preached in order to fulfil a pastoral ministry. It is true his thinking went far beyond that of priestly theology but it was rooted in cultic tradition. So he exhibited a certain theological individualism and this reinforced the independence of his theological approach. He spoke less of doom and salvation than others of the prophetic preachers, and allowed more freedom for his hearers to choose or reject God.

The last of the great preachers in Israel was Deutero-Isaiah, the preacher of the exile, the man whose preaching was so much more important than the preacher that we do not even know his name. He was predominantly the preacher of God's salvation drawing upon

[38] Jer. 15:10–21.
[39] Jer. 1:6.
[40] Jer. 20:7.
[41] Ezek. 1.
[42] Ezek. 1:3.

the three great election traditions of the Exodus, Sinai and Zion, yet relying most heavily on the Exodus tradition. More than any other preacher he proclaimed a new act of God for his people,[43] and developed a doctrine of Creation[44] in God's redemptive activity for his people. Everything depended, in his view, on the creative word of God. It was he who came closest to presenting a theology of the word in the Old Testament.[45] Most striking is his prophecy of a coming world mediator. And the presentation of the Suffering Servant was completely without equal. All this proclamation of salvation, making him the evangelical preacher of the Old Testament *par excellence*, was presented in rich emotional tones, but it was also logical and effective and cast in a mould of majestic rhythmic language.

These three preachers of the seventh century, Jeremiah, Ezekiel and Deutero-Isaiah, sat more loosely to the sacral tradition, thought more theologically, and looked to a new beginning more decisively than did any of their predecessors. And with them the golden age of preaching in ancient Israel passed away. The men who occupied the prophetic pulpit after them are not to be despised. They had a proper ministry to fulfil because they were men suited to the conditions in which they had to minister the word of Yahweh, but in comparison with what had gone before, their age can only be described as the silver age of preaching. These preachers were Trito-Isaiah, Haggai, Zechariah, Malachi and Jonah.

Trito-Isaiah had to grapple with a people discontented because the promised glory of the city of Zion had not come about.[46] With his depressing audience, however, he was faithful in announcing that Yahweh's coming would be a world-shaking event. Haggai and Zechariah preached to people frustrated and turned in on themselves in the wretched conditions which constituted the aftermath of the return from exile. If theirs seemed to be a pedestrian proclamation calling for little else but a resolve to rebuild the Temple,[47] it was what the hour required, and it was linked with the coming of Yahweh and of his kingdom. The anonymous preacher called Malachi spent his preaching ministry handling abuses, carelessness and blasé scepticism.[48]

[43] Isa. 43:18ff.
[44] Isa. 45:18.
[45] Isa. 55:6-13.
[46] Isa. 56:1; 58:8; vv. 10ff; 62:1-3; vv. 11ff.
[47] Hag. 1:8.
[48] Mal. 1:6-8.

Jonah is in a class by himself. Summoned to a preaching ministry with all the flourish familiar to the call of a prophet,[49] he refused to mount the pulpit because he resented the congregation assigned to him. As a result he was made to look very foolish and very small. Jonah, the runaway preacher has no stature, nor for that matter, even existence outside the story, for it must be counted unhistorical, yet the message of the book is important.

As far as the classic mould of prophetic preaching is concerned, Malachi marks the end of preaching in ancient Israel. There was insufficient buoyancy in it to survive. Priestly religion gained ground and the tendency in it as seen in Genesis Chapter One was for nature to be made subordinate to the word and thus be lifted out of the determinism which linked it with history. The word, however, became static in a codified system of law.[50] In the Wisdom literature[51] the word of Yahweh became the subject of poetic description and developed in a speculative direction as a kind of intermediary between God and man, ceasing to operate in the realm of obedience to God speaking. Another significant and popular development was the use of apocalyptic,[52] its characteristic being an intellectual schematisation of history in which all is determined by a transcendent God.

Before leaving this brief survey of the rise and fall of preaching in ancient Israel, three additional points need to be noted. The book of Deuteronomy is cast in the form of sermons, the substance of which is sacral and secular material. In a sense it is expository preaching, not that it explained scripture, for no scripture as such was in existence, but it explained the old traditions and commended them with directness—'the word which I commend you this day'—and with an astonishing range of spiritual insight. It is the product of the reform movement in the time of Josiah, and probably originated in the Northern Kingdom. It may represent Levitical preaching. In any case it is preaching, employed not over against the cultus, but in the service of the cultus, and all with the aim of binding the nation together for the sake of its welfare and salvation. In Deuteronomy we encounter a preacher addressing hearers separated in time from the great events at Sinai which constitute

[49] Jonah 1:1.
[50] See W. Eichrodt, *Theology of the Old Testament* (S.C.M. Press, 1961) Vol. 1, Chapter 8.
[51] See H. H. Rowley, *The Old Testament and Modern Study* (Oxford University Press, 1951) Chapter 7; G. von Rad, *Wisdom in Israel* (S.C.M. Press, 1977).
[52] John Bright, *A History of Israel* (S.C.M. Press, 1960) pp. 443–445. For a full treatment, H. H. Rowley, *The Relevance of Apocalyptic* (Lutterworth Press, 1944).

the burden of his theme, but who uses them as a means for hearing the word of God now.[53]

In three passages[54] in the prophets we encounter not only information as to how prophecies came to be written down, but also a provision for these prophecies to be used as a means for hearing the word of God *in later times*. This provides prophetic insight into the word of God. It applies not only to the situation and the time when first uttered but possesses the potentiality of supplying the word of God for another situation at another time. The meaning of a prophetic oracle is not therefore exhausted, however thoroughly its *Sitz-im-Leben* is comprehended. There are *Sitzen-im-Leben* yet to come necessary to elucidate the truth that lies within it. This is what gives scripture its inexhaustible quality and makes it the stock-in-trade of the preacher.

It is important that attention be given to the synagogue, for it provided a link as regards preaching between the Old and New Testaments. The precise origin is unknown. It is not unreasonable to suppose that synagogue worship developed during the Babylonian exile when the Jewish captives were cut off from the Temple. Since the sacrificial system was no longer available, services involving the reading of the Law especially, though not excluding the prophets, and exposition combined with prayer, took hold. Possibly the spontaneous origin of this synagogue worship is reflected in the account of Ezra mounting a platform of wood (the A.V. has 'pulpit') and reading from 'the book of the Law clearly', making its sense plain, and giving instruction in what was read – a kind of expository teaching or preaching.[55] Whether this was the origin or not, the existence of synagogues in Egypt in the third century is certain, as is also the fact that they appeared soon after in Palestine. By the first century A.D. no sizeable town in the Roman Empire was without its synagogue. In the Gospels and the Acts of the Apostles in the New Testament synagogues are much in evidence, and Jesus and the Apostles after Pentecost conducted their teaching ministries in them. These synagogues were not opposed to the Temple but complemented it, being a people's religious movement. It was an exceedingly powerful movement. It had its popular preachers. Without it the Maccabean resistance to the thrust of Hellenism is unlikely to have taken place. It was a teaching ministry and that its influence was widespread and penetrating has testimony borne to it by the fact that

[53] For another use of this exegetical method see E. W. Nicholson, *Preaching to the Exiles* (Blackwell, 1970).

[54] Isa. 8:16–18; 30:8–11; Jer. 36.

[55] Neh. 8:1–8.

Jesus, brought up in the synagogue in an obscure Galilean town, was thoroughly grounded in the Hebrew scriptures. It was the synagogues, or more specifically, the teaching ministry of the synagogues that kept the unity of the Jewish people in the Dispersion a reality. What above all it proclaimed was the Torah as a way of life, and not as a mere duty but as good news, as a gospel for day-to-day living for every Jew, and in a sense for every man, if he had the wisdom to recognise it. And some Gentiles did. Wherever there was a synagogue there were some 'proselytes of the gate' attracted by the quality of life that was evident. In the light of this history of the synagogue, while it is true to say that the prophetic preaching faded away with Malachi in the Old Testament, the ministry of the word did not cease. Granted the religion of Israel began and continued for centuries without it, and the prophetic preaching came in as it were alongside the cultus, and faded away, nevertheless a preaching-teaching ministry persisted, and with power. Such was the contribution of the synagogue and it was there that the New Testament preaching had roots. It would be hard to conceive of anything more influential for the well-being, even survival, of the Jewish people than this ministry of the word.[56]

What then does this brief survey of preaching in ancient Israel suggest as its chief characteristics?

Preaching is not a ministry in the absence of which there can be no people of God, no Church, no congregation. Israel came into being without preaching, and when preaching did make its appearance, for all its grandeur, it did not save Israel from national disaster. It does, nevertheless, 'save' the people of God in that it operates to keep it true to its calling; not, however, because it is preaching, but because it is a means of encounter with God who wills the salvation of his people. Nor is it automatic in its operation. Preaching reached its peak with Isaiah, but no Israelite audience was as deaf as in the presence of his illustrious ministry. Nevertheless, there is a peculiar merit in words as the medium. In the understanding of the prophets, words were never mere words. They were extensions of persons and instruments of creative or destructive power. When, therefore, these prophet-

---

[56] For an account and assessment of the synagogue see *Hastings Dictionary of the Bible* Art. 'Synagogue'; J. Bright, *A History of Israel* (S.C.M. Press, 1960) pp. 422–445; W. O. E. Oesterley, *The Jews and Judaism during the Greek Period* (S.P.C.K., 1941) pp. 211–218; G. H. C. Macgregor & A. C. Purdy, *Jew and Greek: Tutors unto Christ* (Ivor Nicholson & Watson, 1936) pp. 83–86, 146–147.

preachers spoke God's words, they made actual both the presence and the power of God.

Apparently to plan for preaching is impossible. Preaching happens, or it does not happen. This is because preachers cannot be made, they are born and they are called, and every one is unique. There is no pattern by which to structure them. They must be taken as they are. The call to preach is a sphere in which God pre-eminently exercises his sovereignty. Preachers may, however, have disciples as in 'the schools of prophets' organised by Elisha.

The person of the preacher is important. He labours under the constraint to preach and his message is not his own, it is given him, but he is free to shape that message as seems to him best in order to communicate it. For this every skill he possesses is required. And he must be wholly dedicated to the task, ready not only to speak, but to be and to do. This latter may involve symbolic action leading to the possibility of open ridicule, but he must suffer for the calling's sake. The preaching ministry is nothing if not personally demanding and sacrificial. And the preacher must not only be sensitive to God speaking, that is, the word of God, he must be a keen-sighted observer of his contemporary world; and not only an observer, he must identify with the people to whom he preaches. Judging them, he must nevertheless stay with them, sharing their lot and the consequences of their unfaithfulness to their call to be the people of God. No preacher must be a separatist. Prophetic preaching, and what later came to be called Pharisaism, cannot be combined.

Preaching cannot function independently. It must always be contextualised. It normally operates against a background of the cultus. The only preacher in the Old Testament called to preach apart from such a background was Jonah, and he refused. That he finally obeyed and was astonishingly successful as a preacher with the most meagre of messages, shows the sovereignty of God, and of the word of God. Furthermore, the principles proclaimed must be embodied in the cultus. Preaching by itself is like a flower plucked from its parent plant whose life and beauty is short. Preaching is a proclamation of law, but it is not legalism. It does not seek to evoke obedience to statutes and ordinances in order that salvation may be won, rather it calls for obedience to the will of God as the loving response to a God who has already wrought salvation for his people. It is always radical. It goes to the roots. It tears down subterfuges. Like the surgeon, it probes in order to heal, and never to make way for the hearers to heal themselves, but always to make way for the Divine Healer.

2

The word in the ministry of Jesus

WE HAVE CONSIDERED THE MINISTRY OF THE WORD IN ISRAEL. WE shall also consider it in the life of the primitive Church beginning with the outpouring of the Spirit at Pentecost. Pentecost was the event which initiated the new era of preaching. Its focal point was the gospel of the resurrection of the crucified Christ. The Church did not set about preaching because Jesus had been a preacher. The Church's preaching is not *in imitatio Christi*. Yet Jesus was a preacher. And the early Church was interested in his preaching.[1] It is therefore a proper question to ask, What kind of a preacher was he? And what was his message?

These questions cannot be answered unless we are prepared to jettison the scepticism of the last quarter of a century about the possibility of knowing the historical Jesus on the grounds that we lack the materials, for the gospels are not biographies (a fact which the discipline called Form Criticism has undoubtedly established). Since 1953, however, when Käsemann set on foot a more positive approach there has developed something of a restored confidence even if the four gospels are now recognised as providing four portraits of Jesus, and portraits cannot be superimposed on one another to make one authentic portrait. Difficulties remain[2] in presenting the historical Jesus, but there is not only a new search but an actual rediscovery.[3] It is not, therefore,

[1] The suggestion has been made partly on the basis of a misunderstanding of 2 Cor. 5:16 (R.V.) (but see R.S.V.) that the primitive Church was not interested in the life of Jesus or his preaching. But see G. N. Stanton, *Jesus of Nazareth in New Testament Preaching* (Cambridge University Press, 1974).

[2] For a positive, popular, yet scholarly presentation of these problems see *I Believe in the Historical Jesus*. Howard Marshall (London: Hodder and Stoughton, 1977). The book contains a useful bibliography.

[3] G. Bornkamm, *Jesus of Nazareth* (Hodder and Stoughton, 1960) marks a turning point. C. H. Dodd, *The Founder of Christianity* (Collins, 1971) is also important. The presentation of the historical Jesus by Hans Küng *On Being a Christian* (Collins, 1978) pp. 119–342 is disturbing and important for preachers not least because of this quality.

illegitimate or worthless to enquire how the gospel writers have presented Jesus *as a preacher*.

First, it is evident that Jesus was seen as connecting directly with the classical Hebrew prophets. He was a prophet[4] and known as a prophet. With him and his announcer, John the Baptist, the long era of silence which had overcome prophecy was broken at last. The time of Jesus was the time of the Spirit, and the time of the Spirit was the time of the rebirth of prophetic preaching.

The close of the Old Testament had left behind it a community in which preaching in the form of prophecy was dead. Zechariah declared that the only prophets remaining were false ones,[5] and Psalm 74:9 is categorical: 'We have no prophet now; we have no one who knows how long this is to last', and 1 Maccabees 9:27 takes the dearth for granted, 'It was a time of great affliction for Israel, worse than any since the day when prophets ceased to appear among them.' Rabbinic literature makes the same point.

Nevertheless there was an undying hope that prophecy would rise again. Prophetic preaching would in fact mark the beginning of a new age. It would be the age of the Spirit.

> 'Thereafter the day shall come
> when I will pour out my spirit on all mankind;
> your sons and your daughters shall prophesy,
> your old men shall dream dreams
> and your young men see visions;
> I will pour out my spirit in those days
> even upon slaves and slave-girls.'[6]

But the expectation was more specific than of a general rise of prophecy, it looked for the coming, not simply of *a* prophet, but of *the* prophet. Some identified him as Elijah, and there is strong New Testament support for this.[7] Others identified him with Moses, basing their belief on Deuteronomy 18:17ff. But in whatever way he was conjectured, whether as Elijah or Moses, he would be an eschatological figure.

Into this prophetic expectation the Synoptic Gospels writers show

---

[4] We must remember that a prophet to the Hebrew mind was a man of action. His work was seen as well as heard.

[5] Zech. 13:3–6.

[6] Joel 2: 28–29 (N.E.B.).

[7] Luke 9:8; Mark 6:15; 8:28; 15:34, 36.

that John the Baptist fitted. Jesus designated him a prophet[8] in the line of the Old Testament prophets, and 'more than a prophet', since he was actually introducing the new age.[9] Mark makes clear that he accepts this indentification by inserting Malachi 3:1 before Isaiah 40:3 at chapter 1:2–3 of his gospel. And John himself, by means of his clothes and the simplicity of his message, indicated that he accepted the rôle.

So prophetic preaching returned to mark the new age. It was simple and straightforward preaching. It did not, Rabbinic fashion, expound the intricacies of the Law, but called for repentance lest judgment fall; and there was no protection for being a member of the chosen people. But it was not only a message of judgment called out in strident tones and using metaphors of vipers fleeing from the advancing wrath, an axe ready to fell a tree, or a winnowing fan separating the chaff from the wheat,[10] it told, too, of the 'Coming One', a strong man[11] who would not only act with thoroughness in judgment, but would baptise with the Holy Spirit and with fire.[12] In the light of this the people must repent, but not in order to bring in the kingdom, because it was at hand already.

Yet for all that John is chiefly significant as a preacher, he is known as the Baptist or the Baptiser. He did not therefore only preach, he embodied his preaching in a rite through which those who heard him were able to respond. What exactly the rite was is open to discussion. It did not seem to owe its origin to Judaean lustrations nor to proselyte baptism but to the initiation ceremonies of the sects as described in the Dead Sea Scrolls in the Manual of Discipline.[13] There we are told of how 'all who came into the order of the community shall pass over into the covenant.' Moreover, they were expected to separate themselves from 'all the men of error' and so become the 'sons of Light' and 'the sons of Truth'.[14] John's baptising apparently *symbolised the message* of repentance in readiness for 'the Coming One'.

So John's ministry was two-fold, a ministry of the word, and a ministry of a sacramental act. And although he himself was pre-eminently a prophet, his roots were in his priestly ancestry. And not

[8] Matt. 11:9.
[9] See J. Jeremias, *New Testament Theology* (Eng. Trans. S.C.M. Press, 1971) Vol. 1, pp. 4 & 22ff.
[10] Matt. 3:7–12.
[11] Mark 1:7.
[12] Matt. 3:11.
[13] Q.S. 1:16; 2:2–18.
[14] In a new covenant cf. Jer. 31:31–34.

the least striking was his proclamation of baptism, a ritual act. But it was also a ministry in the Spirit, he himself was filled with the Holy Spirit from birth,[15] and he pointed to the 'Coming One's' baptism with Holy Spirit.[16] And even if this phrase derives from later Christian interpretation, the impression is of John's ministry ushering in the age of the Spirit. So preaching, ritual action and the operation of the Holy Spirit were made to mark John's ministry.

John, it seems, made no use of the synagogue for preaching. All his work, according to the records, was carried out in the wilderness where he operated as a lone voice, setting him therefore closer to the Law and the prophets of ancient Israel.[17]

According to the Gospels John the Baptist preached in the wilderness[18] and nowhere else, except perhaps, in prison.[19] Jesus, however, preached or taught or 'spoke the word' in Galilean[20] and perhaps Judaean synagogues,[21] in the open air, notably by the Galilean lakeside,[22] in private houses[23] and in the Temple.[24] At his trial before Caiaphas he was questioned about his teaching and confessed that he had spoken openly to all the world,[25] specifying in particular both synagogue and temple.[26] Apparently, therefore, he preached and taught in the course of formal worship in public places to an assembled crowd, to small groups of his own followers in houses, and as occasion required, in response to a situation[27] or a question or challenge.[28] His preaching or teaching ministry is presented as having begun in the synagogue and expanded in ever widening circles.

If the contemporaries of Jesus questioned whether or not he was the Messiah, the gospels give us to understand that they were in no doubt that he was a prophet in the lineage of the Old Testament prophets.

[15] Luke 1:16.
[16] No definite article. Mark 1:8.
[17] J. Jeremias, op. cit., p. 49.
[18] Mark 1:4.
[19] Mark 6:20.
[20] Mark 1:21 & John 6:59 (Capernaum); Luke 4:16; Mark 6:2 (Nazareth); Mark 1:39; Luke 6:6; Matt. 9:35.
[21] Luke 4:44.
[22] Mark 4:1.
[23] Mark 2:1,2; 9:33.
[24] John 7:14; 8:2,20; Mark 12:35; Luke 19:47–20:1.
[25] John 18:20.
[26] John 18:20.
[27] Mark 9:33ff.
[28] Mark 10:2–45.

Luke in the third gospel presents two travellers on the road from Jerusalem to Emmaus on the first Easter Day looking back over the whole ministry of Jesus, and offering as their assessment— 'a prophet powerful in speech and action before God and the whole people.'[29] It was a similar verdict to that given by the Galileans when they first heard him (also recorded by Luke), 'A great prophet has arisen among us'[30] and at the close, when Jesus entered Jerusalem and the enquiry was raised, 'Who is this?' they shouted back the same answer, firm and clear, 'This is the prophet Jesus, from Nazareth in Galilee.'[31] There are other similar testimonies.[32]

Luke elaborates this designation of Jesus as a prophet. In the synagogue at Nazareth he describes how Jesus 'stood up to read the lesson and was handed the scroll of the prophet Isaiah. He opened the scroll and found the passage which says,

"The spirit of the Lord is upon me because he has anointed me;
he has sent me to announce good news to the poor,
to proclaim release for prisoners and recovery of sight for the blind;
to let the broken victims go free,
to proclaim the year of the Lord's favour."

He rolled up the scroll, gave it back to the attendant, and sat down; and all eyes in the synagogue were fixed on him. He began to speak: "Today," he said, "in your very hearing this text has come true." '[33] Later, also recorded by Luke (who clearly had a special interest in Jesus as a prophet), Jesus said, 'However, I must be on my way . . . because it is unthinkable for a prophet to meet his death anywhere but in Jerusalem.'[34]

Jesus is presented as exhibiting *the style* of an Old Testament prophet in his preaching. His prepared utterances, as distinct from his spontaneous replies in argument, were for the most part cast in a poetic form of parallelism as were those of all the great prophets in ancient Israel. His language was likewise radical, provocative and disturbing. The message of judgment was not absent from it. With devastating words and unanswerable logic he tore away the religious superficiality which

---

[29] Luke 24:19.
[30] Luke 7:16.
[31] Matt. 21:11.
[32] See Mark 6:15; Matt. 21:46; John 4:19; 6:14; 7:40; 9:17.
[33] Luke 4:17-21 (N.E.B.). On this passage of scripture see J. Jeremias, op. cit., p. 52.
[34] Luke 13:33, cf. Matt. 23:29.

cloaked the hypocrisy of his day. But with the judgment, mercy, and not for some spiritual élite within the community, but for all who would come to him.

He used his tongue as a kind of weapon, thus operating as the Servant of the Lord whom he recognised himself to be, taking on himself the words of the second Servant Song: 'He made my tongue his sharp sword.'[35] Yet he was no ranter, rabble-rouser, or market-square demagogue. Rather he exemplified the delineaments of another Servant Song: 'He will not call out or lift his voice high, or make himself heard in the open street.'[36] Jesus, moreover, in his speech, showed such an intellectual grasp of the scriptures that the Rabbis treated him as a Rabbi. Normally speaking in Aramaic, he both knew the ancient Hebrew scriptures and was conversant with Rabbinic interpretation. Jesus was no amateur carpenter-theologian.

His speech also was action. When he spoke remarkable consequences followed. This was obvious when he began to teach in the Capernaum synagogue. 'What is this?' people asked, 'A new kind of teaching! He speaks with authority. When he gives orders, even the unclean spirits submit.'[37]

So the gospels present Jesus as a prophet in the great prophetic tradition, endowed by the Spirit[38] to speak the words that he received from God,[39] words of judgment[40] and of forgiveness,[41] words that were effective in action, but with one significant difference, he did not point to 'the Coming One'. Instead he opened his ministry with the words, 'The time has come; the kingdom of God is upon you: repent, and believe the Gospel.'[42]

In Jesus we see a signal advance upon John, his immediate predecessor. Both were prophets, both proclaimed the presence of the kingdom of God,[43] both spoke of judgment, but Jesus went beyond, he was also a teacher. He preached *and he taught*,[44] that is to say, he expounded, applied and argued his message, and in so doing, displayed a distinctive style.

[35] Isa. 49:2.
[36] Isa. 42:2.
[37] Mark 1:27.
[38] Mark 1:10.
[39] John 8:26,28,38,40; 12:49; 15:15; 17:8,14.
[40] Mark 12:1–12.
[41] Mark 2:1–12.
[42] Mark 1:14.
[43] Some question the genuineness of Matt. 3:2.
[44] These must not be too sharply separated.

The two most certain facts in the gospel tradition [wrote T. W. Manson] are that Jesus taught, and that he was crucified. In Mark, the verb 'teach' occurs seventeen times, and in sixteen of these Jesus is the subject. In the same gospel he is called 'teacher' twelve times—four times by his disciples, once by himself, five times by persons not of his circle, but not hostile to him, and twice by *his opponents*. Four times also in Mark he is called 'Rabbi', the usual name for a Jewish teacher.[45]

His utterance was cast in a poetic form[46] and it was shot through with short, sharp sayings, often cryptic, allusive and even ironical, on which C. H. Dodd comments, 'they betray a mind whose processes were swift and direct, hitting the nail on the head without waste of words.'[47] There are also similes (one thing compared with another),[48] metaphors (one thing standing for another)[49] and above all, and most characteristic, parables,[50] which are really extended metaphors. Clearly Jesus was a close observer of nature and of people. Possessed of a vivid imagination, he drew word pictures when he preached and taught, he did not speak in the general and abstract, but always in the particular and the concrete. Such a use of imagery was not new, it was a marked feature of apocalyptic literature, and although Jesus may have drawn to some extent on the apocalyptic imagery,[51] it was untypical. His kind of imagery was more realistic, down-to-earth, and taken from the current observable world.

Through all his spoken ministry Jesus revealed a deep underlying concern for people, their needs, their illnesses, their sins. It was this which differentiated him from John the Baptist. He did not withdraw in order to proclaim God's word of judgment, he stayed with those he judged in their cities,[52] with eyes wide open to their duplicity[53] and

[45] *The Sayings of Jesus* (Study Edition S.C.M. Press, 1971) p. 11.

[46] See G. Dalman, *Words of Jesus* (T. & T. Clark, 1902); C. F. Burney, *The Poetry of Our Lord* (Oxford, 1925); M. Black, *An Aramaic Approach to the Gospels & The Acts* (Oxford, 1946); for a summary account, J. Jeremias, op. cit. pp. 8–28.

[47] *The Founder of Christianity* (Collins, 1971) p. 37.

[48] Matt. 10:16.

[49] Luke 12:49.

[50] For their context in the ministry of Jesus see J. Jeremias, *The Parables of Jesus* (S.C.M. Press, 1954) and C. H. Dodd, *The Parables of the Kingdom* (Nisbet, 1935). For an existential interpretation see G. V. Jones, *The Art & Truth of the Parables* (S.P.C.K., 1964).

[51] Mark 13:24–26.

[52] Matt. 11:20–24.

[53] Luke 11:13.

pathetic forsakenness,[54] offering freely God's forgiveness, not from weakness. On the contrary, what singled Jesus out from all other Rabbinic preachers of his day, was his self-authenticating authority[55] derived from his own close communion with God whom he knew as Father, and not from any kind of external and formal authorisation. This was so striking that it was recognised by the public when they heard him preach. John the Baptist had been a strong, rugged, compelling preacher, reminding people of the giant prophet Elijah in the wilderness, but Jesus in the towns and villages of Galilee and Judaea, preaching in synagogues and in the open air, enquiring and counselling, was stronger than he.[56] A preacher is strong when he is learned, imaginative, vivid and thrusting in his speech, tender yet firm, fearless, yet kind, and above all, clearly a man in close touch with God.

What was his message? It was that the kingdom of God was at hand. He did not define it (a fact not unconnected with the enormous literature on the subject), he described what it is like. His method was one of *parabolē*, that is, casting one thing alongside another, and leaving the hearers to make their own deductions. Jesus never handed out theological propositions, he encouraged his hearers to move forward on a voyage of discovery into the truth. Not that there was no truth to be discovered, or that they could make it themselves, or even find it inside themselves. Truth is not a set of packaged ideas, it is a way of living.[57] It must be sought, and it can be found, and the searching is worth all the labour and sacrifice involved.[58]

The kingdom of God which Jesus proclaimed is not an ideal state which men construct, nor even a social ideal to serve as a pattern for such. Nor is it an inward spiritual condition. The kingdom of God is God's real presence now, a sovereign presence, a dynamic presence, a presence which alters people, circumstances and conditions, a presence which rubs out the past and fills the future with promise, a presence which drastically affects the inward aspect of human existence, and its outward aspect as well. God's real presence cannot be defined, delineated, controlled or manipulated, it can only be realised through the human response of repentance and faith, and still it remains sovereign, transforming, remaking and empowering as it will. There is no telling what the kingdom of God will do, but do things it will. So the miracles

[54] Matt. 9:36.
[55] Mark 1:22. See J. Jeremias, op. cit. p. 250.
[56] Mark 1:7.
[57] John 3:21 (R.V.).
[58] Matt. 13:44-46.

operated as disclosure points of the universal sovereign presence of God. There was a necessity about them if the preaching of Jesus was true and the time was fulfilled and the kingdom of God was actually at hand.

The nature of this Divine presence Jesus summed up in one word— Father. This is uninhibited anthropomorphic language, all the more striking because the Jews were cautious about any use of the divine name. Jesus, however, intended God not only to be understood, but approached in the warm and intimate fashion characteristic of the best family life. And he did not, as is too often mistakenly supposed, make much of *commanding* the love of God and love of neighbour, his emphasis was on recognising that God actually is Father, and that men and women should be what they are—his children, and so live obediently and trustingly. They should also imitate, and so reproduce, their Father's generosity, overstepping commonly accepted moral bounds,[59] so that love of neighbour includes even foreigners and heretics,[60] and forgiveness extends beyond any limit.[61]

Nevertheless, no weak sentimentality is implicit in this attitude to the wrong-doer, there is severity as well as kindness in Jesus as a preacher and in what he preached. This being so, the man who does not offer forgiveness to his fellows cannot expect to receive divine forgiveness.[62] If a child of the heavenly Father will not open his own heart the Father will not force it open for his own good, he must suffer the consequences. Thus the twin pillars of the old prophetic preaching[63] took the same weight in the preaching of Jesus— mercy and judgment, and were expressed in similar radical terms and sometimes even extravagant terms. This is a marked feature of that collection of Jesus' teachings brought together in what is commonly called the Sermon on the Mount. Here Matthew and Luke have arranged common material[64] so as to display them in what may be called a discourse on the principles of the Kingdom of God, or better, examples of attitudes characterising those who recognise God as their Father, and live in the light of his real and royal Divine presence. What therefore Jesus preached could be summed up in the one phrase 'the Kingdom of God my Father'.[65]

[59] Matt. 5:45.
[60] Luke 10:25–37.
[61] Matt. 18:21,22.
[62] Matt. 6:14,15.
[63] See J. Jeremias, op. cit. p. 122.
[64] Matt. chaps. 5–7; Luke 6:20–49.
[65] T. W. Manson, *The Sayings of Jesus*, p. 345.

4

There was in addition an element in Jesus' preaching, also to be found in seventh-century prophets of Israel, namely, the fact of suffering. It came to assume fundamental importance and was first spoken about when he was on his way to the villages of Caesarea Philippi. He asked his disciples their views on his identity, and they ventured the reply, 'Elijah, John the Baptist or one of the prophets,' and Peter went so far as to assert that he was the Messiah. Thereafter, 'he began' (note the word), 'to teach them that the Son of Man had to undergo great sufferings, and to be rejected by the elders, chief priests, and doctors of the law; to be put to death, and to rise again three days afterwards.'[66] This element of suffering had been a marked feature of Jeremiah's experience as a prophet; indeed, he was unique among the prophets as a martyr-prophet. According to Matthew's version of the Caesarea Philippi conversation the disciples suggested that Jesus was in fact Jeremiah.[67] But the passage in the prophets which tells most clearly of suffering is the Fourth Servant Song.[68] The First Song had told of the Servant's bearing,[69] the second, of his equipment[70] (both referring to a ministry of the Word); the third Song of the Servant, as a teacher experiencing suffering in his own person;[71] it was the fourth which set out a ministry through suffering.[72] It was these Servant Songs, we may suppose, and especially the fourth, that Jesus had absorbed into his own reflection on his life and which issued in such strong statements as 'it is necessary for the Son of Man to undergo great sufferings'[73] and, 'Whoever wants to be great must be your servant, and whoever wants to be first must be the willing slave of all. For even the Son of Man did not come to be served but to serve, and to give up his life as a ransom for many.'[74] Jesus then presented himself in his preaching, not only as the martyr prophet, but as the Suffering Servant, and St Luke would have the readers of his gospel note that Jesus would not allow the two travellers' assessment of himself as 'a prophet powerful in speech and action before God and the whole people' to stand without this all-important, completing, and therefore correcting commentary of Jesus himself— 'How dull you are!' he answered. 'How slow to believe all

[66] Mark 8:31,32.
[67] Matt. 16:14.
[68] Isa. 52:13 to 53:12.
[69] Isa. 42:1–4.
[70] Isa. 49:1–6.
[71] Isa. 50:4–9.
[72] Isa. 52:13–53:12.
[73] Mark 8:31.
[74] Mark 10:45.

that the prophets said! Was the Messiah not bound to suffer thus before entering upon his glory?'[75]

As the ministry of Jesus progressed, his rôle as a prophet receded, and the more fundamental dual rôle as Messiah and Suffering Servant took over. And that this dual rôle was fundamental Mark makes clear in the prologue to his gospel, where by means of a symbolic event Jesus is designated *Messiah* with a voice from heaven, 'Thou art my Son' and as the *Servant* by the words, 'my Beloved; on thee my favour rests'.[76]

It was not only then as a prophet, preacher or teacher that Jesus is presented as fulfilling his destiny as Messiah, but as God's suffering servant. What is more, he brought into being the new people of God, the new Israel. He did this, however, not by addressing them with the words of God to which they were called to respond, but by giving himself as a sacrifice in death. This then was what he came to do. This was his great work, his supreme work. It was not a sermon that he gave, or a series of sermons, but himself symbolised on the night before his death with the breaking of bread and the outpouring of wine. *So he became the Word of God*, that is to say, what he was and did became God's speech.

What then was the purpose of Jesus' preaching? This is not to ask why the early Church assembled his teaching in the gospels. But why did Jesus preach *to his contemporaries*? Did he expect to win them by his preaching and so bring in the kingdom of God? Or was it to bring into being a new law to replace the Torah? Was not this rather his purpose—so to present the kingdom of God that he himself would be seen as its embodiment, and he a Person, not a programme nor a doctrine, be the heart of the gospel to be preached? This certainly is how the writer of the fourth gospel set out the story of Jesus, inserting such interpretive sayings as, 'I am the door', 'I am the true Vine', 'I am the way, the truth and the life'. Jesus did not advertise himself—this would have been offensive megalomania—but he so preached that after the cross and resurrection it was recognised that in him the kingdom of God, which he had proclaimed, by means of similes, metaphors and parables, and demonstrated by the mighty works, *had indeed already come*. Christ is the kingdom.

There is therefore no contradiction between Jesus the preacher and Jesus the preached Christ. The risen Christ whom the apostles proclaimed is actually the kingdom of God come with power which Jesus

[75] Luke 24:25,26.
[76] Mark 1:11.

proclaimed. The risen Christ is the real and royal presence of God experienced in the present. The works of the kingdom therefore which Jesus performed were of the same kind as the apostles performed in the name of the preached Christ.[77] The book of the Acts of the Apostles, especially in its early chapters, sets out these acts in terms similar to those provided in the gospels for the wonderful works of Jesus. There is a direct line of continuity between Jesus the Christ ministering, and Jesus the Christ ministered[78] passing through the transforming crucifixion-resurrection event. Clearly the same Christ is at work. In proclaiming him therefore the Church is not constructing its own gospel discontinuous from the word of Jesus, it is ministering what he himself came to bring.

[77] On Acts 3:1–10 see C. S. C. Williams, *Acts of the Apostles* (Adam & Charles Black, 1957) p. 74, cf. Mark 3:27.
[78] James D. G. Dunn in *Unity and Diversity in the New Testament* develops this point.

3

The word in the New Testament

WHEN WE TURN FROM THE OLD TESTAMENT TO THE NEW TESTAMENT
we encounter a different world. Preaching entered late into the life
of ancient Israel, but it was there from the start in the life of the new
Israel, the Church. The story of the Church begins on the day of
Pentecost as recorded in the book of the Acts of the Apostles, and it is
there that the study of preaching in the New Testament must be taken
up. But why did preaching begin on the first day of the life of the
Church? What was new about the new Israel (so-called), as compared
with the old Israel? What was there new to proclaim? The book of
the Acts of the Apostles is ready with its answer – the outpouring of
the Spirit of Jesus crucified and risen from the dead. The crucifixion-
resurrection event supplied the content of the preaching and the outpouring the power. No Church existed without, or apart from
preaching; the Church came to birth *with preaching* and preaching
came to birth *with the Church*.

This is not to say that the Church owes its existence to preaching.
The Church owes its existence to Christ, and has its roots in the life of
ancient Israel. The book of the Acts of the Apostles is careful to connect
the outpouring of the Spirit as well as the preaching it evoked, with the
words of a prophet of Israel (Joel).[1] The Church was there in embryo
before the preaching.

The Church also had a distinctive life out of which the preaching
sprang. Luke in the Acts does not allow the chapter which highlights
the preaching of Peter to be concluded without telling of the members
of the Church meeting 'constantly to hear the apostles teach, and to
share the common life, to break bread and to pray'. The primitive
Church possessed its own cultus, flexible no doubt,[2] followed out
against the pattern of the Jewish temple cultus. 'With one mind they

[1] Acts 2:16–21, cf. Joel 2:28–32.
[2] See James D. G. Dunn, *Unity & Diversity in the New Testament* (S.C.M. Press
1977).

kept up their daily attendance at the temple, and, breaking bread in private houses, shared their meals with unaffected joy . . .'[3]

As it happened, the way in which the primitive Church was enabled in practice to fulfil a preaching ministry and be heard, was also provided by a legacy from ancient Israel. This was the synagogue. The exact origin of the synagogue is obscure, as noted in the previous chapter, but it came about that congregations of Jews in any place consisting of not less than ten men could be recognised as synagogues. In these synagogues a distinctive form of worship evolved consisting of prayer, public reading of the scriptures *and preaching*.[4] This preaching was mainly an exposition of the Torah as the way of life, but the prophets were by no means excluded. The early Church, beginning its life within the bosom of Judaism came in time to use the synagogue forms of worship for its own worship, and these pulpits for its own preaching. The facilities of the synagogue are part of the debt the Church owes Judaism for its opportunity to preach.

But what did the primitive Church preach? What was the earliest *kerygma*? Evidence for this is normally sought in the sermons and speeches in the book of the Acts of the Apostles. The first appears in Acts 2:14–36 as a sermon by Peter on the Day of Pentecost. Altogether there are four 'set' speeches by Peter, one by Stephen and seven by Paul. Can it be supposed that these represent the actual preaching as it was delivered? The book of the Acts of the Apostles appeared some fifty years after these events! Is it possible that the contents of the sermons were written down at the time? Or were the main points repeated so often that they were remembered? Jewish teachers and their pupils were accustomed to making considerable use of the memory in their educational methods. This is tantamount to saying that what the speeches in the Acts of the Apostles provide is a summary or gist of the general preaching of the primitive Church. Possibly Luke shaped this up, placing appropriate forms of it on the lips of the preachers on the occasions he was describing.[5] This could even allow for the inclusion of actual distinctive phrases peculiar to the different preachers. There are, however, scholars[6] who reject all such

[3] Acts 2:46 (N.E.B.).

[4] For information on this see Schaff, *History of the Christian Church* First Division, p. 22ff (Edinburgh, 1884), and Schürer, *The Jewish People in the Time of Christ*, Division II, Vol. II, p. 76 (Edinburgh, 1910); W. O. E. Oesterley & G. H. Box, *The Religion and Worship of the Synagogue* (Pitman, 1907); A. Edersheim, *The Life and Times of Jesus* (Longmans, 1900) Vol. I, pp. 430–450.

[5] See C. S. C. Williams, *Acts of the Apostles* (A. & C. Black, 1957) p. 56.

[6] Dibelius, for example.

interpretation and read the speeches as Luke's theological commentary on the history he was describing.[7] On this view they provide no material for assessing what was the preaching of the pre-Pauline Church. On balance it seems reasonable to suppose that this generally reliable historian, Luke, wrote in order to inform his readers what was the Christian faith from the very earliest days of the Church's life, even though he did so by means of his own literary productions and with some element, perhaps, of idealising the various situations and events he was anxious to describe. When therefore we ask the question, what did the primitive Church preach, we cannot surely be wrong to deduce from these narratives that the centre-piece was *the death and resurrection of Jesus of Nazareth*, presented so that the hearers might believe in God.[8] Maybe the Christology of this preaching was primitive. It is not surprising that a later age labelled it 'adoptionist', for the gist of it was that 'God had vindicated his servant or Son' Jesus through the resurrection and *exalted him* as Lord. This certainly is an elementary Christology. In it the risen Christ is conceived of as an individual, identical with Jesus of Nazareth (though transcendent), and very close to God in heaven, from whence he continues his ministry by sending his Spirit. Nevertheless, elementary though such a Christology may be by Pauline standards, it was a proclamation of Christ, and without it there would have been no preaching.

One speech in the Acts of the Apostles might appear as an exception, namely, the defence of Stephen before the Sanhedrin (7:2–53). It reads as a patriarchal history with no mention of either Jesus or Messiah. Foakes Jackson is not the only commentator to label it an interpolation which should be omitted. Rackham, however, pointed out[9] that it consists of an interpretation of Old Testament history designed to show Jesus as Saviour, prophet and fulfiller of the Law, and that though his name was not mentioned, Stephen preached Jesus *in his types*, especially Joseph and Moses. R. P. C. Hanson[10] made the added point that Stephen was saying that God never allowed his people to have a permanent dwelling place for him because that dwelling place was to be Jesus Christ, 'a house not made with hands'. As for Stephen's confession when he was dying— 'Look, there is a rift in the sky; I can see the Son of Man standing at God's right hand!' (7:56, N.E.B.)— it is true the phrase 'Son of Man' occurs nowhere else outside the gospels,

---

[7] Similarly Luke 4:16–30 is Luke's commentary on the scope of Jesus'mission.
[8] See C. F. Evans in *Explorations in Theology* (S.C.M. Press, 1977) p. 107ff.
[9] *Commentary on the Acts of the Apostles* (1900).
[10] *Theology* L 1947.

and on no one's lips but those of Jesus; it is also true that the account bears similarities to Mark's Passion narratives, suggesting that Luke had a copy of Mark's gospel open before him as he wrote; it may be that Stephen was aware of Jesus' confession at his trial, and *echoed* it, or he may have been making use of a Son of Man Christology in current circulation. All in all, Stephen's speech does not destroy the case for asserting Christ as the centre of the primitive Church's preaching, it may even confirm it. And may not the uniqueness and awkwardness of the speech place a question mark against the idea that Luke invented the speeches he included in his book?

The pattern of preaching which emerges from these speeches contains the following elements:[11]

(i) The prophecies concerning the Messiah have been fulfilled.

(ii) The saving acts of God in sending his Son have reached their climax in the crucifixion and resurrection of Jesus.

(iii) The Apostles are witnesses to these facts.

(iv) Jesus is exalted to God's right hand as Lord and Christ, and gives his Holy Spirit, thus opening a new era.

(v) Christ will come again to judge.

(vi) In the light of this men and women everywhere should repent and be baptised in the name of Jesus the Messiah for the forgiveness of sins, and for the reception of the Holy Spirit.

In all that the Acts of the Apostles has to say, attention is focused on the *preaching* (the *kerygma*), rather than *the preachers*. Nevertheless 'prophets and teachers' were soon to be recognised in the Church as men with special gifts of the Spirit *(charismata)* only second in importance to apostles.[12] Among these the two dominant preachers were Peter and Paul, though seven others were named, in addition to those Christians who preached in the countries where they fled as refugees from the persecutions.[13]

These seven others are Stephen, Philip, Barnabas, Simeon called

[11] This is set out in C. H. Dodd's *The Apostolic Preaching and its Development* (1936). It has been criticised by Dennis Nineham in his *Studies in the Gospels & Acts* (Oxford: Blackwell, 1955) p. 223ff.

[12] 'Within our community God has appointed, in the first place apostles, in the second place prophets, thirdly teachers; then miracle-workers, then those who have gifts *(charismata)* of healing, or ability to help others or power to guide them, or gifts *(charismata)* of ecstatic utterance' 1 Cor. 12:28 (N.E.B.).

[13] 'As for those who had been scattered, they went through the country preaching the Word' Acts 8:4 (N.E.B.).

Niger, Lucius of Cyrene, Manaen, who had been at the court of Prince Herod, and Apollos. Nothing is known of Simeon (the Black), Lucius and Manaen, except that they were recognised as 'prophets and teachers' in the congregation at Antioch. Barnabas was remembered more for generosity (Acts 4:36, 37), and for his willingness to believe in Saul's conversion (Acts 9:27), but he preached as well as Saul on the first missionary journey (Acts 13:46) though was soon overtaken in the leadership by him.

Of Stephen and Philip there is more information. Both had Greek names but were members of the Jerusalem Church. They were selected for their administrative gifts with five others, when that Church was experiencing internal troubles arising from language differences (Acts 6:1-7). They were 'men of good reputation' in the congregation, 'full of the Spirit and of wisdom'. These two achieved notoriety, however, as *preachers*. Stephen was 'full of grace and of power' (which means either that he was gracious in his style of utterance as well as effective, or that the grace of God was effective in his ministry) and he was a miracle-worker and subtle debater, being possessed of a remarkable grasp of the Hebrew scriptures. His preaching may have initiated the rift between Church and Synagogue. Anyway, he paid with his life for it.

Philip is presented as a preaching evangelist. He proclaimed Christ in Samaria (Acts 8:5) wielding such an influence by his words that a notorious local called Simeon, a magician and orator, who held great sway over the community, was captivated. Singled out for special mention is his address to a congregation of one in the person of a high official of the Kandake or Queen of Ethiopia, travelling home in a chariot on the Gaza Road. Beginning from 'the Servant Song' of Isaiah chapter 53, Philip 'told the good news of Jesus', as a result of which the official believed and was baptised. But this was not all. Philip went on to preach in all the coastal towns from Azotus to Caesarea where apparently he lived with his family among whom were four unmarried daughters each with the gift of prophecy.

Apollos stands in a class by himself. He was an Alexandrian Jew, described as learned or educated (Acts 18:24-28), which probably had the secondary meaning of eloquent. He was noted for his thorough knowledge of the Old Testament. At Ephesus he encountered Priscilla and Aquila who deepened his knowledge of God. He journeyed to Achaia making a great impression by the force of his arguments. The Greeks, who were by nature great talkers, responded to this. The result was a party gathered round him distinct from Paul. Reference is made to this in Paul's letter to the Corinthians (1 Cor. 1:12; 3:5; 4:6). So the New Testament touches on the danger inherent in gifted preaching. Maybe the trouble arose because Apollos, instead of drawing upon the solid core of testimonies derived from the Old Testament and used in the Church's preaching, experimented with the allegorical methods of interpretation current in Alexandria and applied to Homer and Philo. Here then was intellectualism in the pulpit and Paul denounced it as 'the wisdom of man' (1 Cor. 1:25).

The preaching of Peter is presented in the Acts of the Apostles as standard Christian preaching, indeed, it may be that we hear little of Peter's actual preaching but rather what was the Church's *kerygma* from its earliest beginnings. Peter the indisputed leader is made to utter what the Church as a whole believed. Such was Luke's literary method. This does not, however, mean that Peter was not a preacher.[14] What it does mean is that we know little of his distinctive style. The case is different with Paul. Paul incorporated the basic message common to the Church's preaching, indeed, he made sure that he did incorporate it (Gal. 2:2), but he developed it in a distinctive way, thus causing him to stand out as the preacher *par excellence* of the Apostolic Church. Peter, nevertheless, is credited with three significant utterances in the Acts of the Apostles, marking him out as a preacher of boldness, directness and warmth. He possessed a firm, if not profound, grasp of the implications of the Gospel of Christ's resurrection. At the same time his mind was ready to open out beyond his limitations as well as his prejudices. Peter was a preacher whose own preaching actually developed him (this can happen), and he saw results from his preaching, because he worked for them and expected them. Peter is everyman's preacher in a way that Paul is not.

And now Paul, Paul 'the citizen of no mean city', Paul the Roman, Paul the Jew, Paul the Rabbi, Paul the missionary, Paul the traveller, Paul the Church-builder, Paul the theologian, Paul the writer, Paul the friend of many and the enemy of more, Paul the prisoner; but in addition to all these and never without this other rôle which on no occasion either in season or out of season did he abandon, *Paul the preacher*. To preach was his life, or how could he say to the Corinthians, 'it would be misery to me not to preach'? (1 Cor. 9:16, N.E.B.)

What was the ground-work of his message?

First and foremost, the resurrection of Christ which, plainly he took to be an event within history, that is to say, it was not only a spiritual

---

[14] It is worth noting that Peter (Cephas) is mentioned in 1 Cor. 1:12 in the company of Apollos.

experience nor a speculation, but something which had actually happened at a specific time and place. 'I delivered unto you first of all[15] that which also I received, how that Christ died for our sins according to the scriptures; and that he was buried; and that he hath been raised on the third day . . .' (1 Cor. 15:3,4, R.V.). This meant that those who had 'fallen asleep in Jesus' would likewise be raised (1 Thess. 4:14) and if Paul failed to communicate this he would be a complete failure as a preacher (1 Cor. 15:14). But the preaching of the event was important because the Resurrection of Christ became effective through belief, that is, through dying and rising with Christ as a spiritual response to the preaching made concrete in baptism. Yet it was far more than a spiritual experience, the resurrection had changed the course of human history and a new creation had come into being (2 Cor. 5:17).

This emphasis on the Resurrection received special emphasis in Paul's preaching to the Gentiles. In this connection the First Epistle to the Thessalonians, perhaps the first of all the New Testament writings, supplies a summary of this (1 Thess. 1:9,10) '. . . you turned from idols, to be servants of the living and true God, and to wait expectantly for the appearance from heaven of his Son Jesus, whom he raised from the dead, Jesus our deliverer from the terrors of judgment to come' (N.E.B.). Stephen Neill lists eight points here:

   (i) The folly of idolatry.
   (ii) The nature of God.
   (iii) The necessity of 'conversion' ('you turned').
   (iv) The historic connection with Jesus of Nazareth.
   (v) The death of Jesus.
   (vi) The resurrection of Jesus.
   (vii) The eschatological expectation.
   (viii) The certainty of judgment from which the Church is exempt.

A comparison with Paul's sermon at Athens (Acts 17) reveals the same essential structure and acts as a confirmation of Paul's Gentile preaching. In this the resurrection played an *indispensable* part. In preaching to Jews and in the synagogues, Paul was able to build on a foundation of Law with a liberal use of Old Testament quotations in a way not possible among Gentiles.

The second marked feature of Paul's preaching was his emphasis on the Spirit. The new feature here was his presentation of the Spirit as

[15] Or 'of first importance', so Stephen Neill in *Jesus through Many Eyes* (Fortress Press, 1976 & Lutterworth Press), to whom I am indebted in this section on Paul.

the Spirit of *the risen Jesus*. He, the Spirit, makes the life and death of Jesus beneficial to believers *now* so that Christ becomes the believer's contemporary bringing about in him a transformation of character after Christ's likeness, a possibility open to every man. In this way Paul preached *the living Christ*, one to whom his hearers were able to respond because of the living Spirit, yet it was the same Jesus who had lived in Galilee and Judaea and about whom stories were circulating in the Christian congregations that were growing up.

The *third* strain in Paul's preaching was the theme of reconciliation. This is what God had in mind for mankind – reconciliation, first with God and secondly with fellow-men. Paul saw himself as God's ambassador in this ministry and his preaching was largely a pleading with his hearers to be reconciled to God (2 Cor. 5:20). And the basis of the plea was God's initiative. 'In Christ God was reconciling the world to himself' (2 Cor. 5:19, R.S.V. Marg.). As part of this ministry Paul preached justification by faith – a doctrine easy to misunderstand. But the meaning is not that God *acquits* the sinner (this is immoral), he *pardons* him. It is an act of grace on the part of the Sovereign Lord on whom no claims can be made, certainly not on the basis of merit. But gratitude follows pardon and the beginning of a new life, including works of goodness.

Paul preached Christ according to the tradition he received from the Church (1 Cor. 15:3) but he went beyond this. Christ, far from being an individual exalted to God's right hand who sends his Holy Spirit to continue his work, Paul preached Christ as a corporate person. That is to say, the risen, exalted Christ is more than an individual. Believers are said to be 'in Christ'. In fact Paul spoke more of believers being in Christ than of Christ being in believers. It is the Holy Spirit who is in believers, and it is the Holy Spirit who is the agent of the believers' incorporation into Christ. Not only did Christ's death and resurrection have a universal scope with a 'once for allness' and a continuing activity for all time, but Christ is the new society, even more, Christ is the One 'God chose to reconcile the whole universe to himself, making peace through the shedding of his blood upon the cross – to reconcile all things, whether on earth or in heaven, through him alone' (Col.1: 20, N.E.B.), indeed, 'the whole universe has been created through him and for him' (Col. 1:16, N.E.B.).[16] Paul therefore preached a Christ far beyond that of the primitive Church.

Paul felt himself forced to write *more particularly* about his own

[16] For a detailed study of this see C. F. D. Moule, *The Origin of Christology* (Cambridge University Press, 1977), Chapters 2 & 4.

preaching in his first Letter to the Corinthians (chapters 1-4) because preaching was actually being the partial cause of division within the Church. Apparently the root trouble was the dazzling oratory of Apollos and the Corinthians' innate love of anything showy. What Paul in his letter is at pains to say is that the importance of preaching— and he was second to none in this, for had he not been 'sent by Christ to preach the gospel' (1:17)—lay not in the preacher but in the thing preached *(kerygma)*. He indicates what the *form* of preaching should not be—'the word of wisdom', and in what its content should consist— 'the word of the cross'. The former is foolishness. The latter—God's wisdom. He makes considerable play with these, setting out sharp contrasts between the word of wisdom and the word of the Cross, between the debater and the preacher, between something abstract and something concrete, between something turned in on itself and something concentrated on an event, between a word which leads to perishing and a word which leads to salvation.

Here, then, in the first Corinthian letter something can be learned of the manner of Paul's own preaching—'I came before you weak, as I was then, nervous and shaking with fear' (1 Cor. 2:3, N.E.B.), and something of his method—'The word I spoke, the gospel I proclaimed, did not sway you with subtle arguments; it carried conviction by spiritual power' (v.4), and with it was a clear aim—'so that your faith might be built not upon human wisdom but upon the power of God' (v.5, N.E.B.). And the hidden wisdom of God which he proclaimed was discernible not by human wisdom but by the Spirit (v.10).

So in these chapters there are set out not only hints about Paul as the preacher but guidance about preaching in general, its content, its form, its medium (the Holy Spirit), and its reception, delineated against a background of contrast between wisdom and foolishness.

How far the distinctive preaching of Paul was received throughout the Apostolic Church is unclear. Probably other gospels of Christ, like that encountered by Paul in Galatia, which he roundly denounced as no gospel, were preached by lesser preachers than Paul, and the resulting congregations bore the marks of them.[17] Even within the New Testament there is evidence of the difficulty with which Paul's penetrating Christology was received and few signs of its direct influence. That his thought had to wait for four hundred years and then a millennium for interpreters is not perhaps surprising. Nevertheless the *kerygma* Paul proclaimed reached the high-water mark of the

[17] For a most thoroughgoing study of this subject see James D. G. Dunn, *Unity and Diversity in the New Testament* (London: S.C.M. Press, 1977).

proclamation of Christ by which all subsequent preaching can check its level. Such was the size of the contribution Paul made to the ministry of the word for the Church of all time.

The view has been held, on occasions widely, that Paul distorted the simple gospel of Jesus with theological complexities that did not belong, derived perhaps from current Graeco-Roman thought forms. This is to misunderstand the basic Church *kerygma*. It does not consist in simple teaching of Jesus about God. This is not the New Testament gospel. Nor has Paul inserted into an elementary Christology ideas which are alien to it. Paul's contribution was to develop what was already implicit in the mind of Jesus about himself.[18]

It is evident from the foregoing that preaching was a constituent part of the life of the primitive Church from the very outset and continued as such. Because the Spirit was active in the Church—and this is the theme of the book of the Acts of the Apostles—preaching was a normal part of its life. Its life derived from the Spirit. This was one of its marked differences from the Old Israel. There the Torah was that in which the life of the nation consisted, and preaching came in, in so far as it came in at all, in order to bring about restoration to Israel's true calling, which was to be the elect people of God, rooted and grounded in the law. Not so the Church. Not that this involves an absence of ordered and structural life with a distinctive cultus, but the life is in the Spirit and not in the structure or the requirements of that structure. Wherever therefore the structured and organised Church is alive, it must engage in preaching. It lives by the Spirit and it preaches by the Spirit. Without the Spirit and without preaching its organisation is dead.[19]

There can be no doubt what the message of the Church's preaching should be—the crucified and risen Jesus as Lord. To preach is to proclaim Christ. Preaching which does not proclaim Christ is not preaching in the understanding of the New Testament. Christless preaching does not carry with it the power of the Spirit by which not only the preacher preaches with effect, but the hearers hear in their own language. When Jesus as Lord is proclaimed the Spirit operates, making for communication and community.

It is also clear that the Spirit works with sovereign independence. Peter, the first Apostle in the organised Church, was a preacher, but so were Stephen and Philip, originally set apart by the Church for administrative work. The Church must accept the preachers which the

[18] See C. F. D. Moule, *The Origin of Christology*.
[19] The Spirit is far from being indifferent to administration Rom. 12:7.

Spirit provides, and the preachers must accept the sphere of operation which the Spirit offers, whether a crowd of pilgrims gathered in Jerusalem,[20] a solitary traveller on a desert road,[21] or a small congregation gathered in a room.[22] And even if a preacher is both learned in the scriptures and eloquent, he will not proclaim the way of the Lord effectively till he knows the Spirit's baptism, and not only John's.[23] The message of the book of the Acts of the Apostles is that preaching, intertwined with the life of the Church, is dependent on the Spirit who works as he will.

[20] Acts 2:5–14.
[21] Acts 8:29.
[22] Acts 10:33–48.
[23] Acts 18:24–28.

4

The word in the history of the Church

WE PASS NOW OUTSIDE THE BIBLICAL RECORDS TO OBSERVE LANDMARKS (not more) in the history of preaching, but not without a glance back at the preaching of the Apostles and of the Apostolic Church. Generally it was charismatic in the sense that it was a spontaneous outpouring of the Spirit and not an exercise in structured oratory. As such it was the successor to the early prophecy of ancient Israel, being in fact called 'prophecy'. Paul wrote to the Corinthians (1 Cor. 12:28), 'Within our community God has appointed, in the first place apostles, in the second place prophets, thirdly teachers . . .' (N.E.B.). So a high place in the order of priorities is given to prophecy. It stands second only to apostleship. Paul was careful, however, not least because he was writing to Corinthians, who were bewitched with oratory, to label prophecy as useless without love (1 Cor. 13:2) and as transitory (1 Cor. 13:8), but it edified the Church and was superior to the charismatic gift of speaking with tongues (1 Cor. 14).

In the ministry of the Word there appear to have been an order of priorities. First, apostles and prophets,[1] no doubt representing special ministries. Next (see Eph. 4:11), evangelists, representatives of whom might be Titus, Timothy, Tychicus and Epaphras, men who went about preaching and continuing the work of Paul, particularly necessary when Paul was in prison. Thirdly, pastors and teachers, presumably ministers who stayed with their own community and whose responsibility it was to shepherd the flock they taught. Thus the apostles, prophets and evangelists formed the travelling ministry while the pastors and teachers served the local Church.

The nature of the early Church was markedly charismatic. Eventually, however, prophecy died out because it became discredited.

---

[1] A. E. Garvie, *The Christian Preacher* (T. & T. Clark, 1920), p. 280 suggests that the apostles bear witness to the action (Word of God) in history, and prophets to his action in the contemporary.

Impostors began to appear, as warnings in the Didache[2] show. In the end prophecy lost all favour because of its association with Montanism[3] and also because it was seen as a danger to established order and doctrine. Probably prophecy had indeed become spurious, but the loss with its demise and rejection by the Church was the charismatic element in preaching. Preaching took the place of prophecy[4] but it degenerated into preaching *without a charismatic element,* all too readily becoming subordinate to Church order with a consequent loss of power. It became an office and a regular function of the Bishop. It comprised teaching and exhortation, the former consisting of mediating the tradition, exposition of the scripture and doctrine. But preaching there was and it is salutary to glance at an early picture of the place of preaching in worship as set out by Justin Martyr (circa A.D. 140). What we see is clearly liturgical preaching, preaching in a liturgical context.

On Sunday a meeting of all who live in the cities and villages is held, and a section from the Memoirs of the Apostles (the Gospels) and the writings of the Prophets (the Old Testament) is read, as long as the time permits. When the reader has finished, the President, in a discourse, gives an exhortation to the initiation of these noble things. After this we all rise in common prayer. At the close of the prayer, as we have before described (chapter 65), bread and wine with water are brought. The President offers prayers and thanks for them, according to the power given him and his congregation responds the Amen. Then the consecrated elements are distributed to each one, and partaken, and are carried by the deacons to the houses of the absent. The wealthy and the willing then give contributions according to their free will, and the collection is deposited with the President, who therewith supplies orphans and widows, poor and needy, prisoners and strangers, and takes care of all who are in want. We assemble in common on Sunday because this is the first day on which God created the world and the light, and because Jesus Christ our Saviour on the same day rose from the dead and appeared to his disciples.

When preaching passed from Jewish to Gentile soil it was forced to

[2] *The Teaching of the Lord through the Twelve Apostles.* Date, authorship and origin unknown. Possibly first century.

[3] An apocalyptic movement of the second century.

[4] The so-called *Second Epistle of Clement* represents the change from prophecy to preaching. It is the earliest surviving Christian sermon. For an analysis see *The Apostolic Fathers,* Lightfoot (London & Cambridge: Macmillan, 1869) 1–2 p. 173.

5

adopt new methods of presentation. In the synagogues an appeal to the Hebrew scriptures was effective but not in the market-places and lecture halls of the Greek cities. Furthermore in this environment[5] it encountered preaching of one kind or another as a widespread, even popular, activity. In general this popular preaching advocated a way of life raising questions of religion and morals. Among these preachers there were no doubt some serious-minded philosophers but also sophists whose trade it was to provide rhetorical contests for entertainment at local fairs and festivals, rather like jugglers or fortune-tellers. So although the Christian preachers found themselves with ready audiences, if they were to communicate their message, they were obliged to cast it in a form to which their audiences were accustomed. Thus the rules of Greek rhetoric came to exercise a profound influence on Christian preaching not always to its advantage. This change from one environment to another has its roots in the New Testament where Paul is reported as quitting the synagogue in Ephesus after a period of three months on account of the opposition and continuing for two years with daily discussions in the lecture hall of Tyrannus, apparently with considerable success as far as widespread promulgation of his message was concerned.[6] Writing to the Corinthians, however, he was at pains to distinguish his preaching from that of the sophists.[7]

Preaching as a rhetorical exercise, however, in spite of Paul's warnings, quickly gained a hold in the Eastern Church, indeed, it appears that neither Paul's gospel nor his method of proclamation exerted a widespread influence. Even within the New Testament it stands by itself. And yet throughout Christian history whenever there has been a revival of Christian life, the cause has almost always been a rediscovery of the Apostle Paul. In the third century, however, preaching was being moulded by Greek rhetoric as is evident from the writing ascribed to Hippolytus (died 235), called *In sanctam theophaniam*, and from Origen (185-253 or 4) in whose expositions of Scripture Alexandrine allegorical methods were employed, aiming among other things to show that the scripture contained a wisdom superior to the philosophy of the Greeks.

The victory of Christianity over paganism in the fourth century produced special problems for preaching. Large congregations crowded the churches, but the members were at best only half-Christian. They

[5] See S. Angus, *The Early History of Christianity* (Duckworth 1914) pp. 74-78.
[6] Acts 19:8-10.
[7] I Cor. 1:18; 2:10.

needed evangelising, teaching, and not infrequently, rebuking, no easy task for the preachers. Moreover, it was important that these congregations be held. To a people accustomed to oratory, the Christian preaching had to be attractive. It must compete with the sophists. Small wonder, therefore, that rhetoric was studied and applied, and that discourses, disputations and speeches took over. The preacher, most often a Church official, did not ascend the *ambo*, he sat in his chair of office, the hearers gathered around and applauded his skill. Not surprisingly, some preachers gave way to public display, even becoming itinerant preachers like sophists, earning money for their skills.

The Church was not unaware of these dangers and sought to safeguard its preaching by keeping it close to the scriptures and encouraging it in a liturgical setting. A fixed set of lessons called *Pericopes* was gradually introduced and the sermon was connected with these, though not bound to them. On Saints' Days there was a tendency to forsake expository preaching for topical preaching. Christological controversies also came to form the substance of sermons with less attention to matters of Christian living. This was especially true of the Eastern Church. The Western Church was less attracted to rhetoric, more interested in soteriology than Christology, and more concerned with Church order: in consequence its preaching was more evangelical and practical.

In the Eastern Church the three Trinitarian theologians, Basil of Caesarea (330–79), Gregory Nazianzen (330–90), and Gregory of Nyssa (335–95) were all noted preachers. Basil was the superior as a preacher exhibiting a purity of style, animation in delivery, tenderness and a knowledge of the world around him, whereas extravagance and artificiality marred the work of the other two. The greatest orator was John Chrysostom, 'the golden-mouthed' (374–407). Trained by Libanius in the rhetorical method he was nevertheless concerned to use his skill to nourish Christian devotion. He understood the importance of the introduction to a sermon, how to secure attention by means of observations of life, and how to enrich the production with pictures, epigrams and comparisons. Sometimes he overdid his contrasts of light and shade but he was always arresting. He did not pursue the allegorising fashion of Alexandria favoured by Gregory of Nyssa, but in his exegesis of scripture followed the straightforward Antiochan style. With the exception of Basil, and possibly to some extent Chrysostom, the Eastern Church failed to grasp the essentials of the Pauline message to the great detriment of its preaching.

In the Western Church Tertullian (c. 160–c. 225) could lay some claim to be a Pauline figure, and Leo the Great (d. 461) was a preacher of ability, but it was with Augustine of Hippo (354–429) that Paul's message really came alive and preaching reached one of the great landmarks in its history. Augustine's style was different from the Greek preachers. His imagery was simple but arresting. A master of antithesis and epigram, he combined them with wit and wisdom, rhyme and assonance. He understood how to employ variety in his methods to sustain attention. Some four hundred of his sermons have been preserved, arranged in four groups— de Scripturis, de tempore, de sanctis and de diversis.

Augustine's sermons set a standard for centuries in the Western Church, but the copying of them by preachers lacked originality and power. There was also a growing emphasis on pious works and ritual observances with less attention paid to the scriptures. So the homily fell into the background and was replaced by the topical discourse, and even the sermon itself came to have little importance attached to it.

Preaching gained some impetus where there was a missionary concern and sermons were delivered in the vernacular. The first notable example belongs to Irenaeus (c. 130–200), Bishop of Lyons, preaching to the Celts in his neighbourhood. St Rule (Regulus), too, seeking to convert the Picts near St Andrews in 369 had of necessity to adopt the same practice, and this was followed by St Ninian, St Polladius and St Patrick, but there are no records of this missionary preaching.

Most of the missionaries were monks, not least those who accompanied Augustine to England in 597 at the instigation of Gregory the Great of Rome. These missionaries were instructed to preach in the language of the people or at least to read something profitable for their hearers' souls. From this the Anglo-Saxon homilies originated. In addition to this missionary preaching there was preaching to the assemblies of monks or nuns by the bishop of the diocese, the abbot or a brother monk chosen for the task. These sermons were often delivered at meals and were sometimes called 'collations'. In this sphere the Venerable Bede (673–735) preached most of his sermons. These were in Latin, in homiletical form, commenting on some passage of scripture but sometimes relapsing into the allegorising fashionable at the time. In addition parochial preaching developed for the basic reason that the bishop who hitherto had been the chief executive of this work found the task impossible owing to the increase in size of the dioceses, and so delegated it to the parochial clergy. They were scarcely fit for this ministry with the result that the standard of preaching declined. Charlemagne, the great reformer of the Church in France and in Germany, took great pains to improve the education and character of the clergy, especially their capacity as preachers, as also did King Alfred in England (871–901).

Of preaching in the period 800–1200 we have little information, but the missions in Germany and the reformation movements in Western Christendom must have employed a ministry of the word. The labours of Lanfranc (d. 1089), Anselm (1033–1109), and the reforming work of Hildebrandt (1020–85) are a turning point. The Crusades brought contacts with the learning of the Saracens and a corresponding stimulus to match it. Preaching played a significant rôle in arousing support for the Crusades, and in this the greatest preacher of the twelfth century was Bernard of Clairvaux (1090–1153). Similar to St Augustine, though not his equal, he was often nearer to the heart of the gospel and passionately devoted to Jesus in his earthly humiliation. There are 125 sermons of his on various subjects, most notable are those on the Song of Songs and his Advent sermons. They reflect the living piety of the Middle Ages in contrast to the ecclesiastical ritual and intellectualism. They are more than comments on scripture, they display some understanding of structure, and are presented in oratorical language. Bernard's name must be included among the great names in the history of preaching.

The event of greatest significance in this period was the rise of the mendicant orders of the friars. In them the power of preaching was demonstrated to an extraordinary degree. St Francis of Assisi (1182–1226) although offered churches in which to preach, preferred the open air, and tempered his style to his simple surroundings. He called men to follow Christ after the fashion in which he followed himself. The second order, that of St Dominic (b. 1170–?), also laid great stress on preaching. It was an age of the growth of heretics, united only in their opposition to Rome. Dominic, himself a powerful preacher, encouraged preaching as a means of strengthening orthodoxy and refuting heresy. The members of the Order he founded were expected to be learned theologians and popular preachers. The two most outstanding preachers of the period were Franciscans— Anthony of Padua (1195–1231), and Berthold of Regensburg (Ratisbon in Bavaria, c. 1220–1272). The Franciscan Order did not only aim at producing popular preachers, it paid attention to the theory and practice of preaching as is evidenced by Bonaventura's book, *The Art of Preaching*. So also did the Dominican Order. Its General, Hubert de Romanis, wrote a book entitled, *De Eruditione Praedicatorum*. Preaching also received an outstanding practitioner in Thomas Aquinas (1225–74). Much of his preaching was addressed to the intellect rather than to the heart or conscience, and lacked imagination, but he was able to use homely and lively comparisons, employing short sentences and an overall clarity of expression. Over against the scholasticism of Aquinas was the mystical preaching of Bonaventura (1221–74), and later, the first of a line of the speculative and mystical preachers, namely, Meister Eckhart (d. 1327). What appealed was the 'inwardness' as distinct from the external and mechanical religion of the Church of the period in general.

This new stirring of life represented by mysticism blossomed in four preachers of distinction, John Wyclif (1369–1415), John Huss (1369–1415), Savonarola (1452–98) and John Gerson (1363–1429). All were inspired by a spirit of reform at a time when preaching was being employed mainly to bolster up the Papacy, and encourage the sale of indulgencies. All drew largely upon the scriptures to inform their message. This was true even of John Gerson, the Chancellor of the University of Paris, still to some extent held fast by the scholastic and allegorising methods of the time.

We turn now to Luther and the German scene.

To over-estimate the significance of Luther (1483-1546) as a landmark in the history of preaching would be difficult. He towers above it. With him not only did the content and the style of preaching change, but with it and because of it the history of the whole Church, of the German people and even of Christendom. Luther cannot be estimated apart from his preaching, nor can the Reformation which he initiated. One result was that in Lutheran worship the sermon came to occupy a place of overriding importance, though not set over against the sacraments, nor divorced from the liturgy. A rediscovery of the Apostle Paul lay behind this change of direction and especially of the doctrine or justification by faith alone. This was the burden of Luther's preaching, and what he intended the common people to hear. He had no patience therefore with preaching as an 'art-form', his was a workmanlike approach. Eschewing all artificialities, he spoke in plain and homely words, with all the force of his powerful personality behind them, seeking to explain the scriptures and in doing so to exalt Christ. This latter gave him his principle of selection. Luther's was nothing if not scriptural and Christocentric preaching. For him a sermon was an instrument consisting of the *spoken* word. He did not write his sermons. That we possess many of them is due to the fact that his extempore utterances were 'taken down' and subsequently published. Holding strong views on preaching, as on almost everything else, he did not, however, present them in any systematic form[8] but they can be gathered from his 'Table Talk'. As was to be expected, preachers of less personality than Luther attempted to copy his style but the result was a lifeless rhetoric. A notable exception was Brenz of Wartenburg (1499–1570).

Unfortunately, the revival of preaching in this period coincided with fierce doctrinal controversy with the not unsurprising result that the pulpit was engaged to forward polemics. So spiritual power receded from the pulpit and nowhere so dramatically and swiftly as in Germany where the revival had begun.[9] Soon after Luther, doctrine replaced the Scriptures, abstract presentation in place of directness and concreteness, a parade of learning instead of a persuasion to faith. The homiletical instructions of Hyperius (1511–66) failed to gain a hold and sermons took an almost unbelievable artificiality. In short, the pulpit rapidly died and there were few, though there were some, exceptions. This aridness continued till the rise of the Pietistic Movement in the seventeenth century.

During the seventeenth century, Spener (1635–1705) and Francke (1663–1727) brought back life in a number of pulpits through the Pietistic Movement. There was an insistence on the vitality of faith, the new birth and consecrated life. Spener's preaching displayed no brilliance, poetry or passion, but won complete attention by its earnestness and the variety of his use of the scriptures. He wrote out his sermons in full and committed them to memory. He despised method, but in fact his sermons were complicated structures. Francke was not only a natural orator, but had much wider interests, being both a professor of Halle University and the minister of a town church. He was active in social welfare and in missionary enterprise. In spite of its strength however, this Pietism did not stem the tide of rationalism in Germany, it was too narrow and too subjective. Two notable exceptions, however, were Bengel (1687–1752) and Zinzendorf (1700–60).

Between the Pietistic Movement and the Rationalist was the learned and popular preacher, Mosheim (1693–1755). Without evangelistic or

---

[8] Two systematic treatises on preaching were published during Luther's lifetime, namely, Reuchlin's *De arte praedicandi* (1504) and Erasmus' *Ecclesiastes Concionator Evangelicus* (1534).

[9] Accounts of the German preachers can be read in John Ker, *Lectures on the History of Preaching* (Hodder and Stoughton, 1888), Chapters 9–20.

missionary purpose he saw preaching as leading to the edification of the congregation. He aimed at the cultural classes and produced a standard of eloquence equal to the great French preachers and with as little lasting influence. As a result, Rationalism or Illuminism (*Aufklä-rung*), whose object was to make everything, including Christianity, appear reasonable, quickly affected the pulpit. Bringing forced logic into it quickly killed it, till even the language became turgid and bombastic. In this desert there were exceptions, as always, and men like Spalding (1714–1804), Zollikofer (1730–88) and Reinhard (1753–1812) stand out, but their preaching, containing no evangelical fire, had little religious effect. The opposition between Pietism and Illuminism called for a reconciliation and this was found notably in Herder (1744–1803), but more important is Schleiermacher (1768–1834), who stands as a landmark. He combined piety and philosophy, culture and faith, and to a powerful personality were added the gifts of a speaker. In his preaching he gave the central position to Christ, the sinless Saviour and Mediator between God and man. In his view the source of the sermon is the religious feeling of the preacher stimulated and confirmed by the Bible. The subject must be Christian and the influence of Christ must be applied in manifold ways to life and duty. The purpose, however, is not conversion, but to confirm the faith of the congregation. He aimed at the stimulation of religious emotion by presenting the object of faith. He attached no importance to logical structures. The sermon must be a homily or conversation, a dialogue with scripture and the congregation. The style should not be poetic but elevated prose, moderate and modest in delivery. He preached extempore, after much meditation. In the steps of Schleiermacher there followed the 'Mediating School' which aimed at reconciliation of religion to science, faith and reason. Its most distinguished preacher was Tholuck (1799–1877).

In the Reform Movement preaching continued to hold a dominant place as in Lutheranism. Calvin (1509–1564) was himself a preacher of distinction and like Luther expounded the scriptures, but he did so more systematically. Regarding the Old and New Testament as equal sources of revelation, he employed typology (as distinct from allegorising) as an instrument to draw on both. He insisted that the power of God operates only in extempore preaching, but he spoke such perfect French that in spite of a lack of manuscript when his sermons were 'taken down' they appeared as literary masterpieces. Preaching of a high order developed in the Reformed Church in France during the seventeenth century employing classical modes of oratory for its style. Among these preachers Moses Amyrant (1596–1664) so impressed Richelieu and Mazarin that they looked with favour on the Protestants. He was surpassed by Jean D'Ailly (1595–1670), bitter controversialist though he was. Jean Claude (1619–1687) was respected even by Bossuet, the Roman Catholic court preacher. Among the exiles after the Edict of Nantes (1685) Dubose became famous (died in Rotterdam 1692), but perhaps the greatest of them all was Jacques Gaurin (1677–1730).

Brilliant, however, as was the preaching in the Reformed Church in France in the seventeenth century, it was overtaken by the preaching in the Roman Catholic Church, but only in court circles. This was the source of its strength and of its weakness. Because of the intelligence and culture of those to whom it was addressed, it was able to rise to unsurpassed heights as it combined the French language with classical models of oratory. Its weakness, however, lay in the fact that its hold on the hearers was largely an aesthetic one, though the nation's morals and manners were not entirely overlooked, and in the sermons were passages of rare spiritual quality. The great names are Fénelon (1651–1715), the most attractive as a man, if less oratorical in style than others. The summit of eloquence was reached in Bossuet (1627–1704), Bourdoloue (1632–1704) and Massillon (1663–1762). This impressive attention to the art of preaching had repercussions, if not in national religious life, certainly in pulpits generally. Reformed pulpits in France overtaken by Roman Catholic pulpits attempted to win back what they had initiated, with the result that the preaching, for all its oratory, came to lack spiritual power. Even pulpits in Germany strove to rise above the dullness of the period.

In England the age of preaching dates from the coming of the friars in 1224. Charles Smyth[10] points out how they met and stimulated a growing demand for sermons, revolutionising the technique of preaching and magnifying the office of the preacher. The two outstanding features of their preaching were 'schematisation' and the use of *exempla*. Up to the time of the friars sermons consisted of a spiritual and moral exhortation taken from the gospel for the day. This was replaced by the *schema*, a sermon structure devised in the Universities. The *exempla*, i.e. anecdotes and illustrations, were accommodated to the love of tales and wonders so characteristic of the Middle Ages and flourished in the thirteenth and fourteenth centuries. Collections were made for use in the pulpit. Latimer (1485–1555) was the last Anglican preacher to use *exempla* on an extensive scale.

[10] *The Art of Preaching* (London: S.P.C.K., 1953) p. 17.

In the sixteenth century preaching[11] was deeply affected both by the Reformation and the Renaissance. Cranmer's preaching[12] (1489–1556) was crystal clear, seeking to present Christ as Saviour, even if rather in the style of a lecture on doctrine. There was much apt scriptural quotation and references to the Fathers, but no affectation and no parade of learning. This could not be said of what were called the metaphysical preachers. Their sermons were overcrowded with Latin quotations, affected wit and rhetoric, obscuring the meaning of the text. Lancelot Andrewes (1555–1622) was the supreme example of what was called 'witty' preaching. It was ornate, punning, full of learned allusions and ingenious figures of speech called 'conceits'. His Passion sermon on Good Friday (1604) shows him at his best. John Donne[13] (1572–1631) has left one hundred and sixty sermons able to stand beside some of the finest English literature. They are learned, sensitive and orthodox. This metaphysical preaching was however scarcely suited to parochial use. Good pastoral preaching, nevertheless was carried out, Bernard Gilpin (1517–83)[14] being an example. The kind of situation uppermost in people's minds at the time is reflected in a sermon by Roger Edgeworth[15] of whom little is known except that he died in 1560. He has a word-picture of children playing with images from the dissolution of the monasteries and of the friar's houses. Obviously the Reformation was the worry, and many sermons were preached on it but with caution.

The Puritan preachers[16] had no use for the artificialities of the metaphysical preachers. They believed in a directness of speech with the aim, not of producing a literary masterpiece, but of saving men's souls. Famous among these were William Bourne of Manchester (early seventeenth century), Laurence Chaderton (1530–1640), Thomas William Perkins (d. 1602), and Thomas Goodwin (1600–1671). If their preaching was solemn and dull, it was nevertheless scriptural and convincing by reason of its directness. These attributes were absorbed with advantage by preachers who were not Puritans, notably Joseph Hall[17] (1574–1656), Henry Smith[18] (1550–91), called

[11] See J. W. Blench, *Preaching in the late 15th and 16th Centuries* (Blackwell, 1964).
[12] See Martin Seymour-Smith, *The English Sermon* Vol. 1 (Unwin, 1976).
[13] See Pearsall Smith, *Donne's Sermons, Selected Passages* (Oxford, 1919) and Mueller, *John Donne: Preacher* (Princetown University Press, 1862).
[14] See Martin Seymour-Smith, *The English Sermon* (Unwin, 1976) Vol. 1, pp. 92ff.
[15] See Ibid p. 5ff.
[16] See John Brown, *Puritan Preaching in England* (Hodder and Stoughton, 1900).
[17] Bishop of Exeter 1627, translated to Norwich 1641.
[18] He was lecturer at St Clement Danes' Church, London from 1587.

'silver-tongued Smith, and the prime preacher of the nation', Thomas Adams[19] (d. 1630), and surprisingly enough, to some extent even Tillotson.

Tillotson[20] caused a virtual revolution in English preaching. He broke, not only with the metaphysical, but also with the Puritan tradition. Tillotson did not preach homilies of any kind, liven his sermons with *exempla*, nor repeat over and over again the pious phrases so regularly mouthed by the Puritans. His was a solid appeal to reason, arguing his case for religion without haste and without adornment. There was no emotion, no appeal and no heroism. The sermon under Tillotson's influence—and it was widespread—became a moral essay. So revelation gave way to reason in the pulpit though not without protest from Edmund Gibson, Bishop of London (1669–1748) and Archbishop Secker (1693–1768).[21]

In the seventeenth century there were three styles (or forms) of preaching:

(1) The sermon written out and memorised (*memoriter*).
(2) The sermon preached from (full) notes.
(3) The read text.

No. 1 was favoured by the Nonconformists because it

(a) spoke direct to the heart
(b) was carefully prepared

No. 2 was criticised by the Nonconformists as being ill-prepared.

No. 3 was criticised by the Nonconformists as being more like an essay addressed to the mind, rather than a call to the heart.

In the latter half of the seventeenth century extempore preaching became the fashion and the written sermon fell into desuetude. This was partly due to the fact that after 1640 exiles returned from abroad where they had grown accustomed to the French method of extempore preaching. Moreover, elaborate and learned discourses were not to the liking of Charles II. In 1674 the Duke of Monmouth, as Chancellor of the University of Cambridge censured 'in the king's name' the use of MSS in the pulpit, a course which was also followed by Oxford. Tillotson, however, the most celebrated preacher of the period, continued to read his sermons, due perhaps to his upbringing among the

[19] Called 'The Prose Shakespeare of the Puritans' by Robert Southey.
[20] See C. Smyth, *The Art of Preaching*.
[21] See W. F. Mitchell, *English Pulpit Oratory* (S.P.C.K., 1932).

Puritans. Note-taking of sermons was much encouraged in the seventeenth century as an instrument of education for the young.

Reactions followed in the Evangelical preaching of the eighteenth century, of which the two most outstanding examples were Whitefield (1714–70) and John Wesley (1703–91).[22] It reacted against the intellectualism of the Latitudinarians as represented by Tillotson's preaching, and washed away the last traces of affectation and artificiality that had marked the sixteenth and seventeenth centuries. Its aim was to redeem lost mankind and concentrated wholly on preaching Christ as the Saviour from sin and destruction by means of the Cross. It ran the risk of antinomianism and gave insufficient attention to the duties of living. In the light of the work of the Clapham Sect it cannot be complained as is sometimes done, that it was wholly neglectful of the social reference of the gospel. The preaching both in its Anglican and Methodist form tended to be severe. Only rarely did Whitefield use *exempla* and Wesley even less. Charles Simeon (1759–1836)[23] was the first since the Middle Ages to attempt to *teach* preaching. According to Charles Smyth he was inspired to do so by Robert Robinson's translation of *Traité de la Composition d'un Sermon* by Jean Claude (1618–87), minister of the French Reformed Church at Charenton. True to the evangelical school to which he belonged, Simeon exhorted his preachers not to give way to metaphor and figures of speech. An exception was the Reverend Richard Cecil (1748–1810), a minister of St John's Chapel, Bedford Row, London.

The Tractarian Movement did not give preaching the place the Evangelicals gave it, being concerned for the restoration of the Catholicity of the Church which it saw as gravely threatened. It should not be forgotten, however, that this Movement stepped up on the public stage by means of a sermon, the *Assize Sermon*, preached by Keble in Oxford on July 14th 1833, using the text 1 Samuel 12:23. The background of the sermon was the suppression of ten Irish biographies by the Government. In the preacher's eyes this action in the ecclesiastical sphere was national apostasy, not the dozen or more social abuses of the day. The crying need was for the Church to be the Church. The

[22] Much of the social improvement that took place in Britain in the second half of the eighteenth century owed its inspiration in some way to the changes in public opinion produced by John Wesley's preaching.

[23] See C. Smyth, *The Art of Preaching*, p. 174ff. Simeon was Vicar of Holy Trinity Church, Cambridge. See H. E. Hopkins, *Charles Simeon of Cambridge* (Hodder and Stoughton, 1977); C. Smyth, *Simeon & Church Order* (O.U.P., 1940); A. Pollard & M. Hennell, *Charles Simeon* (S.P.C.K., 1959).

remarkable fact is—or it may not be remarkable—that from this concentration on a spiritual issue grew a movement destined to contribute much, not only to worship and theology but to Christian social concern.

Froude (1803–36), preached as did all the Tractarians, but in his *Essay on Rationalism* he described the effect of preaching as subjective, depending on the merit of the sermon in question while the sacraments have an objective efficiency *because* they are the sacraments. 'To set up sermons as a means of grace to the disparagement of Sacraments is to judge by experience and not by faith and thus "a lower mode of Rationalism". Those who regard preaching as the essence of the service are not making a mere theological mistake, they are putting man in the centre of the worship. In a Protestant Church the parson seems either to be preaching the prayers or worshipping the congregation.'[24] Froude's preaching was reasoned, unfanciful, clear and Church-centred.

Pusey (1800–82) lacked the graces of oratory, but compelled attention by his seriousness. Sara Coleridge wrote: 'He is as still as a statue all the time he is uttering it, looks as white as a sheet and is as monotonous in delivery as possible. While listening to him you do not seem to see or hear a preacher, but to have visible before you a most earnest and devout spirit, striving to carry out in this world a high religious theory.'

Wiseman (1802–65), Keble (1792–1866), Manning (1808–92), Wilberforce (1805–73), and Newman, all prepared sermons that were very serious, solid and scriptural, without *exempla* and without being 'earthed' in the hearers' lives. They do not reveal the times in which they preached but rather the thoughts and aims of the preachers. They *used* preaching to further their different aims *for the Church*.

Among them Newman was the most impressive. A Presbyterian wrote of Newman in his Anglican days:

Each separate sentence, or at least each short paragraph was spoken rapidly, but with fresh clearness of intonation, and then, at its close, there was a pause lasting for nearly half a minute; and then another rapidly and clearly spoken sentence, followed by another pause . . . The most remarkable thing about the service was the beauty, the silver intonation of Mr Newman's voice as he read the lessons . . .

[24] From J. H. Newman and John Keble (eds.), *Remains of the late Reverend Richard Hurrell Froude*, Vol. I, 1838, p. 365 cited in Robert Nye, *The English Sermon* Vol. III, (Unwin 1976) p. 141.

The tone of the voice in which his sermons were spoken, once you grew accustomed to it, sounded like a fine strain of unearthly music . . .[25]

Matthew Arnold wrote:

Who could resist the charm of that spiritual apparition, gliding in the dim afternoon through the aisles of St Mary's, rising into the pulpit, and then in the most entrancing of voices breaking the silence with words and thoughts which were a religious music—subtle, sweet, mournful. Happy the man who in that susceptible season of youth hears such voices. They are a possession to him for ever.[26]

In the nineteenth century the Evangelical preachers and the Anglo-Catholic preachers continued to pursue their different styles and aims, but to the ranks of distinguished preachers were those whose concern it was to bridge the gap for ever widening between the traditional Christian faith and the new knowledge which was steadily gaining ground, as a result of the work of pioneers like Darwin and Freud. Famous among these was Liddon (1829–90),[27] Henry Ward Beecher (1813–87),[28] Archbishop Magee (1821–91),[29] Alexander MacLaren (1826–1910),[30] Dale (1829–95),[31] and F. W. Robertson (1816–53),[32] who stands by himself for excellence as a preacher. For popularity as a preacher probably the prize must be given to Spurgeon (1834–92).[33] Such was the interest in sermons in the Victorian era that Spurgeon's Sunday morning sermons appeared in Monday's newspaper in the United States and even in Australia.

One of the great omissions of the Church of England up to the middle of the nineteenth century was any condemnation from its pulpits of the iniquities of the structure of society which allowed extremes of wealth and poverty to co-exist.[34] The French Revolution

[25] J. C. Sharp, *Studies in Poetry and Philosophy*, 2nd Edition, 1872, pp. 247, 249. From R. Nye, *The English Sermon* Vol. III (Unwin, 1976).

[26] From R. Nye, *The English Sermon* Vol. III, p. 287.

[27] Appointed Canon of St Paul's Cathedral, London, in 1870.

[28] Pastor of the Plymouth Church, Brooklyn, U.S.A., from 1847.

[29] Successively Bishop of Peterborough and Archbishop of York.

[30] Minister of Union Chapel Manchester, 1858–1903.

[31] From 1853 Pastor of Carr's Lane (Congregational) Chapel, Birmingham.

[32] From 1847 Minister of Trinity Chapel, Brighton.

[33] Minister of the Metropolitan Tabernacle (Baptist), London.

[34] For an account of this aspect of Anglican post-Reformation preaching in England see Paul A. Welsby, *Sermons & Society* (Penguin Books, 1970).

had the effect in England of intensifying fear of any reformation of the *status quo* lest complete breakdown ensue. Not surprisingly then the Chartists in the 1830s and 40s saw little hope of support for their cause from the Established Church. This does not mean that charitable relief was not carried out, nor that iniquity at all levels of society went unrebuked. On the contrary, sterling work was done not least in the realm of education and the provision of hospitals. The class structure however was not only accepted but defended.

In the 1840s a significant change came about, a group of 'Christian Socialists' came into being. With this movement two famous preachers were connected, F. D. Maurice and Charles Kingsley. It was in 1851 that Charles Kingsley preached his famous sermon on 'The Message of the Church to the Labouring Man' and for which he was forbidden for some time to preach by the Bishop of London. In 1889 the Christian Social Union was founded. Among its founder members were Henry Scott Holland, a Canon of St Paul's, B. F. Westcott, E. S. Talbot and Charles Gore. Their aim was to apply 'the moral truths and principles of Christianity to the social and economic difficulties of the present time'. Among other activities they organised courses of sermons in London for business men. Gradually the Church began to shake itself free from its three-hundred-year-old attitude to 'the system' till in 1941 there came the Malvern Conference presided over by William Temple, the most significant Church gathering ever to consider whether or not the structure of society should give way to something different in order that the evident ills of low wages, malnutrition, unemployment and lack of educational opportunity be tackled.

The twentieth century began with its pulpits most notable for the variety of its preachers.[35] The First World War produced Studdert-Kennedy, the war-time padre whose gift it was to interpret the mind of the common soldier, and to deliver the Church's gospel in words he could understand. The post-war period saw the rise to fame of the pulpit at St Martin-in-the-Fields through the ministry of 'Dick' Sheppard (1880–1937). To a lesser extent W. H. Elliot at St Michael's, Chester Square, became a national figure. These were popular preachers whose fame reached the ends of the earth because they had mastered the new art of the broadcast sermon. Leslie Weatherhead at the City Temple, London, attracted large congregations partly by using

[35] See H. Davies, *Varieties of English Preaching 1900–1960* (S.C.M. Press, 1963). He distinguishes four main groups: Apologetic, Expository, Devotional, and Ethical or Moral.

psychology, a fashionable interest as a tool for interpreting the gospel rather than as a weapon to destroy it, and by the magnetic influence of his own personality. Campbell Morgan at Buckingham Gate Congregational Church, London, was famous as a Biblical expositor in the conservative tradition. Dean Inge at St Paul's Cathedral, London, could be relied on to impress with his fearless and penetrating analysis of the contemporary scene and with his striking epigrams. Bishop Hensley Henson of Durham expressed his passion for truth in matchless prose; and Archbishop Temple won hearers by the sheer force of his intellectual presentation of a social and evangelical gospel combined. W. E. Sangster at the Central Hall, Westminster (Methodist), drove home his Biblically based message with a rare talent for illustration and force of delivery. Together with Leslie Weatherhead at the City Temple and Donald Soper at the Central Hall, Kingsway, each one of them very different from the other, London in the 1930s offered the choice of three outstanding Methodist preachers. Donald Soper, besides being a fiery advocate of Socialism, was notable for his open-air preaching at Tower Hill, a ministry he continued even after retirement (becoming a member of the House of Lords). James Stewart of Morningside Church, Edinburgh, charmed his hearers with his expository preaching.

After the Second World War preaching began to suffer a decline, though men like Tillich and Niebuhr in the United States appealed to intellectuals. The pulpit of Great St Mary's, Cambridge, built up by Mervyn Stockwood's preaching of a social gospel attracted large congregations of students, backed up by a variety of preachers, not all ordained ministers or clergy. It was an age characterised by weariness with any form of monotony, oratory or paternalism. Public speech had to be conversational. In this situation dialogue preaching was looked to as the appropriate new style. It 'caught on', not least in Germany, but by the mid-1970s was on the wane. Joseph McCulloch, Rector of St Mary-le-Bow, London, achieved a well-deserved fame with two pulpits occupied for a week-day lunch hour service by politicians and other notable public figures who were questioned by the Rector. In the 1960s there was a widespread feeling that the day of preaching was over, though two events[36] contributed to the pulpit holding its own, one was the place given to the ministry of the word

---

[36] A third event of an entirely different kind was constituted by the publication in 1960 by the Faith Press (London) of a volume of Austin Farrer's sermons called *Said or Sung*. This book (it was followed by others) acted like a breath of fresh air in a desert from an unexpected quarter.

in the new liturgies in the Church of England that were drawn up, especially those called Series II and III, the other the setting up of the 'College of Preachers' in 1960 with the aim of encouraging and stimulating preaching, a movement in the Anglican Church which met with considerable success. Star-preachers, however, were rare. Nevertheless a reputation was won by Archbishop Coggan,[37] a teacher-preacher notable for the directness and clarity of his expression; Bishop Cuthbert Bardsley,[38] a spiritual director in the pulpit with a powerful personality; John Stott,[39] a conservative expository preacher with a didactic style; Michael Stancliffe,[40] who developed literary and poetic gifts rare in the pulpit of the age; Colin Morris,[41] whose strength lay in his social concern, product of wide experience, coupled a gospel proclamation with attention to literary style; Harry Williams, a psychological preacher;[42] and Martyn Lloyd-Jones, a remarkable exponent of Calvinistic theology and Welsh eloquence.[43] Curiously enough, the Methodist Church, once famous for its preaching became peculiarly disenchanted with it, and the Roman Catholic Church, rarely enchanted with preaching, began to exhibit an enthusiasm for the ministry of the word—partly as a result of a rediscovery of the Bible—surpassing many a Protestant Church. There were several causes for the weakness of preaching in this period among which must be placed the growth of the parish Communion movement, which, in spite of the place carefully assigned to the ministry of the word in the Eucharist, nevertheless in practice seemed to provide little time for it, the underrating of the monologue as a serviceable educational tool partly based on confusion as to what is the nature and function of a sermon, and the general theological uncertainty of the age, fostering a crisis of authority on the part of the Christian ministry. This resulted into something resembling an escape from the pulpit into the counselling chamber, the discussion group and the clinic for the relief of social needs.

[37] Bishop of Bradford, 1956; Archbishop of York, 1961; Canterbury, 1974.
[38] Bishop of Croydon, 1947; Coventry 1956–1976.
[39] Rector of All Souls' Church, Langham Place, London, 1950–1975.
[40] Rector of St Margaret's, Westminster, 1957–69; Dean of Winchester, 1969.
[41] Superintendent of Wesley's Chapel, City Road, London in 1970, General Secretary of the Methodist Missionary Society from 1973.
[42] Dean of Chapel, Trinity College, Cambridge, 1958–69; House of the Resurrection, Mirfield 1969– .
[43] Succeeded Campbell Morgan at Buckingham Gate, London, in 1943.

6

Preaching has been a particularly influential factor in the development and history of the United States of America.[44] It operated as a powerful influence in the Calvinistic Churches of New England in the seventeenth century. Both before the Revolution of 1776 and after it, experienced a number of fresh impulses and reactions, oscillating in the main between two poles, a concern for the conversion of the individual to present and eternal salvation, and a concern for the social betterment of the community. Underneath both these differing concerns, however, there has always lain the urge to build that better life in America which its citizens felt they were free to build and could build, and which would prosper those who were willing to gird themselves to work for it. This optimism and self-reliance has operated as an important factor in shaping American preaching.

The following are some of the landmarks in this history.

In spite of the rigid and strenuous activity of the Right Wing Protestant Churches of New England in the seventeenth century, more likely because of it, piety and Church membership sadly declined and the compromise Covenant produced by the Synod of 1662 did nothing to improve the situation. Irreligion increased until Jonathan Edwards[45] arose by means of whose preaching the 'Great Awakening' took place in 1734. His message was one of justification by faith, the justice of God in the damnation of sinners, the excellency of Christ and the duty of pressing into the kingdom of God. Moving his hearers partly through fear he won a considerable following. This was the beginning of Revivalism in America, a method which he defended in four treatises. Running to extremes, especially of emotionalism, has always been the danger of Revivalism, and it quickly showed itself in a contemporary of Jonathan Edwards called Davenport. His sermons became completely chaotic and his hearers hopelessly unruly. For all its defeats, however, Revivalism produced a number of changes in preaching, not least in completely disrupting the Puritan method. It paid scant attention to style and abjured all manuscripts, notes and anything that savoured of a well-prepared oration. The sermon was judged by whether or not it led to conversion.

Opposition to Revivalism quickly developed and one form it took was the rise of Unitarianism. The first Church was opened in 1785.

[44] For a comprehensive survey see De Witte Holland, *Preaching in American History* (Abingdon Press, Nashville, N.Y., 1969) and Ralph G. Turnbull, *A History of Preaching* Vol. 3 (Baker Book House, Michigan, 1974) pp. 15-318.

[45] Ralph G. Turnbull, *Jonathan Edwards the Preacher* (Baker Book House, Michigan, 1958).

Unitarianism did not come about in the first place in America as a criticism of the doctrine of the Trinity. This was one of the reasons why its supporters were reluctant to use the same title as its counterpart in Europe with a different background. Unitarianism arose in America because of the innate conviction that man is potentially good as well as potentially evil, and is able, with the assistance of God, to overcome evil. Soon the necessity for God's assistance was soft-pedalled, and man's freedom became the overriding interest. Later still the doctrine of the Trinity was rejected and Christ was interpreted in an Arian sense. Unitarian preaching took the form of carefully structured orations which leaned heavily on human reason with scant attention to anything resembling emotion in the shape of metaphors, literary allusions or illustrations. Over against this Lyman Beecher (1775–1863),[46] one of the great American preachers, sought rather to impress his hearers than to argue out reasonable propositions (which is not to say there was no structure or cogency in his preaching).

At the beginning of the nineteenth century the great trek westwards began providing a new challenge and a new opportunity for Christian preaching. At this time it was reckoned that ninety per cent of the American people was unchurched. In the rugged life of the frontier the situation was met in the form of the 'Camp Meeting', a kind of social gathering and revivalist mission notorious for its vitality and crudity. In this period revivalistic preaching received a new impetus from C. G. Finney (1793–1875). His preaching was popular, and in it he sought for favourable verdicts like the lawyer he once was. His message was — men made right with God will make society right. He preached extempore and used homely illustrations. Lyman Beecher supported him but pleaded for moderation in revivalist methods, as did also Aschal Nettleton (1783–1844) and Edward Griffin (1770–1844), the greatest as an oratorical preacher in this group.

The Revivalist religion being propagated by preachers at a time when Americans were excited with the prospects opening up before them, and their new-won freedom, strengthened the sturdy individualism so characteristic of the nation. It also conditioned the soil out of which the humanitarian movements of the later part of the century grew. But as a method it was questioned, not least by Horace Bushnell (1802–76), another distinguished preacher. He rejected it because it dislocated normal pastoral work and its excessive emphasis on men's freedom to respond or reject the gospel overlooked the organic laws

---

[46] A series of lectures called the Lyman Beecher Lectures at Yale on preaching was founded to commemorate this giant of the American pulpit.

of life. His concern was to build up relationships between parents and children, so that the American people were nurtured into the Christian faith almost unconsciously. This he regarded as a more safe and sure way avoiding the lapses which Revivalism was never able to avoid. Bushnell's sermons were carefully constructed, written out in full, and read in the pulpit. The general effect on his preaching was to free theology from the stranglehold of rigid Calvinistic theology, but objections were raised against it because it smacked of naturalism. All in all, New Birth versus Nurture constituted the great divide in American religion during the first half of the nineteenth century. Both sides, however, were alike in their wish to build the American way of life after a Christian pattern, and both have survived in strength to this day, Revivalism in Billy Graham, and Christian Nurture in the social gospel.

Problems other than theological affected preaching. From 1830 onwards slavery in America began to be seriously questioned. It was taken up as a moral issue by Abraham Lincoln, and the pulpits of the New England State thundered against it and against their preachers in the South who supported it as an ordinance of God and part of the natural order. The problem reappeared in the middle of the twentieth century as the problem of race. In 1954 segregation in schools was forbidden as contrary to Civil Rights and the struggle began. Martin Luther King championed the cause of the Blacks and suffered martyrdom.[47] It was a struggle which has transformed the situation of the coloured population of America.

Another problem to be faced was of a different order. The period 1875 to 1915 saw a rise in American wealth and a slackening of interest in Church life. The attendant evils of industrialisation aroused a concern about social conditions, and in particular about the Christian message for economic conflicts. Gradually social reform became the subject of American preaching, and by 1915 the social gospel was the major influence in America. Not without protest, however, and one of the forms protest took was a proliferation of sects claiming to present a more 'spiritual' gospel. After the Second World War there was a further development towards a this-world concern in what may be described as the gospel of the secular associated with the names of Altizer, van Buren and Harvey Cox.[48] The latter saw preaching as

[47] A book of his sermons called *Strength to Love* was published by Hodder and Stoughton in 1964 and republished by Collins in the Fontana series in 1969.

[48] For a brief assessment of these writers see William Hordern, *New Directions in Theology Today* Vol. I (Lutterworth, 1968).

man's commentary on what God is doing on the stage of secular history.

The problems raised by evolution in the late half of the nineteenth century, by Modernism in the 1920s, and the response of Neo-Orthodoxy in the 1930s, were not peculiar to America, and they caused their stir chiefly in theological and Church ministerial circles. Nevertheless, the names of great preachers were connected with them.[49] The contribution to preaching from the Episcopal Church was small with the notable exceptions of Bishop Phillips Brooks (whose eight lectures on preaching delivered in 1877 are still available),[50] and of Dr Theodore Wedel, second Warden of the College of Preachers in Washington (dedicated 1929) and more recently of Bishop Terwilliger.

A large amount of preaching in America must be labelled 'popular' in that it confines itself to matters of Church, home and personal efficiency (Norman Vincent Peale is an example), avoiding intellectual problems and a deep involvement in external affairs. A reaction against preaching altogether exists, small but significant. Following the study of 'group dynamics' and other psychological researches emphasis is now being placed on small group discussion and counselling. This approach sees God's concern for people expressed not through the proclamation of his Word, but as persons reacting to the events of life. Yet orthodox Christian proclamation continues as an influence in Church life of which Dr David H. E. Read (1910–) of Madison Avenue Presbyterian Church must be considered an outstanding exponent.

No summary of American preaching would be complete without notice being given to 'Black-American preaching'. This has received attention in recent years through the publications of Professor Henry H. Mitchell.[51] His contention is that white European/American preaching fails to appeal to the whole man because it is too cerebral and this accounts for its decline. Afro-American preaching on the contrary relates to the hearers 'transconsciously', it speaks from the depths to the depths of the entire personality, it is 'gut-preaching'. Preaching for the black preacher is both celebration and proclamation, it is joyous, interpretative of experience, and keyed into folk culture and language.

---

[49] Henry Ward Beecher (1813–1887) preached a significant series of sermons in 1885 confirming Evolution.

[50] The fifth edition (1879) was republished by the S.P.C.K. in 1959.

[51] A Baptist Minister, Director of the Ecumenical Center for Black Church Studies in the Los Angeles area, and Lyman Beecher Lecturer at Yale in 1974. His publications include *Black Preaching* (New York: J. B. Lippincott, 1970) and *The Recovery of Preaching* (San Francisco: Harper and Row, 1977).

The black preacher is articulate for his people and they honour him for it. His method is largely that of the story-teller, the Bible story-teller, to which the hearers can respond emotionally and vocally. Identification with the people's deepest feelings is perhaps the secret of the black pulpit's strength. Dr Mitchell is of the opinion that such identification is necessary for the recovery of preaching generally. No doubt preachers of other races could learn from it even if they could not, because of difference of temperament, copy it.

We return to Europe. In Scotland preaching has continued with strength, stimulated not only by the preaching tradition in that country, but by the five Warrack Lectures delivered annually by some notable preachers on the subject of the ministry of the word. There are great names among many famous Scottish preachers such as Alexander Whyte[52] and G. H. Morrison,[53] and in the mid-twentieth century James Stewart[54] and William Barclay.[55] The two latter were University Professors in Theology and combined preaching with academic discipline. James Stewart is possessed of a rare magnetic charm in the pulpit, whereas William Barclay was more successful as a broadcaster and popular religious writer. A concern for social conditions more characteristic of the last quarter of the twentieth century than formerly in Scottish preaching appeared in the preaching of Murdoch Ewen MacDonald.[56]

In Germany the concentration on the sermon, characteristic of the Lutheran Church, has continued. The need to produce shorter and more popular sermons for week-day broadcasting has assisted to some extent in taking some of the heaviness out of German preaching.[57] There has also been a concerted attempt to reach the public outside the regular congregations of worshippers with sermons. These have appeared in paper-backs as 'Pocket-book sermons'.[58] In the 1960s dialogue preaching

[52] 1836–1921. He made his name as 'Whyte of Free St George's, Edinburgh'. His two volumes of *Bible Characters* republished by Oliphants (London) in 1952 are famous.

[53] 1866–1928. He accomplished a notable ministry of twenty-six years at the Wellington United Free (Prebsyterian) Church, Glasgow.

[54] Minister of North Morningside Church, Edinburgh and subsequently Professor of New Testament, New College, Edinburgh. See Bibliography.

[55] 1907–1977. Professor of Divinity and Biblical Criticism, University of Glasgow.

[56] Minister of St George's in the West, Edinburgh.

[57] Helmut Flender in *Bibeltext und Gegenwartsbezug in der Predigt* (Guterslob, 1971) is concerned to bring the Christian proclamation and reference to the contemporary world.

[58] *Taschenbuch Predigten* (Laetare Verlag, 1970). The sermons are the work of theologians and lay people of different generations and varied walks of life.

came to be valued as a way of giving freshness and participation by the laity to the German pulpit.[59] Up-to-date reflections on preaching have been published in a student book series,[60] and preparation classes of considerable size have been organised in parishes to assist the pastor with his sermon so that it is grounded in needs which they understand and can make explicit to him.[61] Various fresh approaches to the sermon have been published called 'Preaching Studies',[62] providing a relief from books of the old style such as *Homiletik* by Fendt.[63] As elsewhere the names of the well-known preachers, as distinct from those who speak and write about preaching, tend to belong to the older generation. It is for example, the preaching of F. G. E. Niemöller (1892–) and Karl Barth (1886–1968) that is on sale on records; and other famous names are Hans Lilje (1899–), Karl Friedrich Otto Dibelius (1880–1967), Rudolph Bultmann (1884–1976),[64] and Helmut Thielicke (1908–).[65] Since Vatican II the Roman Catholic Church in Germany has organised a series of conferences to encourage preaching, counting the ministry of the word as an activity in which God himself is at work, and not merely as an edifying exercise on the part of the Church.

In France preaching is not in the ascendant though Père Bro (O.P.) has attracted attention as the preacher of the annual Lent sermons at Notre Dame in Paris. In Protestant circles Brother Roger at Taizé has considerable influence as a preacher especially with young people; so too Max Thurian, a Lutheran.

In the Orthodox Church in France, a layman, Oliver Clement[66] is widely known for his preaching, as also Fr Boris Bobrinskoy[67] and Father Cyril Argenti.[68]

In the Orthodox Church in general although the sermon forms an

---

[59] Hans-Wolfgang Heidland has discussed this in *Das Verkündigungsgespräch* (Stuttgart, 1969).

[60] For example, Manfred Mezger—*Verkündigung heute* (Hamburg, 1964).

[61] See *Die Predigt Zwischen Text und Empirie* by Herbert Breit, Leonhardt Goppelt, Jürgen Roloff and Manfred Seitz (Stuttgart, 1969).

[62] *Predigtstudien zur Theorie und Praxis der Predigtarbeit* (Kreuz-Verlag, Stuttgart-Berlin, 1968).

[63] Revised by B. Klaus and republished (Berlin, 1970) Stuttgart, 1968.

[64] For a sample of his preaching see *Marburger Predigten* (Tübingen, 1956) E.T. *This World and the Beyond* (Lutterworth, 1960).

[65] For a sample of his work in English Translation see the Bibliography, page 240.

[66] A teacher at the Institute St Serge, Rue de Crimée, Paris 19.

[67] The Orthodox Cathedral, Rue Daru, Paris 17.

[68] In Marseilles.

integral part of Eucharistic worship, its importance has not been much appreciated. The ideal however is recognised that the sermon is not an expression of the priest's personal views on morality but the Word of God speaking through the words of the preacher. He must however pray urgently for the guidance of the Spirit both as he prepares and delivers his sermon. Many Orthodox prefer not to write out their sermons beforehand, or even to speak from the notes they have prepared so as to leave themselves more open to the action of the Spirit. In the words of a Russian priest, 'The creative process should itself be performed aloud in front of the people . . . One must keep in mind a precise theme divided according to its essential ideas. But the real creation must take place, not in the study, but in the actual sermon; otherwise one is burnt out during the preparation and offers one's listeners only cold ashes.'[69] No note on the Orthodox Church and preaching, however brief, would be complete without a reference to Anthony Bloom, Metropolitan of Sourozh, who has achieved a remarkable reputation in England as a spiritual guide through his sermons and retreat addresses.

[69] From Alexander Elchaninov, *The Diary of a Russian Priest* (1881–1934) (Faber & Faber, 1967) p. 220.

II
Theological

1

Word and Spirit

THE FOUNT OF ALL PREACHING IS THE HOLY SPIRIT. THERE CANNOT BE
a ministry of the word of God apart from the ministry of the Spirit of
God. Jesus did not begin his preaching ministry in Galilee until he was
endowed with the Spirit at the Jordan river. There was no preaching
until Pentecost on the part of the followers of Jesus, except on the
experimental mission where they were deployed as recorded in
Matthew chapter ten. And no mission, no preaching mission, was
allowed until the waiting period for the outpouring of the Holy Spirit
was over.[1] Preaching apart from the Spirit is unthinkable in the New
Testament. Without the Spirit the message would not be communicated, but with the Spirit men would hear it each in his own native
language.[2] This is because the Spirit is the medium of the real presence
of Christ within or between the members of the fellowship making
for communion and for communication. In the matter of the proclamation of Christ communion and communication belong together
through the Spirit.

What or Who is the Spirit?[3] How is the Spirit presented in the
Bible?—as the outreach of God. God (so to speak) approaching people
and touching them. Parallels to this are the angel of the Lord, the
finger or hand of God, the arm of the Lord and Wisdom. Both Wisdom
and Spirit express God's outreach and also his immanent presence.
God comes out, he enters in and he quickens. In the Book of Wisdom,
Spirit and Wisdom are almost identical.[4] From the idea of reaching out
and indwelling there follow notions of inspiring and possessing. The
Spirit of God takes possession of a man without, however, destroying

[1] Acts 1:4,5.
[2] Acts 2:8.
[3] I am indebted to Professor G. W. Lampe, Regius Professor of Divinity at Cambridge for some of the points in the first section of this chapter. For a full treatment see
his *God as Spirit* (Clarendon Press, 1977).
[4] Wisdom 1:4–6; 9:17.

his natural faculties, but rather enhancing them. In such an experience a man realises his freedom. Examples in the Old Testament are judges,[5] warriors,[6] artists[7] and prophets.[8] With the latter the work of the Spirit was unpredictable and spasmodic, but with the King the Spirit of God rested more permanently.[9]

All this is distinctively Hebraic, that is to say, the conception of the Spirit is expressed in personal terms. The Hellenistic view on the other hand embraces the Stoic idea of the Spirit producing a cosmos out of chaos.[10] Such is the presentation in the book of the Wisdom of Solomon.

In the New Testament it is the Old Testament conception of the Spirit which is portrayed. The outreach and indwelling of God reached a climax at the baptism of Jesus. It was then that the Spirit possessed him, and it was then that he knew his Sonship. Spirit-indwelling and Sonship are identical. Thereafter Jesus became not only like a prophet in whom the Spirit dwelt—in his case permanently and not spasmodically—but he was also the bearer of the Spirit. References to the Spirit in the Synoptic Gospels, are, however, rare, but this in fact may be evidence of a more faithful reporting of the historical Jesus than is sometimes allowed. He hid his unique possession of the Spirit as he hid his Messiahship.

In the New Testament as a whole the Spirit stands out as a distinguishing feature. It is the Spirit who witnesses to Christ and presents Christ to men and women, and men and women to Christ. The Spirit assures believers of their sonship, but not a sonship as in the experience of Jesus, but a sonship in *Christ*. And the witness of believers to Christ and their representation of him through the work of the Spirit makes for their sonship. And here the fourth gospel provides a special contribution in asserting that the Spirit renders the historical Jesus contemporary and understandable, more understandable than was ever possible for the people who actually lived with him.[11]

Paul taught that the indwelling Christ and the indwelling Spirit are interchangeable terms. Life in Christ and life in the Spirit are identical. It is the Spirit who presents Christ for man's inward life and conforms

[5] Judges 6:34.
[6] Judges 11:29.
[7] Exod. 31:2–6.
[8] I Sam. 19:20.
[9] I Sam. 16:13.
[10] Wisdom 1:7; 10:1–21.
[11] John 16:12–14.

it into the likeness of Christ. He also reproduces the character of Christ in the Church, especially love, the first 'fruit of the Spirit'.

So to the question (as it relates to our special interest), who or what is the Spirit? We can answer, the Spirit is God proclaiming Christ in the Christian mission; God making Christ real to the preacher so that he can assimilate his Word and communicate it; God attesting the Word to the hearers so that they can accept Jesus as Lord. All effective preaching then, is the work of the Spirit. The preacher by the Spirit understands Christ, mediates this understanding by words, which in time produces understanding of Christ on the part of the hearers in the congregation, but only because the Spirit is active there between the preacher and the hearer, making the current of communication. And the result of such preaching and hearing is the Spirit-filled Church.

The story of Pentecost then in the Acts of the Apostles is a picture of the Church embarking on its mission. It is taken hold of by the out-reaching God and equipped to proclaim Christ effectively, the symbolism of which is a tongue of fire for every one gathered in the Christian assembly. It is to be a mission prompted, pushed on, and even on one occasion at least, restricted by the Spirit of God.[12] It is a story punctuated with preaching because this is a prime part of the work of the Spirit, but not without healing also *and* nurture of the congregations.

We turn now to consider the relation of the Spirit to the word, or to use the appropriate technical phrases, the relation of RUACH to DABHAR.

Sometimes in the Old Testament, Spirit and word are interchangeable as is clear from a comparison of Numbers 23:5 (N.E.B.) – 'The Lord put words into Balaam's mouth and said . . .', with Numbers 24:3 (N.E.B.) – 'The spirit of God came upon him, and he uttered his oracle.' And in the story of the rejection of King Saul we read, 'Samuel answered, "I will not come back with you; you have rejected the word of the Lord and therefore the Lord has rejected you as king over Israel"' (1 Samuel 15:26). Then when the rejection is further described we read, 'The Spirit of the Lord had forsaken Saul' (1 Samuel 16:14).[13]

There is, however, a distinction between Spirit and word. Spirit is less specific than word. It represents God's all-pervading power in operation. God breathes out what is actually the breath of life, and not

[12] Acts 16:8.
[13] See also the parallel use of *dabhar* and *ruach* in Psalm 33:6 and Psalm 147:18 (R.V.).

only man becomes a living soul thereby, but the created order generally depends on it for existence, and when it fails, they fail. So Psalm 104:29, 30 (N.E.B.), 'When thou takest away their breath *(ruach)*, they fail . . . but when thou breathest into them, they recover; thou givest new life to the earth.' Spirit then is the divine life pulsating throughout the whole cosmos. It could almost be described as crude or naked power. *Ruach* caused the waters of the flood to subside,[14] dried up the sea-bed for the Hebrews,[15] and shattered the rocks on Mount Carmel.[16] It is also spiritual power without moral purpose.[17]

Word, however, is more precise.[18] It represents power canalised. *Dabhar* is like a funnel, it receives *ruach* and narrows it for particular purposes. In the Old Testament *ruach* is active in the lives of the Judges and the ninth-century prophets, but figures far less in the eighth-century 'writing' prophets. There the divine power, or in-breathing (inspiration), has been channelled into the word *(dabhar)* of the Lord which the prophet is bidden to utter. When, therefore, attention is drawn to the *person* of the prophet, as in the case of Elijah and Elisha, *ruach* is mentioned, but when attention is drawn to the *message* which the prophet proclaims, as with Amos and Hosea, then *dabhar* dominates the narrative. Thus Spirit can be said to be concerned chiefly with inspiration, and word with revelation. And when the Spirit is withdrawn the reference is to a general abandonment by God, and when rejection of the word is described, the reference is to some specific act of disobedience.[19]

The prophetic-preacher then in the Old Testament is one who has been called by God in an individual way, and who has accepted that call, and who has been equipped with the Spirit or power of God. One result of his experience, and that an important one, is new ability to see. Before he is a speaker he is a seer. He sees himself, he sees the hand or Spirit of God at work in contemporary events, he sees his own task in relation to those events, and he sees something of God's purpose for the future. Sometimes he sees by means of an external event,[20] sometimes by means of an inward vision.[21] So the coming of *ruach* provided

---

[14] Gen. 8:1.
[15] Exod. 14:21.
[16] 1 Kings 19:11.
[17] Jer. 5:13.
[18] J. Taylor, *The Go-Between God* (S.C.M. Press, 1972) p. 61.
[19] 1 Sam. 15:26.
[20] Jer. 1:11-13.
[21] Isa. 6:1.

the prophet with power and insight. Thus Micah confesses . . . 'I am full of power by the spirit of the Lord, and of judgment and of might, to declare unto Jacob his transgression and to his Israel his sin.'[22] What then the prophet sees becomes a revelation, indeed *the word* of God for the time, and this he feels compelled to declare. Prophetic preaching has very little reference either to a natural or acquired facility for utterance, a point emphasised in the case of Jeremiah,[23] nor has it in the first place a concern how, or even whether, people hear, the over-riding necessity is that the word of God shall be received by the prophet and passed on whether 'they listen or whether they refuse to listen'.[24] This is an entirely different emphasis in the matter of communication from that which obtains in the modern world where the concern is to extend the facilities by which people see, hear, and generally receive the message. Part of the reason for the change is the advances made in the fields of science and technology *without* a matching confidence in what life itself is about. Even in Church buildings the proliferation of public address systems has corresponded with a growing uncertainty as to what ought to be preached and whether preaching ought to be engaged in at all. If to assert that the Old Testament prophets were not concerned with audition would be an overstatement, it would not be incorrect to assert that their almost exclusive concern was with the word that had to be uttered. This is not surprising in the light of their understanding of words as effective instruments capable of changing the course of events.

Spirit takes possession of the prophet, without destroying his indi-viduality, but rather enhancing it, with the result that he has the power to see and hear the word which he is then bound to utter. In this way he becomes a channel both of the Spirit and of the word, that is to say, the Spirit and the word have entered into him. But he has also entered into the Spirit and the word. He has taken his place within the divine energy so that he himself becomes part of what God is doing and saying. The prophet is therefore a man set apart. He is one who has responded to a call to a new stance. Henceforth he occupies a place at the point where the eternal now impinges upon the sequence of con-temporary events. The prophet therefore in one sense *is* possessed, all that is represented by his experience of *ruach* refers to this, the Spirit working in his spirit, that is to say, the bond pervading his whole unconscious and subconscious, holding him together as a person; in

[22] Mic. 3:8. See also Isa. 48:16; Ezek. 2:2; 3:12; 11:1,5,24 (R.V.).
[23] Jer. 1:6.
[24] Ezek. 2:5 (N.E.B.).

another sense he is *not* possessed, and all that is represented by *dabhar* refers to this, the mind free to think, evaluate and shape the revelation which he has both seen and heard. It is no wonder the prophet was counted as a man of God, a person to be held in awe wielding a self-authenticating authority which was not his but God's.

It is in the light of such understandings as this of the Old Testament prophets that Jesus must be seen. When he was categorized[25] as a prophet (though more than a prophet), awesome authority would be implied; and when his authority was recognised,[26] his assignation to the category of prophet would be natural. The Synoptic Evangelists are careful to introduce Jesus as in the prophetic succession, and to make clear that before he preached 'he saw the heavens torn open[27] and the Spirit, like a dove, descending upon him.'[28] He was a seer. Possessed then by the Spirit and conscious of his unique Sonship he began (and not before), his ministry of the word,[29] *seeing* men in a new way and with new possibilities[30] and healing with a word.

The same pattern is repeated in the Acts of the Apostles. There is no ministry of the word until there is possession by the Spirit. With this there goes the ability to *see* people in a new light, and also the ability to heal them — with a word.[31] And here once again the emphasis is not on improving or enlarging the range of human vision and audition, but on the message, the *kerygma*. It is the word of God, the crucified and risen Christ, proclaimed in the power of the Spirit which will accomplish the saving work that God purposes. The Spirit is the interpreter operating within both speaker and hearer, and what is equally important — between them both.

Does the conclusion follow that no attention need be paid to rhetoric? Can the whole technique of delivery in preaching be ignored? As well might the question be asked, must there be no preparation of the *content* of preaching? But reliance on the Spirit is no substitute for human effort. The Spirit works through the preacher's consecrated labour both as regards sermon preparation and delivery. Everything

[25] Mark 8:28.
[26] Mark 1:22.
[27] Isa. 64:1.
[28] Mark 1:10 cf. Luke 4:1.
[29] Mark 1:14.
[30] Mark 1:16–20 (note the word 'see').
[31] Acts 3:1–10.

depends on where reliance is finally placed; on the Spirit and the word? Or on the expertise of the preacher? The former does not cancel out the need for the latter, but the latter alone can block out the working power of the former.

2

The word of God

UNLESS THERE IS A WORD OF GOD THERE CAN ONLY BE PREACHING OF
the word of man. The word of man is not to be despised. It is capable
of rising to supreme heights, none greater than in philosophy. It can
be stimulating, not only academically, but practically, and buoyant,
not only intellectually but morally and even spiritually. What is more,
there have been martyrs among those who have preached it, justifiably
inspiring a following. Least of all ought Biblical theologians to underrate the preaching of the word of man, for is not man made in the
image of God? Which being so, how can logic allow the Barthian
position which consists in denying any ability on the part of man as
man to know God and to speak of him? We assert therefore that the
word of man is worth preaching, not omitting his word about God,
but we are bound at the same time vigorously to make the faith
assertion that there is a word of God to be preached, and this is what
the Church is peculiarly called to undertake.

What is this word of God? Tillich lists six different meanings.[1]
'There is the principle of the divine self-manifestation in the ground
of being itself. The ground of being is not only an abyss in which
every form disappears. It is also the source from which every form
emerges . . . it has *logos* character. *Secondly*, the Word is the medium
of creation; that is to say, a spiritual force, and not a mechanical operation; it brings out from the silent mystery of the abyss the rich variety
of developing and developed forms. *Thirdly*, there is all that which
can only be described as the product of inspiration. It does not arise
from the human reason, it enters from outside it, yet it is not irrational,
it is not *a-logos*, it proceeds from the non-human *logos*. This too
can be called the Word of God. *Fourthly*, the Word of God is the manifestation of the *logos*, the divine life, in Jesus as the Christ. The reference
here is not the sum total of the words of Jesus, but to the being of Christ
himself of which the words are an expression, implying an acceptance

[1] *Systematic Theology* (Nisbet, Combined Vol. 1968), Vol. I, pp. 175, 176.

of the doctrine of the Incarnation. *Fifthly,* the Bible is the Word of
God in the sense that it is the book, or collection of books by means of
which the knowledge of the ultimate revelation of God in Christ is
conveyed, and which also partakes of that revelation. *Sixthly,* the
word of God is that message which the Church is singled out to
preach, but which is only the word of God in so far as it has divine
manifestation within it, otherwise it is the word of man, even though
about God.'

The preaching then which the Church is called to undertake is the
proclamation of the word of God in the power of the Spirit. So to
define preaching is both to narrow it and to broaden it. It narrows it
by limiting its content to the word of God as opposed to the word of
man; it broadens it when it recognises that word to be encountered
not only in the historical Jesus as the Christ, but in the corporate and
cosmic Christ (as presented by Paul),[2] and also 'in the fragmentary
and varied fashion' in which God has spoken apart from the historical
revelation in his Son.[3]

The preaching to which the Church is committed is rooted in Jesus
as the Christ. His Person and his work is the point where it begins and
with which it must never lose contact. It is the point at which it began
historically.[4] To preach, as the New Testament understands preaching,
is to proclaim Christ and to do this is to preach the Word.[5] Not only
was this true of the pre-Pauline Church which Luke described but
even more so of Paul's ministry. In a strong defence of the gospel
which he preached, in writing to the Galatians, he roundly declared
that he had been set apart from birth in order that he might proclaim
God's Son among the Gentiles.[6] In point of fact he began his preaching
ministry among the Jews,[7] but the aim was always the same, it was to
proclaim Christ, and proclaiming Christ was the ministry of the Word
of God[8] or the gospel of God,[9] or the gospel of Christ.[10]

To preach the Word, however, that is, to proclaim Christ, is not

[2] Col. 1:15–17, cf Eph. 1:10. And see C. F. D. Moule, *The Origin of Christology*,
pp. 47–96.
[3] Heb. 1:1.
[4] Acts 2:14–36.
[5] Acts 8:4,5 (R.V.).
[6] Gal. 1:15,16.
[7] Acts 9:22, cf 17:2,3.
[8] 2 Cor. 2:17; 4:2; Phil. 1:14.
[9] 2 Cor. 11:7; 1 Thess. 2:8,9.
[10] Rom. 1:16; 1 Cor. 9:12; 2 Cor. 2:12; 9:13; 10:14.

according to the New Testament only to provide information about what Christ is or has done. It is to introduce into a situation something which is dynamic. Having life in itself it can both increase and it can transmit life. Of the history of the early Jerusalem Church Luke wrote, 'and the Word of God *increased*,'[11] and to the elders of the Ephesian Church summoned to Miletus Paul said, the Word is 'able to build you up'.[12] To the Thessalonians he described it as a *working* word. 'When we handed on God's message, you received it, not as the word of men, but as what it truly is, the very word of God at work in you who hold the faith.'[13] According to Paul, therefore, when Christ is preached the action is not to be interpreted in terms of explaining or implanting an explanation of the ministry of Christ in the hearers' minds. Preaching is much more than an educative exercise. It is speaking so that in and through the words of the proclamation Christ himself is *made present* together with the redemptive power of his resurrection.[14] The word of life[15] communicates life, and the work of reconciliation actually reconciles men with God.[16] Preaching handles a working, an effective, a creative word. Preaching has to do with the real presence of Christ in the congregation of the faithful at work for their welfare. Writing to the Corinthians Paul designated preaching as the power (Greek *dunamis*), of God.[17] Preaching (in the New Testament understanding of that word) is God's effective instrument for man's salvation entrusted to his chosen servants. Preaching is the action by means of which the ministry of the Christ is prolonged as Paul understood it.[18] Christ acted in and through his preaching. Since he, Paul, was 'in Christ' his preaching was 'in Christ', and Christ was in his preaching. So in function, he, the preacher and Christ were united. Therefore he could say that he spoke to the Gentiles that they might be saved,[19] and that he became all things to all men so that in one way or another '*I may save some*'[20] and that when he spoke the

[11] Acts 6:7. See also 12:24; 19:20; Note the imperfect tenses. The Greek could be translated 'Was growing'. It is used of plants in Matt. 6:28, Luke 12:27; 13:19; and of infants in Luke 1:80; 2:40.

[12] Acts 20:32.

[13] 1 Thess. 2:13, cf 2 Thess. 3:1; Phil. 3:12; Gal. 5:7; 1 Cor. 9:24,25; 1 Thess. 1:6.

[14] 1 Cor. 15:45.

[15] Phil. 2:16.

[16] 2 Cor. 5:19.

[17] 1 Cor. 1:18.

[18] See Jerome Murphy O'Connor, o.p. *Paul on Preaching* (Sheen and Ward, 1964).

[19] 1 Thess. 2:16.

[20] 1 Cor. 9:22.

Word of God it was *'as of God'*.[21] Viewed in this way the words of the preacher are never 'mere words', they are integral to God's redemptive purposes for mankind.

This dynamic understanding of the word is in line with the Hebrew understanding of the word *(dabhar)*, rather than with the Greek *logos* as taught by Philo and the Stoics where it is used to denote the rational principle by which the world is sustained.[22] In short, *dabhar* is dynamic, *logos* is static. For the Hebrew, word is not merely the expression of thought, it is the making real of what is in the heart.[23] There is a close relationship between word *(dabhar)*, heart *(lev)* and spirit *(ruach)*.[24] Word is the going into action of the very essence of the person, and its effectiveness is conditioned by that person. Blessings and curses of a man in touch with God are words which must be taken with deadly seriousness because results are bound to follow.[25] The word of God as God speaking, and speaking with creative power was an idea destined to be submerged in the concept of the Word as the written word of the Torah forfeiting its dynamic quality. It was one of the most striking characteristics of the ministry of Jesus that he rescued this aspect by means of the personal authority by which he preached and through which situations were changed and people were healed and demons exorcised.[26] It was such a ministry of the word that the early Church assumed at once[27] and which became part of its theology.[28] To struggle for this dynamic conception of the word has always been necessary. All too easily the word of God is thought of as a document or a theological proposition, but periodically times of refreshing have come whenever the spring of the Hebrew understanding of language has bubbled through the ground again, sometimes through unexpected channels as it has in the twentieth century by means of the philosophy of Heidegger and the presentation of the word as an event,

[21] The Greek is *'ek theou'*. 2 Cor. 2:17. *'Praedicatio Verbi Dei est Verbum Dei'*. See K. Barth, *Church Dogmatics* (1975) Vol. 1, Pt. 1, p. 52.

[22] Jewish thinkers (probably influenced by Greek philosophy) reached a very similar conception of the divine 'wisdom' cf Prov. 8. esp. vv. 22–31 where the personification is more than a literary device. A. Richardson, *A Theological Word Book of the Bible* (S.C.M. Press, 1950) p. 285.

[23] 'To say in the heart' is a distinctive Hebraism. See Gen. 17:17; Ps. 14:1; Eccles. 2:15.

[24] Isa. 32:6; Ps. 39:3.

[25] Gen. 12:3; Num. 23:8.

[26] Mark 1:21–28.

[27] Acts 3:6.

[28] 1 Pet. 1:23–25.

an *Ereignis-sprache*, as the Germans call it. Father Aloysius Church S.J. lights up this view of the word as an event when he wrote,

If you come across a road accident you either help or walk on; in either case you are committed. Christian preaching announces events, the wonderful works of God in sacred history, particularly the paschal mystery of our Saviour. This very announcement is in itself an event. It is a new moment in that sacred history—for it brings the people before a decision of faith. The Lord who is ever present in mystery in his Church becomes present to the consciousness of the hearers and invites them to a new participation in his mystery.[29]

A dynamic in place of a static interpretation of the word of God leads to an understanding of the relation of the Bible to preaching. In an often-quoted passage Barth[30] brings the Bible and preaching into a relation with the revealed word of God which we know only from the scriptures adopted by Church proclamation. The revealed word has the priority and from it there stems God's word written (the Bible), and God's word spoken (the preaching of the Church). We may say then that the Bible is man's account written of God's word in action. It is a human proclamation on parchment, and subsequently on paper printed by a machine, of the divine initiative for man. It is a written-out sermon telling of what God has done and what he is, what man can be and should be and even will be in consequence. The Bible is a basic and primary document and for this reason is indispensable. No account for example exists apart from the four gospels which tell as they do of Jesus of Nazareth. But in as much as no words are ever mere words, as if they were dead counters, words about God's word must partake of the potential of that word causing the scriptures to stand in a class by themselves. Tillich is therefore able to say not only that the Bible is the word of God in the sense that it is the book by means of which the knowledge and the final revelation of God in Christ is conveyed to us, but also because it participates in that revelation.[31] It follows that the Bible is the essential and indispensable tool for the Church's preaching of the word of God. The Bible therefore and preaching are possessed of an essential connection grounded in the word of God. As a result the Bible is assisted by preaching to give it a voice, and preaching

[29] See Karl Rahner, *Theological Investigations* (Darton, Longman & Todd, 1966) Vol. lv, p. 256.

[30] *Church Dogmatics*, Vol. 1, Pt. 1, 2nd Edition, p. 121.

[31] *Systematic Theology*, Pt. 1 (1968) p. 176.

requires the Bible to give it its message (*kerygma*). Predominantly therefore, though not exclusively, the Bible *becomes* the word of God in preaching, and preaching *becomes* the word of God when it is informed by the Bible.[32] The connection between the Bible and preaching has been demonstrated in the history of the Church in that when the Bible is neglected, preaching loses its power and in a Church where there is little preaching there is little study of the Bible. Nor is it without significance that the liturgical revival consequent upon the Second Vatican Council of the Roman Catholic Church has shown itself not only in enthusiastic Bible reading, but also in a marked revival of preaching and the pursuit of a study of its theology.[33]

There is need to touch on a further question here, the relation of the Bible to the Church. It would be easy to read Barth's order of priorities, namely, the word revealed, the Bible, preaching, as if the Bible possesses a certain independence of the Church. Not so. The Bible is the Church's book. It is the Church's book even though the Church is the creation of the Word of God (which is not to say that it only exists where there is preaching, and even less only *when* there is preaching, for the Church is an ontological reality). It was the Church that brought forth the scriptures. They were brought forth by the Church and for the Church within the life of the Church, that is to say, not as the result of an ecclesiastical policy. Viewed from this angle the Church has a priority over the Bible. But this assignment of orders of priority is dangerous. Wisdom counsels that the word of God as the Bible, the word of God as preaching and the Church be seen as belonging together in a relationship which if broken can only distort the true nature of each of the separate parts. So preaching is proclaiming Christ from the scriptures, a ministry of the Word specifically entrusted to the Church and which operates for the wholeness of the Church itself, but is also an instrument for the furtherance of God's will to reconcile all men to himself.[34]

Understanding the word of God which is preached as something dynamic and not static has a direct bearing on the verb used for preaching in the New Testament, it is the Greek word *kerusso*, that is, to act as a herald. There are other Greek words used as well, the most common

---

[32] This is not the whole picture. See P. Tillich, *Systematic Theology*, Pt. 1, p. 176.

[33] A significant article was that by Charles Davis in the *Clergy Review* No 45 (1960) entitled 'The Theology of Preaching'.

[34] In different ways all three Synoptic Gospels are made to end with some kind of great commission to preach the gospel to all the world. Matt. 28:19; Mark 16:15; Luke 24:47.

being *evaggelizo*, *kataggello* and *laleo*.[35] To proclaim as a herald is however the most distinctive metaphor for preaching. A herald, be it
noted, does not proclaim the impending presence of philosophical or
theological propositions, an idea, a thing, least of all a corpse, but of a
living person, or of news; what is more, a *significant* living person, most
likely a king. And if what the herald announces is good news, or for
that matter, even bad news, it is news that has *immediate important
consequences*. 'There is a voice that cries,' wrote the second Isaiah,[36]
'Prepare a road for the Lord through the wilderness.' 'Here is my
herald' (Greek— *kerux*) wrote Mark,[37] 'whom I send on ahead of you,
and he will prepare your way. A voice crying aloud in the wilderness,
"Prepare a way for the Lord; clear a straight path for him." And so it
was that John the Baptist appeared in the wilderness proclaiming
(Greek-*kerusso*) . . .' Preaching is acting like an announcer at a reception, a messenger running on ahead of an approaching army or even a
town crier. What is proclaimed is someone or some new situation
which will 'take over', because an event has already occurred which
must have consequences. In the case of the second Isaiah's proclamation
it was the edict of Cyrus telling the Jewish exiles that they were free to
return to their homeland. In the case of John the Baptist it was the
impending appearance of one mightier than he who would baptise
with the Holy Spirit. Preaching is not preaching in the New Testament
understanding of it if it lacks this element of heralding news, news of a
living person, changing the current situation.

Consequently, preaching is not to be confused with lecturing, nor
with diagnosing a situation, nor with providing homiletical advice.
Preaching is being a herald because what it proclaims is the Word of
God which in itself is dynamic. That is to say, the power of preaching
lies not in the act of preaching, be it never so vigorous, but in the
thing preached (the *kerygma*), which is the crucified and risen Christ.
And the preacher who has personal experience of what he preaches is
a preacher indeed. Perhaps one of the most striking stories the early
Church employed to illustrate this was that of the cured Gadarene
demoniac. 'The man went off and spread the news [Greek— *kerusso*] in
the Ten Towns of all that Jesus had done for him.'[38] To do this is to
preach.

An emphasis on heralding as the essential element in preaching does

[35] A list of some thirty verbs could be provided.
[36] Isa. 40:3.
[37] Mark 1:2-4.
[38] Mark 5:20, cf 7:36.

not mean that teaching is excluded. The *kerygma* has consequences. Because there is a changed relationship on the part of man to God brought about by the cross and resurrection of Christ, there is harmony and a changed relationship on the part of man to his fellow-man. Reconciliation with God calls for reconciliation with men and the preacher becomes a minister of reconciliation.[39] What this implies is not so obvious that teaching is unnecessary, on the contrary, those who have responded to the gospel need to be shown what the gospel requires of them. So the *kerygma* calls for distinctive conduct.[40] It calls for a new relationship between men and women, between husband and wife, between those who govern and those who are governed, between employer and employee, and the attitude to money, time, and those of another race. So there comes about the form of preaching called the homily. There is also a need for teaching the content of the faith, the nature of the Church, and the eschatological hope, and a need for doctrinal preaching and apologetic preaching. But, and this is where the emphasis must lie— *the teaching arises out of the preaching*. *Didache* is the consequence of applying the *kerygma* to the life-situation in which we find ourselves. *Kerygma* without *didache* leaves the word of God isolated from life. *Didache* without *kerygma* is most likely to be the word of man, be it never so replete with wisdom. *Kerygma* and *didache* go hand in hand. In all preaching of the word of God there is teaching, and in all teaching of the word of God there is preaching. What in fact the New Testament provides is *proclaimed teaching*.

Proclaimed teaching is a characteristic of the Synoptic Gospels. Jesus 'went round the whole of Galilee teaching *(didaskōn)* and preaching *(kerussōn)* the gospel of the kingdom.'[41] This statement, combining teaching and preaching, Matthew followed with what is commonly called 'the Sermon on the Mount', closing with a formula repeated in part after all five blocks of teaching presented in his gospel— 'When Jesus had finished this discourse . . .' *(logous)*.[42] Clearly Jesus is represented by Matthew's gospel as *proclaiming didache*. It is what this evangelist meant by preaching.

Luke for his part also presented Jesus' pulpit ministry in the same light. He taught *(didaskōn)* in the synagogues, but when Luke gave

[39] 2 Cor. 5:18-20.
[40] Col. 3:16ff 'Let the word *(logos)* of Christ dwell in you richly in all wisdom, teaching *(didasko)* and admonishing one another . . . Wives, be in subjection to your husbands', etc . . .
[41] Matt. 4:23 (N.E.B.).
[42] Matt. 7:28, cf 11:1 (note the words 'preach and teach'); 13:53; 19:1; 26:1.

an example of Jesus' teaching in Nazareth he fastened on the words
'announce' *(evaggelizo)* and 'proclaim' *(kerusso)* found in Isaiah[43] to
describe it. And appending an example of his preaching in the Capernaum[44] synagogue, he specifically labelled it *didache*. It even wrought
deliverance in so remarkable a fashion that it was declared to possess
authority and power. What is more, it was designated *logos*[45] — the
word. And when this ministry of the word continued it was called
proclamation[46] *(kerussō)*. It is for these reasons that Jesus' ministry of
the word can be called *proclaimed teaching*. It did not provide directions
but rather direction, and being proclamation, it possessed and conveyed
liberating power.

The phrase 'word of God' is used sparingly in the gospels[47] to describe
the teaching of Jesus, but it is clear that the early Church understood
it in this way. 'The seed is the word of God.'[48] It was no small part of
the ministry to proclaim the teaching *(didache)* of Jesus. It was to be a
universal mission,[49] and the purpose was to act as a pastoral guide to
believers and also as a *praeparatio evangelica* for the serious-minded who
were as yet outside the membership of the Church. The fact ought
not to be overlooked that proclaiming the teaching of Jesus was a way
of commending Jesus. Gentiles had been attracted to the synagogues
by the teaching of the Torah. They would likewise be attracted to
the Church by the teaching of Jesus. *Didache*, therefore, formed an
important part of evangelistic preaching.

In general it may be said that preaching consists of the proclamation
of Christ with an evangelical aim *(kerygma)*, it also consists of the
proclamation of the teaching of Jesus with the aim of edifying the
Church *(didache)*, and thirdly of proclaiming it as the word of God for
the nation or nations (prophecy). Jesus himself was a herald, a teacher
and a prophet. If Mark fastened on the first aspect of Jesus' ministry,
Matthew fastened on the second, and Luke on the third. Luke went
even deeper, he recognised that Jesus as a prophet was doomed to
perish at the hands of his own people.[50] Rejection had been the fate

[43] 61:1,2.
[44] Luke 4:31,32.
[45] v. 36.
[46] v. 44.
[47] It has been suggested that when the gospels were written Jesus himself was
understood as the Word of God.
[48] Luke 8:11, cf Matt. 13:19; Mark 4:14.
[49] Matt. 28:19.
[50] Luke 13:33.

of the Old Testament prophets who proclaimed the word of God as it pertained to the people of their time; rejection, too, would be the experience of Jesus.

There are times when the word of God as teaching *(didache)* assumes a particular relevance. Such was the fourth century when Christianity became the official religion of the empire and untaught half-pagans filled the churches. A different time was the situation in England at the end of the nineteenth century when the revivalist campaigns of D. L. Moody brought in waves of new converts to the churches.[51] There may be a cry for Christian teaching in the last quarter of the twentieth century to meet the ignorance of the masses about even the essentials of the Christian faith. Preaching is essentially proclamation, it is the proclamation of Christ, but the content will vary according to the requirements of the time and the place where it is exercised.[52]

The spoken word we have had in mind possesses a peculiar aptness for being the medium of the revelation of God. To this we shall return; yet the word of God did not, does not, only let itself be heard, it lets itself be seen. *Verbum* is more than *oratio*.[53] Not to recognise this is a mistake the twentieth-century theologians of the Word have made, resulting in an exclusive concern for an existential Christ, coupled with an undue scepticism about the historical Jesus. The word of God was seen in the works of the prophets, in the Word made flesh, in the increase of the Church and in the lives of its members. This awareness of the word of God as *'Verbum Visibile'* necessarily leads on to a consideration of preaching and the sacraments, a subject which calls for a chapter all to itself.

When the word of God is understood in a dynamic sense, that is, as having power *(dunamis)* within it, the preacher is not its master but its servant. The preacher cannot control the word of God, he cannot even forecast what his preaching of it will accomplish. Results may follow contrary to his expectation. He cannot even be sure that the Word of God will actually be in his preaching, but he must preach in the faith and expectancy that such will be the case. As it happens, this attitude gives the preacher confidence, for in a sense he is not responsible for

---

[51] Campbell Morgan (1863–1945), Minister of Buckingham Gate Chapel, met this situation.

[52] For a consideration of teaching from the pulpit see D. M. Baillie, *The Theology of the Sacraments* (Faber & Faber, 1957) pp. 141–155.

[53] 'Word is not only present when it is spoken and conceived, but word is also present when it is made present and actualised in powerful symbols. *Verbum* is more than oratio. Protestantism has largely forgotten this.' *Kirche und Kultur* 1924, p. 19ff. (Tillich) quoted by Barth in *Church Dogmatics*, Vol. I, Pt. 1, p. 63.

his preaching. He has been called by God to preach, been licensed by the Church, given the *kerygma*, and when he preaches, the word of God will accomplish what it will.[54] Such is the faith in the word of God peculiar to the preacher, who, when he lives by it and preaches by it, discovers it to be the victory by which he overcomes[55] the enemies of fear, nervousness and futility. Conversely, the consciousness of being the servant of the word and not its master, promotes a desirable modesty, reliance and humility in the preacher. He the preacher stands under the judgment of what he is preaching, no less than the hearers, indeed, what he speaks in public he has first heard in private;[56] he passes on a message as a herald does, he gives what he has been given.

It cannot be denied that the message will to some extent be conditioned by the messenger, just as the playing of a symphony is conditioned by the quality of the orchestra, and the instruments at their disposal. There is Beethoven's 'Fifth' according to Furtwängler, Klemperer, and Henry Wood. There is the gospel according to Matthew, Mark, Luke and John. There is the word of God as Father Smith, the Reverend A. B. Jones and Pastor Brown preach it, no doubt differently conditioned by each in his preaching, but in as much as the word of God is too great and too powerful for any one preacher to comprehend it wholly, or to contain it, there is an inevitability about the way it is conditioned. In the last resort, it is only *the whole Church* that is sufficiently comprehensive to be able to be the servant of the Word and to proclaim it.

For completeness something needs to be said about the relation between preaching (proclamation), teaching and prophecy. All three may be included under the general heading of preaching. Sermons may belong to any one of these groups and a full pulpit ministry would embrace all three. How then are they to be distinguished?

Preaching is basically the proclamation of the goods news of Jesus Christ to the Church and to the world. It is made to the Church for its own welfare but also in order that the Church may preach to the world. What it proclaims is God's historical achievement in Jesus for the whole world's ultimate restoration to God's design.

Preaching also includes the teaching which is a consequence of the basic proclamation and is not independent of it. It uncovers what must be the nature of God in that he so acted in and through Jesus Christ for

[54] Isa. 55:8–11.
[55] 1 John 5:4.
[56] Matt. 10:27.

the world. It also tells what those who live by faith in the God proclaimed are to think and do in the world they inhabit. It requires close attention to the situation of the hearers, indeed all preaching which is teaching presupposes listening and a sympathetic sharing of the hearers' lives.

Preaching should also include prophecy. Were it not so, it would have nothing to say to the world. Such silence in the face of the world's bewilderment, or even rebellion, would be a denial of the Gospel. But *what* is to be said? A word of judgment certainly, but not only of judgment, there must also be an indication of the right way to go. But can the Church know this? It can only know it in so far as under the guidance of the Spirit it applies the revelation of God in Jesus Christ to the predicament in which the world finds itself. This, however, it is bound to do for the Church has been chosen to play its part in the redemption of the world. And if teaching requires listening and sharing the common life of those who hear it, how much more true is this of prophetic preaching. The prophetic preacher must even suffer with the world to which he preaches, and in this shared suffering speak the word of God that comes to him. All this calls for involvement though not absorption, in the social and political aspirations of the day.[57]

[57] See Trevor Beeson, *Britain Today and Tomorrow* (Collins 1978), pp. 251–269.

3

The Word and words

'WORDS ARE TO THE PREACHER WHAT PIGMENT IS TO THE PAINTER AND stone is to the sculptor.'[1] Words are his *materia operandi*, he cannot work without them, and if he is to succeed he must love them, understand them and know how to employ them to achieve his purpose. A man may possess a gift with words, not always recognised until he finds himself responding to words, then he may develop his gift, but there will still remain a technique to be learned.

What are words? Technically speaking they are verbal units of meaning called *morphemes*, composed of units of sound, that is *phonemes*, able to be regulated in modes of association by a grammatical system which modifies and arranges vocabulary. Words are the smallest units of meaning. Not that every unit has only one meaning. Meaning is modified or even changed by context and this context may be the sentence structure where the word occurs, or the personality of the speaker and his mannerisms, or even the life-situation where the word operates.

Words are sometimes conceived of in terms of clothing covering a body.[2] There is a vast literature illustrating the view that a speaker's thoughts can be separated from the words in which he clothes them. On this interpretation what the speaker needs to do is to find the adequate words in which to express his thoughts, and what the hearer needs to do is decode the message so as to arrive at the thought of the speaker. Successful communication involves this double process of thoughts into words and words back into thoughts.

This understanding of the matter is too tidy. Thought does not precede speech, nor does speech succeed thought in such a neat step-by-step process. Thought and speech get born together, for thought immediately urges forward into symbolic and linguistic expression. If this situation is not recognised but an insistence is made on the idea that

[1] I owe this phrase to the Very Reverend Michael Stancliffe, Dean of Winchester.
[2] See Max Black, *The Labyrinth of Language* (Pall Mall Press 1968), Chapter 4.

in some prior fashion thoughts operate independently of words, then words have no meaning in themselves, and meaning can only be sought in some unchartered territory called thought. A better model is that of a melody consisting of the actual sounds of which the melody is composed; that is to say, thought is immanent in the words which express it.

A speaker cannot, however, make or choose his own words. If he is to communicate with others he must use the words they also use; he must employ a common language. This however means a harness on his freedom. Language therefore makes communication in thought possible, but it also controls what is communicated.

What is the origin of language? Where does it come from? It is not something we make, it is 'out there' already. Nor can we be taught it or even learn it. All parents can do is to expose their children to human beings who are constantly speaking and wait for them to latch on. Children will talk when they want to talk. After this they can be instructed how to talk correctly.[3] So then language *comes to us*. It comes to us as life comes to us. It comes along with the physical and the material. Not that it is the product of the physical and the material any more than life is the product of the physical and the material. On the contrary it shapes the physical and the material. Language then is a gift to every man. It is the gift that makes him a man. It is what differentiates him from the animals. It can almost be said that language is his life. It is the light by which he thinks, the means by which he is able to reason. This is why language can be called *logos*, that is, word or reason, and why (because language comes to us), the prologue to the fourth gospel could be paraphrased:

> In the beginning was language . . .
> all things were made by it . . .
>   in it was life,
> and the life was the light of men . . .
> there was the true light which illuminates
> every man who comes into the world.[4]

This constitutes a recognition of language as creative, as light, as life, and as the characteristic of every human being. Moreover, the

[3] See Ian Robinson, *The Introduction to the Survival of English* (Cambridge University Press, 1973).

[4] It is recognised of course that the prime reference of these verses is to Christ as the Word.

range of these verses can be extended if *logos* is translated not only by 'language', but by 'communication' and by 'reason'.

Language is thus closely connected with meaning. By means of language we put things together, comparing them and contrasting them. And when we share this meaning by means of language with others we make contact with a meaning that transcends the two individual points of view. So language reaches out to ultimate meaning, and because things can only exist in so far as they have a meaning or significance, language is intertwined with existence. Heidegger taught that language is the mark of authentic being. All this sets language on a higher plane than does 'language naturalism' and the views of the scientific semantics.[5] If these views are more like mathematics, then what we have been describing are more like poetry. And if the former are comparable to a closed television circuit, the latter are like a set open to receive messages from outside. Part of the wonder of language is that it is able to register mystery.

There is a particular example of the general principle we have been presenting in the case of the language of the Bible, important for preachers. I. T. Ramsey[6] asserted that the Bible presents a distinctly 'odd' or 'improper' kind of language because it handles those peculiar kinds of situations in which 'the penny drops' and which 'come alive' offering both discernment and commitment. They are disclosure situations. The significance of the language of the Bible therefore which handles them is not the facts underlying the narrative (*wie es eigentlich gewesen ist*), nor even the event plus interpretation, but the events as disclosure points of what, in the last resort, we can only call God. Language then discloses, it even brings into being ultimate meaning or ultimate reality. So the 'odd' language of the Bible is able to be a means of making possible the real presence of God. It is what makes the language of the Bible especially significant for the preacher, and why he cannot wholly dispense with it, whatever problems it may pose for him as a communicator in the modern world. At the level of language as well as at the theological level, the Bible and preaching are together in a marriage which should know no divorce.

None of this makes sense, however, if words are merely transitory tools. The Marxist takes this view. He reckons that words only have the meaning attached to them which politics requires, there is no intransitoriness about words, they are not 'given', but are subject to a

---

[5] Protagonists are Ogden, Richards, Korzybski and Wittgenstein. For an introduction to semantics see F. H. George, *Semantics* (English University Press, 1964).

[6] *Religious Language* (S.C.M. Press, 1957).

continual flux brought about by our modern world of change. The neo-Freudians, for their part, recognise no '*logos*' in the cosmos, and so their use of words does not rely on any concept of order. All this represents an opposite view from that which sees words as media of revelation or as acts or events. In this case words are related to the Word, and therefore must be treated with a certain respect, if not reverence. According to C. S. Lewis all words are blasphemy unless they are tied to the Word, though they eventually break down because they are but the stammerings of the human tongue.

But what are the uses of language? What are words for? Wittgenstein used the expression 'language game' in order to emphasise that the use of language is part of an activity or form of life.[7] It can of course be purposeless, but is usually purposeful. There is some aim in uttering words, perhaps to express thoughts, to provide information or to give orders. This could be called the cognitive use of language. But there is also the non-cognitive, we might call it emotive language, using emotive words, what Bentham calls 'passion-kindling epithets'. Then thirdly, there is a use of words designed to be *effective in action*. This is of particular interest to the preacher who observes how the words of Jesus were employed to perform cures. 'I say to you, stand up, take your bed, and go home.'[8] Whatever the purpose behind the speaking however, its efficacy does not rest on the words alone but on the trans-mission of non-verbal signs of credibility. To a greater extent than is often realised words depend for their reception by the hearers on the context in which they are spoken. This is a point to which preachers must pay attention. It is not only what they say or even how they say it, but who they are making the utterance to, what they look like at the time, and where they are saying it. The writer of the Proverbs was aware of the importance of context for speech when he wrote, 'A word fitly spoken is like apples of gold in pictures of silver.'[9]

This recognition of the context of language giving life to the language[10] at once connects language with existence. Words are embedded in life and life is embedded in words *as they are used*. This is why it is imperceptive to talk about 'mere words'. Words in use are the key to being. They are as Heidegger expresses it, 'an existential

[7] *Philosophical Investigations* p. 11. An introduction to the thought of Wittgenstein can be read in David Pears, *Wittgenstein* (Fontana, 1971).

[8] Mark 2:11 (N.E.B.).

[9] Prov. 25:11 (A.V.).

[10] 'Every sign by itself seems dead. What gives it life? In use it is alive. Is life breathed into it there? Or is the use its life?' Wittgenstein, *Philosophical Investigations* p. 128.

8

phenomenon'. They may be an event. This then is why the preacher is justified in a *ministry* of the word. He is concerned about 'being', about 'Ultimate Being', and about New Being (Tillich), no wonder he uses words in context as his material and treats them with reverence, counting them sacred to life.[11] Unfortunately this existential nature of language has been at something of a discount in recent years owing to the preoccupation of logical analysis with the meaning of language insisting first on the verification principle and more recently on the principle of use, that is to say, the meaning of language is to be looked at in the way it is used. From these angles of criticism the speech of theologians and more so of preachers, has been written off as meaningless.[12]

We turn now to the spoken word as distinct from the written word.[13] This is of special importance to the preacher for it is in spoken words that his ministry predominantly consists. Is there any special virtue in spoken language for this purpose?

Before attempting to answer this question wisdom counsels that we show an awareness of how in recent years there has been a flight from words, and a boredom with language.[14] There may be historical reasons for this. From its earliest beginnings, Christianity has fostered education, indeed discipleship, that is, learning, has been its life. And so in Europe and wherever Christianity spread, the promotion of schools, colleges and universities has been in the forefront of its activities. Moreover, wherever Christianity has been in a dominant position as in Europe, almost all learning has been in the Christian mould. What is more, it has been mediated with the tool of Christian language informed by the Bible. When, however, secular education developed, informed largely by the scientific movement, the old language tool was rendered inapt. Thus two languages developed, one informed by Christian insight, another informed by scientific insight, and not many people were bilingual. Gradually, therefore, what was said in Christian proclamation was meaningless, and inability to understand spells boredom. Added to this is the fact that modern educational method relies more on seeing, that is, on experimentation, than on learning by hearing. All of which poses a sharp question for the

[11] From this point of view the blasphemous use of language is a serious matter.

[12] For an approach to this subject see J. Macquarrie, *Principles of Christian Theology*, pp. 111-114.

[13] In this section I am greatly indebted to Walter J. Ong S.J., *The Presence of the Word* (New Haven and London: Yale University Press, 1967).

[14] See Gerard Ebeling, *Introduction to a Theological Theory of Language* (Collins, 1973).

theologian and for the preacher—is it possible to have knowledge of God by seeing and doing, if not by experimentation? The answer is yes, but the fact stands out that in the Bible hearing is the faculty most often used for contact with God, and the very first instance is presented in terms of sound—'The man and his wife heard the sound of the Lord God walking in the garden.'[15] So maybe Eugen Rosenstock-Huessy was right when he wrote, 'Experiences of the first order, the first rank, are not realised through the eye.'[16]

All too widespread is the notion that the written word is primary and the spoken word secondary. This is not so. What is written is actually at one remove from the reality which the word symbolises. The spoken word is primary. The point is demonstrable historically. If mankind has inhabited the earth for five hundred thousand years, he has only been writing words for three and a half thousand years. Words as symbols therefore and not as sounds are comparatively new in the history of mankind. The alphabet was invented about the year 1500 B.C. in near Eastern lands (there had been picture words before), thus bringing about one of the greatest turning points in history. Up to that time the word was known for what it essentially is—*sound in time*. Words in this form are spoken and heard. That is all. They cannot be 'looked up'. They have no history in the modern sense. They come and they go. They can in fact only be known *as they are going*. So they are events in time. They are existential and they carry meaning because of their context, that is the speaker, the person addressed, and the situation in which they are uttered. Words, therefore, belong to the community in life and from this they draw their significance.

In contradistinction from the spoken word, written words are arrested in the present. *Verba volent, scripta manent.* But when they are written down, they can be dissected and their parts studied in separation from their flow between person and person. So words, instead of being sounds in time become *visual objects in space*, and as such can be studied in isolation. Then they no longer belong to the community as relationship instruments, nor are they events, nor effective instruments, but counters, labels and things.[17]

[15] Gen. 3:8 (N.E.B.).
[16] 'Erfahrungen ersten Grades, ersten Ranges, werden nicht durch die Auge gemacht.' *Die Vollzahl der Zeiten* (1953), p. 33.
[17] 'The spoken word . . . is a very different thing from the written word. What is effective or allowable or desirable in the one may be quite the reverse in the other . . .' Sir Ernest Gowers, *The Complete Plain Words* (Pelican, 1976) p. 26.

This transition was greatly accelerated by the invention of printing by Gutenberg in Mainz in 1448. Thereafter, words as printed symbols on paper could be, and were, multiplied *ad infinitum*. Not that the oral-aural period was *completely* overtaken by the literary, but certainly eighteenth-century culture was one of literary activity. It was the great age of dictionaries, apophthegms, adages and colloquies, not least from the pen of Erasmus. By the time of Descartes, learning had become a process of individual enquiry, an activity of silent cerebration, almost dehumanised, replacing an involvement with persons in vocal exchange. And in 1751 James Harris wrote a book which explained how writing *causes* reading and reading *causes* oral communication. This is standing the truth on its head.

What then is there about sound and the spoken word that makes it a suitable medium for communicating what we mean by 'God'? – a point of obvious relevance to preachers.

First, sound is always involved with the present. It emanates from something happening now, from an event in the contemporary, even from force operating somewhere in the vicinity. Cultures therefore which know words as sounds know them as dynamic instruments possessing power to do things. It is wise to beware of words, they are never empty. This accounts for the reverence accorded the words of the prophets in the Old Testament as media conveying the dynamic presence of God himself. It also draws attention to the suitability of the spoken word in preaching as a primary tool for the ministry of the active presence of the risen Christ in our contemporary environment, creating, reconciling and healing.

Secondly, spoken words cannot be 'captured', examined and compared with other words as is possible with written words. Spoken words address us as persons. The action is first of all on their side, and whatever we do is first of all in the nature of response or re-action. There is therefore an appropriateness about the ministry of the word being in the first place a spoken ministry. God is not a thing to be 'captured', examined and compared. God takes the initiative and we must respond to him while he is speaking, while he is near.

Thirdly, spoken words presuppose community. A man speaks because there is someone to hear. Communication, community and communion belong together. The spoken word therefore rescues from isolation, and to be rescued from isolation is the first step towards wholeness, if not salvation. The case is different with the written word. Literary people, 'booky' people, can be isolationist with all the consequence of an unhealthy inwardness. Basically, the ministry of the *saving* word of the gospel uses speech as its medium.

Fourthly, sound is associated with mystery. It is not for nothing that cathedrals are made resonant and that liturgical chanting occupies a considerable part of the activity in them. The origin of sound in actual experience, quite apart from the technical study of sound waves, is mysterious. We hear a sound at night and we are puzzled, perhaps frightened. 'Listen to the wind,' said Jesus in effect, to Nicodemus, '. . . thou hearest the sound thereof, but canst not tell whence it cometh, and whither it goeth . . .'[18] And the mystery is heightened because sound 'comes at us' from all sides. There is no space in front as with vision. We are in the midst of sound, a principle which operates in 'stereo'. The hearer is set therefore in *the midst* of acoustic space. And when this recognition is coupled with that of sound representing *dynamic* presence, then we are aware of dynamic presence *all around us*. We do not occupy a two-dimensional world, nor even a three-dimensional world, but one with another mysterious dimension all around us. Sound then, and the spoken word *as sound*, is appropriate for the communication of the mysterious and dynamic divine presence.[19]

Fifthly, words as sounds and not symbols on paper, that is, spoken words, are always attached directly to persons and cannot exist apart from them. Even electronically recorded speech or electronically transmitted speech is only at one remove from persons. Spoken words are personal words, and when 'the Word became flesh',[20] it came into its own. So the spoken ministry of the word is appropriate to the service of the God whom we (as persons) recognise as (at least) personal. God addresses us in personal terms and we answer correspondingly.

Sixthly, the spoken word is less open to misunderstanding than is the written word in spite of its transitoriness. Take the sentence, 'The Queen rode on a horse in Hyde Park today.' It may conceal ten shades of meaning depending on which of the ten words in the sentence is given accentuation, and more than ten if more than one word is accented. Which of these meanings is to be counted the correct one? It is impossible to tell from the sentence *when written*, but (unless the speaker is gifted with a remarkably dead-pan voice), there will be very

---

[18] John 3:8 (A.V.).

[19] In my association with the Imperial College of Science and Technology (London) for many years, I was always impressed by the number of scientists who found recreation in music. It was as if they needed this mystery to counter-balance their preoccupation with the abstracted world of science.

[20] John 1:14 (R.V.).

little doubt when the sentence is spoken. In this case it will carry over-
tones and undertones indicating the speaker's own convictions, even
if only to admit 'I couldn't care less what she rode or where.' The way
the speaker speaks turns the speech into a confession or testimony.

Seventhly, speech is universal. An astonishing number of people live
and have lived full lives who are illiterate, not forgetting leaders of
whole nations in past history. Reading and writing are acquired skills,
but speech comes naturally. The ministry of the word *spoken* then is
for every man, helping to underpin the universality of the gospel.

We have drawn attention to the oral-aural period in the history of
language followed by the literary period. This began with the invention of the alphabet, developed by writing and was vastly accelerated
by the technique of printing. With the modern invention of electronically recorded and transmitted sound, a new era for the spoken word
has begun, not that the skills of rhetoric have ever completely ceased
to be practised. There has always been a live theatre, a live political
platform as well as a live pulpit. A new situation however, providing
a new opportunity has arrived with sound radio, calling for new
techniques. To some extent even this has already been superseded by
television. No doubt sight added to sound increases *impact*, but it
actually decreases *personal involvement*. The play of the imagination is
not required since everything for eye and ear is provided. As a result
television fails to touch persons in depth, and on this account is less
effective for religious broadcasting than sound radio. Unfortunately
to some extent sound broadcasting has been set back by the introduction
of the tape-recorder which only succeeds in deadening programmes
with chunks of dully presented material, but its general superiority
for the presentation of religion remains. 'Two in the eye is worth one
in the ear' – so television and sound have been compared. But it all
depends on what it is that is to be communicated. If something
about God who is mysterious, whom for centuries we have been taught
to close our eyes the more readily to appreciate, then sound is ahead of
television, and this tells us something important about the *spoken*
ministry of the word.

4

Word and Sacrament

IN PART II CHAPTER TWO A HIGH DOCTRINE OF PREACHING WAS EXPOSED. The words of the preacher, it was asserted, could become the word of God, and the preacher's voice the voice of God. This possibility is dependent on the free choice of God with whom therefore the realisation of the possibility remains. God is always the sovereign of his own word and the preacher no more than its servant. When, however, the possibility is realised, it is realised through the action of the Holy Spirit in the congregation of faithful men and women, that is, men and women of faith. So there is able to be a real presence of God in the ministry of the word, and a means of divine grace. Moreover, grace is experienced there for what it is, namely, the influence or constraining power of a God who is (at least) personal.

The question may now be raised as to why any further ministry is required. Why does there need to be a ministry of word *and sacrament*, constituting together the ministry of the Church? Why the introduction of a material element in the encounter between God and man, which is precisely what sacramental religion provides? Does it not represent a decline from a level of mental and spiritual awareness when a resort is made to something able to be touched, tasted and felt? Can we not maintain that the ministry of the word is on a higher plane intellectually than the ministry of the sacraments, requiring more in the way of expertise on the part of the preacher, and more in the way of mental capacity on the part of the hearer?

The short answer to these questions readily provided by some is that Christ instituted the sacraments, and therefore we are in duty bound to observe them. But are we sure that Christ did institute even the Dominical Sacraments, that is, Baptism and the Holy Communion? There are scholars who deny this, though there are others who affirm it. What cannot be gainsaid is that these two sacraments are integral to the New Testament and informed the very life of the early

Christian Church.[1] Even so we can scarcely remain content with ministering the sacraments simply because we are bidden so to do, and because the early Church observed them. We are bound to ask why?

We turn therefore to note that the universe is sacramental.[2] Beauty is conveyed to us through things, through the autumn tints in the woods, through the arrangement of pigment on the artist's canvas, through the striking of the taut wires in the piano by felt-covered hammers. And latent patriotism is aroused by the sight of a flag, and love by the impact of lips upon lips. We live in a material universe and cannot know our fellow human beings apart from their material bodies. The material is largely the vehicle of all the experiences we have, whether pleasurable or painful.

Furthermore, the Christian belief is that God made matter, perhaps it is more true to say God makes matter. He is the sustainer of the material. And does not Jesus' use of parables from nature to teach men and women about God imply this view of the natural order? It is not simply that the parable of 'the seed growing secretly'[3] formed a suitable illustration of the way in which the kingdom of God operated, but that there actually exists an essential harmony between the working of the spiritual and the working of the natural, because they are both the handiwork (or handiworking) of the same God. So Jesus can point to the material and natural in order that people may recognise the spiritual and transcendent.

This use of matter to reveal spirit does not only belong to the Christian religion. In Judaism unleavened bread, the Ark of the Covenant and various ritual actions operated a sacramental principle, and not only Judaism but Greek mystery religions, and even primitive cults; and in almost all, water and food played a considerable part.[4] What the Christian gospel does then is to concentrate our universal sacramental experience into two primary sacraments which have a historical root in the Christ event, namely, Baptism and the Eucharist. And for this reason, that Christianity tells of something that happened in the life, death and resurrection of the historical Jesus which alters our relation to God. This is the gospel. So we have sacraments *of the gospel,*

---

[1] See O. Quick, *The Christian Sacraments* (Nisbet, 1927, Reprinted 1944), pp. 118–120.

[2] See D. M. Baillie, *The Theology of the Sacraments* (Faber, 1957) p. 42f.

[3] Mark 4:26–29.

[4] See W. F. Flemington, *The New Testament Doctrine of Baptism* (London: S.P.C.K., 1948) p. ix.

sacraments that relate to us, and to what God did in Christ and still does. They bring us into communion with the Divine gracious and real presence now.

We must be careful therefore not to imagine that hearing is the only means of receiving the word of God. It is true that 'faith cometh by hearing, and hearing by the word of God',[5] and there is a certain priority about it. Even so we must not imagine that speaking and hearing is non-material activity. Both speaker and hearer are flesh and blood. And the scriptures in addition to hearing use seeing, feeling and tasting as well as hearing in describing the experience of the Divine presence. There is therefore a natural aptness about the use of water, bread and wine in seeking communion with God.

We may go even further. There is truth in the claim that the sacraments—and here we are thinking chiefly of the Eucharist—are able to be a vehicle of the divine grace to more people than is the case with preaching.[6] Sacraments appeal rather to the senses than to the mind. They call for less effort on the part of the recipients. Hearing sermons can be an exhausting business. There is an argument to be followed. Constant attention is required or the thread will be lost. The mind is stretched, and there are decisions to be made. By comparison, the reception of the sacramental elements is a relief. It is possible to be wearied with arguments, worn out with words. In the Eucharist, however, the worshippers can relax into the presence of God and simply receive. And the very inexplicable nature of the sacraments encourages this simple trust, indeed, almost makes it inevitable and so demands it. Moreover, to give up the human mental struggle and fall into the hands of the self-giving God—'This is my body—this is my blood'— makes for our salvation.

If it is true that the Eucharist requires only a minimum ability on the part of the communicant to receive the Word of God sacramentally, it is also true that the Eucharist does not depend on the ability of the *celebrant* in the same way as preaching requires it. That is to say, the Eucharist provides an objective structure able to operate more effectively and more consistently than is the case with the ministry in the pulpit. There is not the same dependence on the officiant. People do not talk about a good celebrant or a bad celebrant as they might talk about a good preacher or a bad preacher. In general then sacraments can be relied upon to minister to a wider range of people than does preaching. Women are more at home with them than with preaching.

[5] Rom. 10:17 (A.V.).

[6] See J. Macquarrie, *Principles of Christian Theology* (S.C.M. Press, 1966) p. 399.

Perhaps the strongest commendation of the sacraments is that they supply the element of incorporation and communion in a way the ministry of the word does not. Preaching can leave the hearers high, dry and isolated. In those churches where preaching dominates the enduring outcome has too often been an intellectual élitism. R. H. Fuller has pointed out that preaching divorced from its proper context in liturgical action degenerates into intellectualism as in seventeenth-century Lutheran orthodoxy, moralism as in Tillotsonian Anglicanism or emotionalism as in the Pietism of all the Protestant churches including Evangelical Anglicanism.[7] 'All three are too individualistic. They leave man in isolation. They do not draw him into the Church. The hearer of the sermon goes home maybe a better person intellectually, morally and emotionally, but still an individual.'

In the last resort it must be admitted that the sacraments are the safeguard of the Church's Christocentric and saving message. Much else might be stripped away, but if the sacraments are stripped away there is no guarantee that there will remain a doctrine of cleansing from sin, or that there is sin that needs cleansing, and no message of body broken or blood outpoured 'for us men and for our salvation'. The pulpit can be occupied without a proclamation of the need for cleansing or of Christ's self-sacrifice. It is impossible however to function at the font without water, and impossible to preside at the table of the Lord without breaking bread and pouring out wine. The sacraments therefore *protect* the Word of God, they operate as the sheet anchor of what is proclaimed, or should be proclaimed, from the pulpit. And because the sacraments carry this responsibility, the ministers of the sacraments must be ministers of the Church of God, and not only of one congregation, otherwise the Holy Communion will become a mere fellowship meal and not a sacrament of the universal Church.

Having now set out the importance of the sacraments, we turn to enquire what is the relation of the word to the sacraments. This aspect can be examined by reference to different Church traditions.

In the Church of Rome the Mass is the ministry *par excellence*. Uniquely it mediates the real presence of Christ. Preaching is both desirable and valuable, but traditionally (though not in the same way since Vatican II), its nature lies in instruction or exhortation rather than in proclamation. The work (*opus*) is done by the Mass, the preaching is commentary.

In the Reformed Churches, by contrast, preaching is basic. It

[7] *What is Liturgical Preaching?* (S.C.M. Press, 1957), p. 11.

occupies the centre and the furnishing of the Church building frequently emphasises the fact. This does not mean that the sacraments are either underrated or neglected, nor could they in fairness be labelled as secondary, with preaching as primary, not in the official Church formularies at least. Their function is to act as seals or verifications of the proclamation and to root the proclamation firmly in history. The real work however is done by the preaching.

Anglicanism, over against both the Roman Catholic and Reformed tradition, sees the ministry of word and sacrament as *a dual ministry* (though the sacrament is not understood as in the Catholic tradition). The Word of God is mediated along the parallel lines of word *and* sacrament. The sacrament is not therefore a seal or confirmation of the Word of God conveyed by the preaching, it is a means of conveying that Word itself *apart from* the preaching. The Book of Common Prayer directs that a sermon shall be preached at the Eucharist, and only directs it for that occasion, but Hooker argued strongly that it is not absolutely necessary that a sermon shall be preached at every act of worship, and this applies to the Eucharist. Cranmer, Ridley and Jewell, as well as Hooker all interpret John chapter 6 so as to promote feeding on Christ in the sacrament *and* feeding on Christ in teaching and meditation on his words. The mode of feeding is different but the food is the same. These two modes are parallel modes of Christ's self-communicating to the believer. They are not, however, to be separated from each other in the Church's *total* ministry because they each need the other. A Church's ministry with the ministry of the word only would be unsafe, and a Church's ministry with the ministry of the sacraments only would likewise be unsafe. Preaching without the sacrament omits salvation by incorporation into the body of Christ, and the sacrament without preaching lends itself before long to magical interpretation. Furthermore, the ministry of the word and sacrament belong together not only because they safeguard each other, but because they both proclaim the same gospel. 'For every time you eat this bread and drink the cup, you proclaim the death of the Lord, until he comes.'[8]

We have said that the Anglican understanding of the sacrament is not identical with the Roman Catholic. The difference is that the Anglican view of the Real Presence is neither corporal nor substantial. On the other hand it is not purely subjective, it is not created by the faith of the recipients. It is received by them. In this way it is a true or real presence in a spiritual sense, mediated by the Holy Spirit. The bread

[8] I Cor. 11:26 (N.E.B.).

and the wine are the pledges given by Christ, and to those who receive them in faith the Holy Spirit makes them efficacious.

The question which can properly be asked at this point is, what can the ministry of the sacrament teach us about the ministry of the word if they really are parallel means of receiving the grace of God?[9]

First, perhaps, to remind us of the real or true presence of Christ in the preaching. Preaching (and with this must be included 'proclaimed teaching'), is not a lecture, nor is it a means of communicating religious information, preaching is a means of bringing about the real presence of Christ in the congregation. The congregation is necessary for this. Preaching requires a congregation at least of one. So does the Eucharist. In this preaching is different from praying which can be solitary. Preaching requires corporate action. It requires faith and speaking on the part of the preacher and it also requires faith and hearing on the part of the congregation. The faith, and the togetherness of the preacher and congregation, provide the sphere in which the Holy Spirit can take the words of the preacher in order to mediate the real presence. This brings about the possibility of communion through preaching, which is much more than communication. In the sacrament Christ is there seeking to be received, and in the preaching whenever it is in alignment with the sacraments, Christ is there also seeking to be received. The alignment with the sacraments is important because only when Christ is proclaimed by means of words in the preaching as also by means of actions in the sacraments can we know that the Spirit will be at his work, whom Bishop John Taylor calls being 'the go-between God'.

Secondly, we can learn from the sacraments of the 'two-way traffic' in preaching. There is in the Eucharist the proclamation of the Lord's death 'till he comes'. There is in preaching the same movement from God to man though with greater emphasis. But there is also in the sacrament the movement from man to God. In the offertory he brings the products of his labour to offer to God who then takes them, consecrates them and uses them as a means for meeting man where he is. There is also in preaching the same man-to-God movement. The preacher brings his sermon, the product of his labour in preparation and delivery, and the congregation offers its attention and its devotion

[9] In Romans 15:16 Paul calls his preaching ministry his priestly service. The Greek word for service used here is '*leitourgon*' and it is employed definitely and technically as in the LXX of a priest. (See I.C.C. Commentary on Romans.) Here is New Testament support for letting the priestly ministry illustrate the prophetic.

which God takes, consecrating it and using it as a means for meeting
the congregation where it is. Herein lies the principle of the Incarnation.
God reveals himself to man, but he takes a man, he takes our flesh,
through which to make himself *be present*. The doctrine of the Incarnation has reference to the sacraments,[10] it also has reference to
preaching. The Word is enfleshed in the preacher, a particular person,
and this does not exclude, but includes personality. Personality is not
therefore to be deliberately suppressed in preaching. Neither of course
is it to be paraded. But if it is suppressed then the Word is not really
being enfleshed in the preacher, there is no full Incarnation, but a strange
kind of docetism, the Word only seems to have taken on the garment
of the human.

Thirdly, in the sacrament we expect something from what in the
last resort we instinctively know to be inexplicable. Somehow sacraments open out on to a different dimension of existence where faith is
the only means of approach. So with preaching. How the words of a
man can be the medium for realising the presence of God is inexplicable whatever our theory of language. Yet the preacher's faith is, or
should be, that when words are used to convey the Word of God,
God himself will be there, which is not far short of saying a miracle is
expected. Such is the mystery of the sacrament, and such is the mystery
of preaching, and the result of each ministry, and of both, is new life
through communion with God in Christ.

What insight does this ministry of word and sacrament provide
about the operation of grace? Surely that it works as personal influence
and not as a mechanical force. This is the weakness of all '*ex opere
operato*' theories of the sacraments. Personal influence requires the
presence of the person, it requires action and it requires words. The
presence of a person is entirely different from that of the proximity of
a lifeless object. There is a wealth of subtle meaning in the remark, 'He
might as well not have been there.' Personal presence is always effective
even though it be negative, but if there is action and words, the influence is powerful, and nowhere with greater intensity than in a shared
meal with friends. And if it be a time of food scarcity, as was the case
in the life and times of Jesus, the occasion is potent indeed. Then the
personal presence of the host presses on his table guests. In sharing
what is not an unending store of food, it is the very sustenance of life
that is being shared, if not life itself. Such was the occasion when Jesus
instituted the Last Supper, and it is in the remembrance of this that the
Eucharist is always celebrated. Looking therefore through this glass

[10] See Evelyn Underhill, *Worship* (Nisbet, 1936) p. 278.

we can see grace for what it is—personal influence, and looking from the sacraments to the parallel means of grace, namely, preaching, we can begin to appreciate how its effectiveness does not depend on the automatic excellence of the medium employed, but on the real presence of Christ who is being proclaimed. And we may also understand that however right and proper may be the arrangement of occasions after the sermon when its contents may be discussed, argued over and questioned, nevertheless it is right for the word of God through preaching on many occasions simply to be received, as in the sacrament.

Earlier in this chapter a brief reference was made to the fresh interpretation of the ministry of the word in the Eucharist as a result of the Second Vatican Council. Some amplification is called for. What has come about is a new awareness of the Mass as a celebration of the word. So the liturgy of the word is seen as inseparable from the liturgy of the sacrament. The wording of the Council's statement is specific. 'The two parts which in a certain sense go to make up the Mass, namely the liturgy of the word and the Eucharistic liturgy, are so closely connected with each other that they form one single act of worship.'[11] Strictly speaking this is not a new development but a rediscovery of what belonged to the Eucharist from the very first. Christ instituted it in a context of dialogue and conversation. This idea has never been wholly lost from the best Catholic tradition. Nevertheless, all too frequently and in all too widespread a fashion, the word has been regarded in Roman Catholic circles as an intrusion into the liturgy of the sacrament. The sermon has been entirely omitted at Low Mass and treated perfunctorily at High Masses. Altogether preaching has been at a discount. This situation is passing, if it has not already passed. Far from the word in the Eucharist being a subsidiary, perhaps an explanation or a moral exhortation, it is understood as the light which gives meaning to the whole Eucharistic symbol. The word evokes faith so that by means of the preaching and the faith response, the Word is encountered who becomes bodily present in the bread and the wine. The word saves the liturgy from automatism and makes the liturgy 'an encounter with God through which we enter the redeeming work of Christ'.[12] It is not surprising that with this understanding of the Eucharist as a *celebration of the word*, serious attention is being given to the homily. The preached word is recognised as dynamic, capable of

[11] *Constitutua of the Sacred Liturgy*, 56.
[12] J. D. Crichton, *Christian Celebration. The Mass* (Alpha, 1971) p. 23. See also p. 77.

operating as the Word himself, and being of the nature of an event, contributing an essential part to the event of the Mass, indeed, normally the Mass is incomplete without it.[13] The word becomes incarnated in the sacrament, and there is celebrated.

[13] Expositions of this viewpoint can be read in the published works of J. D. Crichton. See also *The Ministry of the Word* edited by Paulinus Milner, O.P. (Burns & Oates, 1967). Other publications are R. Gantoy, *Le Ministère du Celebrant* and J. Champlin, *The Priest and God's People at Prayer*.

5

The word in worship

IN THE INTRODUCTION TO THIS BOOK THE CATEGORICAL STATEMENT WAS made that the basic concern was with Church preaching, that is, the ministry of the word in Church. It was recognised that this could not be said to represent the whole of preaching, nevertheless the assertion was made that if preaching were weak here, it would probably be weak everywhere. The concentration has therefore been on the ministry of the word *in worship*.

We have to admit, however, that a great risk is run in basing it there. It cannot of course be denied that from the earliest days in the Christian Church, preaching formed a regular part of Christian worship. It was preaching based on the Bible, indeed lections were drawn up, so that the preaching covered the whole range of the Christian revelation with the result that preaching was liturgically controlled. Suppose, however, worship fails. Suppose there is a general disenchantment with it. Suppose it comes to be thought that our reasonable service[1] is not worship in Church but service of the hungry, the thirsty, the naked and those in prison. Suppose the cultus is thought to be expendable. Suppose 'religionless Christianity' takes hold, what then becomes of preaching?

To this we would reply that there cannot be Christianity, as we know it, without worship. A religion can exist without preaching. As has been shown above the religion of the Old Testament developed over a long period despite this lack; nevertheless, a religion cannot exist without a cultus. Worship is religion's primary duty, its essential function, and that which keeps it alive. To incorporate preaching therefore into worship, to relate preaching to it, and even to make it *an act of worship*, is to secure it as long as religion lasts.

What is worship? Worship is bowing down,[2] certainly of the mind and spirit, but possibly also of the body. It is the recognition of a

[1] The Greek is '*latreia*' meaning 'worship'. See Romans 12:1.
[2] Ninian Smart, *The Concept of Worship* (Macmillan 1972), p. 6.

Superior, an 'acknowledgment of Transcendence; that is to say, of a Reality independent of the worshipper, which is always more or less coloured by mystery and which is there first.'[3] It is more than recognition, it is confession of a relationship. The worshipper confesses his dependence and inferiority *in the presence of the Other*, so he approaches with humility, in short, he bows down and worships, rejecting independence, self-sufficiency and rebellion, and substituting instead, surrender, submission and a search for help, and all in the belief not only that help is there, but is able and willing to be imparted, and is therefore worth while seeking. When preaching is undertaken in this context it comes into its own.

There is more to be said. When the object of worship is conceived not only as superior but as holy, there is engendered in the consciousness of dependence the conviction of unworthiness. This aspect is perhaps brought out nowhere more clearly than in the classical expression of Isaiah's Trisagion[4] with its response:—

> 'Holy, holy, holy is the Lord of Hosts:
> the whole earth is full of his glory. . . .

Then I cried,

> Woe is me! I am lost,
> for I am a man of unclean lips
> and I dwell among a people of unclean lips;
> yet with these eyes I have seen the King,
> the Lord of Hosts.'

This consciousness, or more accurately, this conviction of personal unworthiness (for there is an element of guilt involved), over against God's transcendent holiness, is not only individual. Isaiah, the worshipper, recognised that he was involved in *corporate* uncleanness.[5] It is this that separates *the whole people* from God, and this separation from the whole people that makes for God's holiness, or 'otherness'. Worship is a corporate activity and not simply an individual one. When the individual worships he worships with the people of God. He *joins* in praising God, *joins* in confessing the sin of his fellow human beings and his own sins, and what is most important, for it safeguards him against an unhealthy individualistic pietism, *joins* in receiving that pardon, reconciliation and newness of life which God offers.

[3] Evelyn Underhill, *Worship* (Nisbet, 1936) p. 3.
[4] Isa. 6:3,5 (N.E.B.).
[5] Isa. 6:5.

9

Prayer, of course, is part of worship, but in worship it is common prayer, prayer not by the individual worshipper for himself, this belongs to the sphere of private devotions, but intercession for others, for the people of God, and for all whom God is perpetually seeking. So the Church of God, and the individual as a part of that Church, becomes the instrument of God's purposes of good for all men, with the result that mission becomes the product of worship. Mission begins in worship and mission returns to worship. The worshipping Church, like the seventy-two sent out from Jesus' presence, returns full of praise at its accomplishments in his name.[6]

There is one other element so prominent in the history of worship as exercised by man that it seems to be inseparable from worship, and that is sacrifice. From primitive forms to the highly systematised worship of Israel, sacrifice plays a prominent part. It can be grossly misused. It can be exercised to propitiate an angry God. It can even be transferred to the cross of Christ to become Christ's propitiation of the wrath of God on man's behalf, a terrible doctrine. And if the word propitiation be banned and expiation be substituted, as is proper, nevertheless man is still prone to reckon that he himself is both able, and under an obligation, to expiate his own sins by his own sacrifices, or perhaps the sin of the whole community by the same means. But for all the misuse of sacrifices the principle of sacrifice is unable to be excluded from worship, it is a constituent part of any cultus. Nevertheless, in Christian worship[7] it needs to be enlightened by the New Testament *kerygma* or it will distort the word of the cross and the resurrection of Christ.

Worship is a form of proclamation. The coming together (congregation) of a group of people in any locality to worship God as known in Jesus Christ, cannot be anything else in the first place, but a witness to the existence of faith in him. The worshipping congregation therefor preaches. The building in which the worship is carried out preaches. It may be evangelical preaching. It may even be a means of conversion.[8] Its distinctive architecture is significant. Its cruciform structure. Its spire. Its bells. All this is a form of communication. Most significant

[6] Luke 10:1 & 17.

[7] Perhaps the sacrifice of the Mass has been one of the most sensitive points. One of the greatest encouragements, however, is the fact that there has been something of a reconciliation of Catholic and Protestant interpretations of the Eucharist in this matter of sacrifice.

[8] There is a remarkable illustration of this in S. Vanauken, *A Severe Mercy* (Hodder and Stoughton, 1977) p. 82.

of all is the congregation actually bowing down there. This presence and this action is a proclamation of the sovereignty of 'otherness', a proclamation of the insufficiency of man and of his search for, and (it is to be hoped) his experience of the saving power of the One he worships. The congregation therefore preaches long before, and whether or not, a ministry of the word is exercised from any pulpit, and what it says may be a preaching into life or a preaching into death.

The actual form or structure of the worship also preaches; it would be more accurate to say that it ought to preach, and this it will do if it follows the liturgical patterns that have become traditional in Christian worship, and nowhere more forcibly than in the Eucharist.[9] Here we have the drama of God's action 'for us men and for our salvation'. The broken body and poured-out blood of Christ is at the centre, prefixed by praise, confession of sin and absolution, and with actual participation in the central act. So the drama is more than a drama, it is a means of making available in the present the sacrifice of the action by Christ that took place in the past. The Eucharist is not the only pattern of worship, but the elements it has should always underlie whatever patterns of worship are followed and there are three: the humble approach, the service of the Word of God (liturgy of the catechumens) and the liturgy of the faithful (the communion).

Worship requires ritual. The simple bowing of the head, or of the knee, even the closing of the eyes, is elementary ritual. There may be an elaborate ritual as in Catholic worship, or a simple ritual as in Presbyterian worship, where the Bible is ceremoniously carried to the reading desk, but ritual of some sort there must be to sustain the worship. And ritual needs symbols, making possible symbolic acts which have the capacity to speak where words fail, and where words of necessity are better not employed.[10] So the ritual of worship has a message to proclaim which, wherever there is proper Christian worship, is a message of God's sovereignty, man's need and God's provision. Here then is a test to apply. Is the form of worship too elaborate, or too bare, to convey the message? Where, however, the message is clear, and where there is music, movement and colour in the setting of worship, power exists, able to speak to those who encounter it.

[9] See T. H. Keir, *The Word in Worship* (Oxford University Press, 1962) pp. 30–60; also R. H. Fuller, *What is Liturgical Preaching?* (S.C.M. Press, 1957).

[10] An example of such a situation is bereavement, or some other overwhelming tragedy. Words on these occasions are out of place. See Job 2:13.

A church then is a stage for the re-enactment of the drama of God's redemption of mankind. The re-enactment has to be planned. It cannot happen without planning, sometimes not even without rehearsals. There are actions to be thought out and lines to be learned. The planning and the rehearsing are necessary because the drama has to convey a message, it has to be shaped and staged in order to be both a celebration and a proclamation. Without planning, the outcome is a pointless ritual and a confused stammering, helpful to none and irritating to all. And if the objection be that planning produces a performance lacking in sincerity, the point may be met by referring to the aim, which is so to proclaim God that we may worship him, and also by the reminder that in great art excellence is reached, not by complication but by simplicity. Planned worship should be restrained, purposeful and meaningful, engaging the mind, the emotions and the will of the worshippers, reaching its perfection, as far as its human aspect is concerned, when it is so planned as to appear unplanned, and even *becoming* unplanned, so wholly have the structures entered into the minds of the worshippers.

Worship is the place where the ministry of the word is primarily undertaken. This is its proper place, which is not to assert that it is its only place, but that it is the place where it fits. In worship preaching does not stand by itself. It is supported by its context and it communicates, as does all speech, largely because of its context. To concentrate on preaching without its context is to fail. Of course objections will not be wanting ready to assert that the worship-context is designed to 'soften-up' the hearers of the word; and no diligent research would be required to discover occasions when this possibility has been exploited to the full, as for example, in evangelistic campaigns, with startling, if short-lived, results. But so to understand the relation of worship to preaching is to misunderstand. Christian worship is both celebration and proclamation. It proclaims as it celebrates, and when there is included the ministry of the word, the preacher is saying in words what the hearers are celebrating in worship. So preacher and congregation act together in the ministry of *the word in worship*.[11]

[11] 'You would hardly expect a roustabout, non-reading, careless clergyman to produce a useful sermon, neither can you expect to be in tune with a good sermon if you are a roustabout, non-reading, careless member of the congregation. The ten minutes or so of a service called the sermon is probably the time when priest and people should be working together in closest rapport. God has been involved, especially to bless the activity—and that involves both them and us, as it were.' Norman Ingram-Smith, *St Martin's Review*, May 1978.

He proclaims against a background of their proclaiming. A preacher is not like a singer, performing solo as he wanders aimlessly along the streets, but more like a soloist performing with a choir in an oratorio. His solo is of a piece with their choral singing. He contributes to their performance and they contribute to his. Their work is in fact integrated both in aim and execution and together they present the message of the oratorio, not least when they sing separately.

This togetherness of preacher and congregation in worship is expressed theologically by saying that faith addresses itself to faith. To understand this is to appreciate the part played by the congregation in the ministry of the word. What the hearers bring to their hearing conditions what they hear. Jesus gave warnings about this.[12] Communication of the word of God is not possible to those who for all the faith they bring to the hearing of it might as well be absent. Yet there is always the possibility of awakening because the Spirit of God, 'the author and giver of life', as well as the interpreter, is at hand in the congregation assembled for worship. This assembly, for this reason, is ever the most potent place both for evoking and nurturing faith, converting those who enter and stay in its company.[13] The word *in worship* is the Spirit's agent.

If it is true that the ministry of the word in worship is the primary place for that ministry whatever extensions and developments from it may be exercised, and rightly so, then it follows that a preacher belongs to a particular congregation. He by his preaching has made that congregation what it is, and they by their faith have made that preacher what he is, in neither case wholly, but in both cases significantly. A preacher, to be appreciated therefore, must be heard preaching in his own worshipping congregation. It is *with the preacher's own flock* that preaching reaches its full development. The name of Father Stanton is not thought of apart from St Alban's Church, Holborn, nor F. W. Dale apart from Carr's Lane, Birmingham. All great preaching belongs somewhere to a worshipping community. And there it is nurtured and there it blossoms, and only there. This is why a preacher cannot be taught preaching in a seminary and sent on tour preaching. He has to be grown in a worshipping congregation over the years. Parish churches and congregations are the places to look for preachers.[14]

12 Mark 4:24,25.
13 Those churches which practise infant baptism understand this.
14 There are exceptions, such as Austin Farrer, but his delivery lacked that which belonging to a congregation would have provided.

At this point a difficult question has to be faced, namely, what is the best form of worship for preaching? Is it the Eucharist, or is it Morning or Evening Prayer, as the Book of Common Prayer calls these offices?

Let it be established at once that preaching properly belongs to the Eucharist. In that ministry of the word and that ministry of the Sacraments there is the full ministry of proclamation and celebration together with the opportunity for participation in a spiritual and physical act of reception of that which is offered. What could be more complete? All the riches of that which God offers through worship are there. But the question arises, is a rich banquet always the best way of feeding the multitudes?

There is also a practical point to be considered. The ministry of the word in the Eucharist brings into play two focal points in the act of worship, both powerful. It is unlikely that both *can be* sustained.[15] History has shown that both *have not*, with exceptions, been sustained. In the Roman Catholic Church with its emphasis on the Mass, preaching has been almost at a discount, though there are signs since the Second Vatican Council, of a revival. In the Church of England the Parish Communion Movement which came to birth in the 1930s has flourished sufficiently in forty years to see Morning and Evening Prayer virtually disappear and with it the decline of preaching, not, let it be noted, because the Church of England has developed in a Catholic direction, quite the reverse, but because the Eucharist as an act of worship is faced with the problem of sustaining two focal points. In this situation one has to be restricted, and the one cannot be the ministry of the sacrament. So the ministry of the word finds itself with a subordinate function, a rôle emphasised where the officiating minister proceeds after the sermon to robe himself in Eucharistic vestments. The question of two focal points and the impossibility of giving full emphasis to both, is what lies behind the shortening of the sermon in the Parish Communion to ten minutes or less. The Church of England in the last quarter of the twentieth century presents a picture of a Church in a predominantly secular, yet spiritually hungry age, recognising the ministry of the word in its worship but affording it no room to develop, with the result that the work of fortifying the faith of the faithful is reduced in many parishes to ten minutes a week, which, be it never so skilfully employed, is unlikely to be a bulwark against the forces of unbelief. What is equally significant is that the multiplication of Communion services has cheapened the sacrament, forfeiting

[15] Any preacher who has made the mistake of preaching at a musical festival will know the force of this argument.

the sense of awe in the presence of the Transcendent which is proper
to it. What would appear to be required is not only a recovery of the
ministry of the word to its proper place, but a recovery of the majesty
of the sacrament of the Eucharist.

A place for the ministry of the word in the Eucharist must be kept
though it need not always be filled with preaching, because the reading
of the scriptures safeguards this element. It is a misplaced enthusiasm
which feels bound 'to offer a few words' at every celebration of the
Holy Communion, neither beneficial to preaching nor to the Eucharist.
What is more, the Church of England sees the two ministries as
parallel means of grace. What is called for in the current situation is a
working towards the establishment on occasions of forms of worship
where the ministry of the word can be the one and only focus.[16] This
will take time. The capacity to preach has been lost by the Christian
ministry, and the capacity to hear has been lost by the worshipping
congregations. A vicious circle exists. What needs initiating first is an
improvement in the preaching at the Parish Communion. If this is
maintained and an extension of preaching is also developed on other
occasions of worship, an overdue advance will be possible. The growing popularity of what are called 'family services' is an indication of
the need; not a few of these are far less satisfactory than a simplified form of Mattins or Evensong imaginatively presented because it
is properly structured.[17]

We return to the preacher himself. Can his ministry of the word
be an act of worship? If it can it will preserve his preaching from the
offensive forms of that exercise. Worship means bowing the head in
the presence of the Transcendent Being, and not only the head but the
mind and spirit. The preacher who sees his work as part of the congregation's act of worship will not display himself. Be he never so competent, he will refuse the title 'master of the pulpit', replacing it with
'servant of the Word'. He will not seek to entertain, harangue or
indoctrinate. Instead he will offer his tribute of praise to the One he
(*mirabile dictu*) has been called to proclaim, conscious of his own
unworthiness, a tribute which it has cost him to prepare and to offer,
but which is his sacrifice, a sacrifice so far as he can make it, without
blemish. Confidence he must have as a preacher, and confidence must
be apparent or the hearers will find it hard to hear however acceptable

[16] The history of the Anglican pulpit has not developed at the Eucharist but on
other occasions.

[17] A good example is the worship at St Martin-in-the-Fields, London, under the
leadership of Prebendary Austen Williams.

the words. His confidence, however, will be grounded in the gospel he proclaims and not in himself as the proclaimer, and in the Spirit who communicates that particular proclamation and what flows from it.

The preacher will also see himself as the spokesman for the congregation. The whole world-wide Church is God's preacher of his gospel, not one man or one woman. What individual preachers are called to do is speak on behalf of all. Ways should be sought in congregations to give expression to this truth. There could be a weekly prayer meeting when members of the worshipping community gather with the preacher to seek the guidance of the Spirit concerning what *the Church*, that is the local Church, ought to be saying. The current climate of opinion would be taken into account and the needs of the community of which the Church forms a part. This sermon prayer group could develop into a discussion group (it should not meet apart from prayer), in which the dialogue between preacher and hearers of the sermon, under the inspiration of the Spirit, move towards the proclamation of the word of God by the Church through the mouthpiece of the preacher. The final preparation of the sermon, however, like its delivery, must be the work of the preacher alone. When the congregation assembles for worship and the sermon is preached, that praying group will be present interceding during the preaching for the power of the Spirit to implement the words spoken. In such circumstances the preaching will assume an entirely new significance.

6

The word of the Cross

SO FAR IN PART II OF THIS BOOK IT IS THE THEOLOGY OF PREACHING THAT has been under consideration. The *fons et origo* of preaching, namely the Holy Spirit; the word of God which the Church is commissioned to preach; words written and spoken constituting the material the preacher employs in his task; the sacraments which are complementary proclamations of the Word; and then worship as the primary, though not exclusive, context for preaching. The question '*what is to be preached*' must now receive attention. What can be preached in the last quarter of the twentieth century?

There can be no Christian preaching without the word of the Cross. This does not simply mean that there can be no Christian preaching without including among the sermons preached some sermons on the Cross. It means that Christian preaching *is* preaching the Cross. The Cross informs Christian preaching. The Cross is what makes preaching Christian preaching. The word of God is the word of the Cross.[1] Even though Paul preached nothing else among the Corinthians but 'Jesus Christ and him crucified',[2] he was not corrupting the word of God. Such preaching was indeed a stumbling block (scandal) to the Jews, and foolishness to the Gentiles,[3] yet it was in reality the good news, it was the gospel, not to be written off as clever human oratory, but rather recognised as the instrument of the power of God. When the word of the Cross is preached, Christ is actually at work in it.[4]

This centralising of preaching on the Cross is no more arresting than that the Cross should have become the symbol of the Christian Church. Jürgen Moltmann writes,

When archaeologists dig up a place of worship in the desert sand

---

[1] Cf 1 Cor. 1:18 & 2 Cor. 2:17.
[2] 1 Cor. 2:2.
[3] 1 Cor. 1:23.
[4] 1 Cor. 1:18.

and find in it the sign of the cross, they can be virtually certain that it is a Christian Church. Today, too, we find the Cross in Christian churches as the centre symbol. The worshipper gazes upon the crucifix. The word of the Cross is preached to the congregation. They are blessed and sent from the church with the sign of the cross. Many make the sign of the cross as the Holy Trinity is named. In Passiontide in many churches, devout Christians follow the course of Jesus' passion in the Stations of the Cross, and meditate on the reasons for his sufferings and the redeeming effects of his death. In other churches, even today, Good Friday is the central Christian festival of the Church year. There is little that expresses Christian fellowship with God better than passion hymns. Even in the world of Islam, Christianity is represented by the symbol of the Cross.[5]

We shall not, however, penetrate the significance of the Cross unless we first strip away the protective coat of piety that prevents it from being seen for what it is, and also the interpretations that are so piled high on top of it that we fail to observe it as a thing of horror and profanity. Without the stripping we do not hear what God is saying there, we do not encounter the Word of the Cross.

A crucified man is an embarrassment. No one without a warped mind, having once looked at a victim impaled on a cross, would enjoy looking again. The exhibit (because that is what it is), is repulsive. 'A dead man, twisted by torture, every bone protruding from his bruised body, his tongue too swollen for his mouth any longer to contain it. Blood, sweat and excrement exuding a stench offensive to all but the flies which settled in droves.'[6]

The cruelty of the crucifixion was not, however, the terror of the crucifixion of Jesus, but the fact that he was done to death as a *blasphemer*. According to the Bible, such a man dies under the curse of God.[7] He is excluded from the fellowship of God and man, a reject from the congregation of the faithful and from human society altogether. The fourth gospel represents the Jews as retorting to Pilate, 'We have a law; and by that law he ought to die, because he has claimed to be Son of God.'[8] Tragic as it is to record, the Romans crucified many freedom fighters when they overran Israel, but those

[5] *The Crucified God* (S.C.M. Press, 1974) p. 32.
[6] See my *New Preaching from the New Testament* (Mowbrays, 1977) p. 70.
[7] See Deut. 21:23; Gal. 3:13.
[8] John 19:7 (N.E.B.).

men on those crosses died as heroes for what the nation took to be a just cause, not as rejects from religious and respectable society.

The Romans, for their part, kept crucifixion as the punishment for escaped slaves and for rebels against the State. Crucifixion was the ultimate deterrent in the classical world. No one mentioned it in polite society. Small wonder that worship of the crucified Christ was treated with distaste, if not with mockery. On the Palatine in Rome there is a *graffito* representing a crucified figure with a donkey's head, and this caption, 'Alexamenos worships his god.'

Less forcibly than the Israelite laws, and with more reverence than Roman society, the Christian Church has nevertheless softened the harshness of the crucifixion of Jesus in order to make it tolerable.[9] It has become golden, even studded with jewels—and the rationale of this metamorphosis?—because it was transformed by the resurrection. We must, however, see the Cross in history as well as in faith. Christian faith is only faith and not the projection of desire when it forces itself to look at the *horrible* and historical Cross. What we see there is Jesus rejected and killed *in the absence of God.*

Why was Jesus crucified as a blasphemer? Because of the scandalous message which he preached. He proclaimed the justification of sinners. For him the kingdom of God was not the falling of judgment on the unrighteous and the vindication of the righteous, as every one believed, but the reverse. And as if saying it was not dangerous enough, he freely associated with tax-collectors, sinners and outcasts of every kind, indeed, the riff-raff of the town. All this was offensive to the law (the Torah), but then he set himself up above the Torah, even above the authority of Moses. 'You have learned that our forefathers were told . . . but what I tell you is this.' Six times this unbelievably provocative assertion is repeated in the Sermon on the Mount.[10] So Jesus elevated himself above every Rabbi who drew his authority from Moses, even above the Torah itself. But no one could be above the Torah except God who gave it. So Jesus was guilty of self-deification. This was blasphemy. Incident after incident demonstrated his guilt — his cavalier attitude to the Sabbath,[11] his scorn of the tradition of the Pharisees, his deliberate omission of their ablutions and food laws,[12] but above all the company he kept.[13] And all this by

[9] Some of the ways are set out in *The Crucified God*, pp. 41ff.
[10] Matt. 5:21,27,31,33,38,43.
[11] Mark 2:23; 3:3 etc.
[12] Mark 7:1ff.
[13] Mark 2:16.

a poor man, whose very poverty proclaimed him according to Jewish understanding as one on whom the favour of God did *not* rest. That *he* should assume authority was the last straw. Nothing could discredit him and re-establish the Torah, but his public rejection as one cursed by God which meant 'hanging him on a tree'.[14] No wonder the disciples fled[15] when they saw the inevitable outcome. Who could exercise faith in a crucified man? Who could have faith in the curse of God? the thing was impossible. Jesus must be *God's rejected servant*. This was the satisfaction the religious leaders of the day drew from his crucifixion. This was the nightmarish mystery haunting the disciples. If *this man* were a reject, what then is goodness?

So the Cross tells of the deadly conflict between the righteousness which derives from observing laws and the righteousness which derives from the exercise of faith. Jesus proclaimed God's free pardon of sinners — he even pardoned himself[16] as if he were a sovereign (because only a sovereign *can* pardon), and they killed him for it, counting it blasphemy. Jesus' preaching stood the law on its head, it played havoc with morality, it undermined society, and knocked down the moral credit privileged men had proudly piled up for their own acquittal. Where would Israel end if such preaching were accepted? Was not the stability of the State itself in danger with such an affront to established religion? So it was the preaching and teaching of Jesus which brought him to the Cross. The upholders of the law were mortally offended at almost everything he said. The word of God on his lips was the thing that killed him.

But are we sure? Are we sure that it was not for political reasons rather than for his preaching that Jesus was crucified? What interest could the hard-headed Romans have in *kerygma* and *didache*? Were not all religions equally superstitious and unworthy even of investigation? This position cannot, however, be sustained. The ancient world knew nothing of our modern separation of religion from politics. All religions, Judaism especially, had a political face. And the preaching of Jesus could only have been empty of political reference had it been confined solely to matters of internal piety, which clearly was not the case, otherwise it could never have provoked the strong opposition it did from politically orientated parties.

This matter has come to a head in recent years in claims put forward that Jesus was a political Messiah, in fact a member of the Zealot

14 Deut. 21:23.
15 Mark 14:50.
16 Mark 2:5.

party. It is true there are similarities between what Jesus was and taught and the Zealots, but there were also marked differences. These have been set out by no one so clearly as Jürgen Moltmann[17] and the conclusion is that in spite of the similarities, Jesus was no Zealot. Yet Jesus *was* killed by the Romans[18] for religio-political reasons. So he stands with all those down the ages who have resisted all forms of tyranny on grounds of faith.

We have said that the Cross will fail to speak its word unless we sense its horror. The terrifying horror was not, however, in the last resort, the rejection of Jesus by Israel as a blasphemer, nor his unjust condemnation by the Romans in the exercise of power politics, but the fact that at the last he was *abandoned by God*. All his ministry he had lived in the closest possible union with God. Had he not confessed him as 'Father', employing the word 'Abba' for which perhaps the nearest equivalent can only be found in the homely word 'Daddy'? This intimacy was the source of his strength of personality, the origin of his extraordinary powers, even the ground of his uniqueness, and yet on the Cross when he most needed it, he lost it, 'My God, my God, why hast thou forsaken me?'[19] the only saying from the Cross which Mark's gospel, our basic Christian document, records, and which, because of its shocking unexpectedness, must reflect at least an authentic interpretation of the crucifixion event, if not Jesus' actual words.

This divine forsakenness in dying was the ultimate horror of the Cross of Jesus, and why there was no nobility in his death compared with that of Socrates committing his teachings to his disciples up to the last. Jesus had taught the real presence of God as Father and lived it. This was the kingdom of God come. Now he was dying with that which constituted the spring of his life and work snapped. And he was alone. His disciples had forsaken him and fled. And the secret of his life perished with him.[20] 'My God, my God, why hast thou forsaken me?' This was the end.

It is tempting at this point to remark, 'But was it? Was the crucifixion the end?' Is there not another chapter called Resurrection? Did

[17] See *The Crucified God*, pp. 138–144.

[18] Moltmann, following Oscar Cullmann suggests that they were Roman cohorts who arrested Jesus in the garden of Gethsemane, and that he was from the first a prisoner of the Romans who feared revolt in Jerusalem. The trial before the High Priest was a consultation.

[19] Mark 15:34.

[20] John Austin Baker, *The Foolishness of God* (Darton, Longman & Todd, 1970) p. 244.

not everything turn out well in the end like some Victorian novel? But so to pass on hurriedly from the horror of the Cross counting it as an episode contributing to the build up of the final resurrection truth is to miss hearing the word of the Cross. The Cross, the horror, the abandonment *is* the word of the Cross. The message is here at Calvary where God speaks to the whole world, and not simply to the righteous or the religious. God left Jesus at Calvary, but where did he leave him? This is the important question. Not alone, and not with the God-fearing, and not with his own disciples. He left him between two reckless freedom-fighters; and nearby none but callous soldiers, mocking priests and a vulgar, ignorant mob. Jesus reached the climax of his ministry outside the Holy City, cast out, out among the outsiders to everything considered orderly, respectable and sincerely religious. Jesus ended up among the aliens, the kind of people with whom he had never spurned to associate, alienated among the aliens, the companion of the *un*righteous, and alone with them, utterly alone . . .

This is the word of the Cross. *Jesus with sinners to the last,*[21] alone with sinners, alone as they are alone, their fellowship with God nonexistent, men and women without faith to justify them, and certainly without works, people sitting in darkness, who expect no light to shine on them, hopeless people, warped people, defiant people. Jesus was left alone with the sinful. That is where he belongs by his own choice. He said so in Capernaum when the Pharisees complained, 'he eats with tax-gatherers and sinners. Jesus overheard and said to them, "It is not the healthy that need a doctor, but the sick; I did not come to invite virtuous people, but sinners." '[22] But Jesus was with the sinners *as a sufferer*, not as a lighthearted observer. This is what the Cross says.

It is impossible to see the Cross and not to see the sinners. Sin and sinners is what the Cross is about. It is about separation from God, about alienation, and about bondage to everything in life which drags down, degrades and deadens. The Cross is there for men and women who imagine that they are free, but are actually bound, some without even the will to break the bonds, let alone the power. The Cross is for people without a sense of God, and almost without a sense of goodness.

[21] Perhaps there are no words more stark than Paul's to the Corinthians, 'Christ was innocent of sin, and yet for our sake God made him one with the sinfulness of men.' 2 Cor. 5:21 (N.E.B.).

[22] Mark 2:16,17. (N.E.B)

Paradoxically, the Cross is also for the self-righteous, for they too are caught, caught in the coils of their own self-centredness, without knowing it. The Cross is for Pharisees, as well as for tax-gatherers, for the respectable as well as the disreputable. When Jesus entered the house of Simon the Pharisee who complained that Jesus allowed a former prostitute to anoint his feet, he told a parable about two debtors, one representing the Pharisee and the other the prostitute. The point in the story is that he forgave them *both*.[23] The Cross is for all who are separated from God even by religion, for this can stand between a man and his Maker, it does so when it is composed of moral credit reckoned to put God in man's debt. *Whatever separates is sin*, and the Cross is there to deal with it.

How? We have to confess we do not know. Not that we are wrong to propound what are called theories of the Atonement, but theories of the Atonement do not atone.[24] At best they are attempted rationalisations of *the experience* of atonement, that is, of the consciousness of being made at one with God, the chasm of separation bridged, bridged by Christ, who came where sinners are living in alienation. To choose to be with people is to accept them as they are. The Cross shows Christ accepting sinners, a costly acceptance, an acceptance so costly it cost him his life in self-sacrifice. This is what he did. This is why there *can be* a word of the Cross saying to *sinful men*—you are accepted.

But how is this message proclaimed? How is the word of the Cross preached? First by telling the story. This is what the gospels do. The gospels are not biographies, they are proclamations of Christ using historical material about Jesus. They are portraits, portraits of the man who was crucified. Mark's gospel is the supreme example. It has been rightly described as a Passion narrative with an introduction. It introduces us to the Christ who was condemned to a horrible death for blasphemy so that we may know him; and interspersed in that story are hints here and there by way of interpretation.[25] This *is* proclaiming the Cross of Christ. It is proclaiming it in such a fashion that the word of the Cross which the Spirit would have proclaimed proclaims itself. Faith on the part of the preacher is faith in the narrative, faith that when the narrative is exposed, the miracle of preaching, by the power of the Spirit, will take place and (as in the Sacrament), the real presence of

[23] Luke 7:42.
[24] But see P. T. Forsyth, *The Cruciality of the Cross* (Hodder and Stoughton, 1909) p. 45.
[25] Examples are: Mark 10:45; 14:24; cf Matt. 26:28.

Christ will be effected. Thus the hearers will know existentially that
Christ is identifying himself with the sinners, justifying them, reconciling them and leading them on to a sense of being at home with (or
at one with) God. This is the Atonement. Bultmann was right. We
are brought home to God by the existential word of the Cross, but
he was wrong in separating it from the historical Cross itself. The
preached Christ cannot be separated from the historical Christ because
we can only respond to the Cross *we know*.

There are, of course, difficulties in telling the story. Difficulties
occasioned not only by the limitations of the storyteller, but difficulties in the gospel accounts themselves of the trials and crucifixion
of Jesus, especially of the trials, the figure of Barabbas and the character
of Pilate. There are many would-be guides through these difficulties—
Knox, Dodd, Blinzler, Paul Winter, Barratt, Brandon, Sherwin-
White, Bammel and Catchpole.[26] But there are some certainties. All
four gospels give the same order of events. Each gospel gives at least
some independent information, for example, Matthew tells about
Caiaphas, Luke about the trial before Herod Antipas, John the longer
trial before Caiaphas. This suggests that no gospel should be omitted.
And all the passion narratives are set in the context of the life of Jesus.
The difficulties lie in two main areas. First, what was the intention of
the evangelists in providing the passion narratives? Brandon draws
attention to the progressive amount of blame laid upon the Jews and
less upon the Romans. Bauer affirmed that the purpose was to prove
the innocency of Jesus in the eyes of the Romans. If, however, there
really was tendentiousness it seems to have affected the narratives
surprisingly little. The second area of difficulty concerns the trials of
Jesus. It is asserted that the Jewish court scene is unlikely because its
order of events is unlike the Mishnah, but the Mishnah developed after
the time of the trial of Jesus. All in all, we cannot be wrong to assert that
although we cannot make an hour-by-hour reconstruction of the trials,
a solid, historical basis lies behind the accounts as a whole, and if we
attempt to remove the Jewish trials, a great deal of explaining will need
to be done about the earlier life of Jesus and his conflict with the Jews.
And this in turn forces us to ask more than historical questions about
him.

Must there not, however, be some interpretation in preaching the
word of the Cross? Preachers cannot simply tell the story and leave it
there! This is true, and the overriding question for preachers is to

[26] A scholarly introduction to the problems can be read in *Theology* Feb. 1972 in an
article by William Horbury entitled *The Passion Narratives and Historical Criticism*.

decide what to fasten on as appropriate to the time and situation in which they preach. Is it to be the Cross as a sacrifice for sin,[27] the means of reconciliation[28] with God, and flowing from it reconciliation with men, or the shedding of blood for sins forgiven?[29]

We offer the suggestion that any interpretation provided must convey the message that God not only *showed* something in Christ for mankind, but *did* something for them. That is to say, the Cross is not only a revelation of God's love (and indeed of his wrath) but actually altered the status of mankind before God. 'The feeble gospel preaches, "God is ready to forgive", the mighty gospel preaches, "God has redeemed". It works not with forgiveness alone, which would be a futile amnesty, but with forgiveness in a moral way.'[30]

We also suggest that the message should be conveyed that God did something for mankind *in his solidarity*, and not only for the individual. The whole world is included in what he achieved.

We also suggest that the horror of the crucifixion and especially of the abandonment of Jesus by God in his last hour points to a theology which is liberating. God is not impassible. He actually suffers with the human race. He knows darkness, he knows heartbreak and he knows rejection. He identifies with the horrible aspect of sin and suffering, and so there is no horrible depth where he will not reach to accept the human race. The appeal of the word of the Cross is therefore (as Paul Tillich so finely expressed it), *to accept that we are accepted*.[31] This is the liberating response to the new status humanity has acquired through Christ's free action. It is the proper place to begin, the place from which new life springs up, life of a different quality, eternal life, the gift of God in Christ, a life no man can make, a life he can only receive.[32]

The word of the Cross derives from something sufficiently horrible to match the blood-drenched horror of the story of mankind. Nothing less will speak to that total condition, certainly no tinkling humanism, only the daring word of God's acceptance.

---

[27] In the twentieth century in Europe there will be some understanding of sin-bearing in the light of the Jews in Auschwitz and other concentration camps, having the sins of Europe heaped on them.

[28] Another word able to be understood in the light of modern industrial troubles.

[29] Probably a most difficult interpretation for modern man, but see Austin Farrer, *Said or Sung* (Faith Press, 1960), Sermon on Atoning Death, p. 65ff.

[30] P. T. Forsyth, *The Cruciality of the Cross*, p. 52.

[31] The whole sermon where the words occur is worth reading in *The Shaking of the Foundations* (S.C.M. Press, 1954), pp. 153–163.

[32] Romans 6:23.

Sooner or later every preacher who takes his pastoral responsibilites seriously will have to preach on suffering.[33] He may well quake at the thought, and he should not attempt to preach on it unless he does quake. Insensitive preaching on suffering is offensive. But why do people suffer? The Bible raises but does not answer the question, and it will not go away. Individuals will cry out of bitter anguish—'What have I done to deserve this?' And some will be oppressed at the massive-ness of suffering in the age-long story of man's inhumanity to man. Truly, suffering is the biggest single obstacle to belief in God. John Hick puts the point sharply, 'Can the presence of evil in the world be reconciled with the existence of a God who is unlimited both in goodness and in power? This is the problem equally for the believer and for the non-believer. In the mind of the latter it stands as a major obstacle of religious commitment, whilst for the former it sets up an acute internal tension to disturb his faith and to lay upon it a perpetual burden of doubt.'[34] No serious-minded preacher can avoid this issue, but what shall he say? He will offer such explanatory assistance as he can. He will point out that in a family all the members profit by the good things that come its way, they must not be surprised therefore if all suffer by the bad things that come its way. Human beings are bound together for good *and* for ill. He will also explain that if God suspended the laws of working in his universe so that fire did not burn the saint at the stake nor the seas drown the life-boat crew engaged on an errand of mercy, where would the reliability of nature be on which life depends? James Stewart set out some of these simple considerations in four sermons which may serve as a guide.[35] He comes closer to the distinctive contribution of the Christian preacher and the problem of suffering when he stresses the fact that *Christ* suffered. How then can anyone any longer nurse the notion that all suffering must be God's punishment for personal sin? What sins had Christ committed? And so a careful path is able to be opened to the awe-inspiring concept of one suffering for another, one even suffering for many others and that one chosen for that particular ministry. There is such a thing as God-like suffering, mysterious and ineffable but real. Only the good can suffer this suffering. And now we are left with the problem on our hands as to why the bad suffer pains in no way commensurate with their sins. The preacher sooner or later will have to confess his own bewilder-ment and abandon explanations altogether. Indeed, he will offer what

[33] See Hans Küng, op. cit. pp. 570–581.
[34] John Hick, *Evil and the God of Love* (Collins, 1968) p. 3.
[35] *The Strong Name* (T. & T. Clark, 1940) pp. 125–168.

the God revealed in the crucified Christ offers—his own reinforcing presence:

> When you pass through deep waters, I am with you,
>   when you pass through rivers,
>   they will not sweep you away;
> walk through fire and you will not be scorched,
> through flames and they will not burn you.
>   For I am the Lord your God,
>   the Holy One of Israel, your deliverer.[36]

[36] Isa. 43:2,3 (N.E.B.).

7

The word of the Resurrection

PREACHING HAS NO CONTENT WITHOUT THE RESURRECTION OF CHRIST.
This assessment Paul made in writing to the Church in Corinth, 'If
Christ hath not been raised, then is our preaching (*kerygma*) empty.'[1]
At the beginning of the same letter he stated that the sole content of his
own preaching was, 'Jesus Christ and him crucified.'[2] According to the
Apostle therefore the word of the Cross and the word of the resurrection
supply that without which there cannot be preaching. It is the event
of the Cross and resurrection together which supplies the ground of
Christian proclamation.

This estimate was not peculiar to Paul. There existed an orthodoxy
of preaching of which the Church in Corinth was well aware. It contained as its two basics the Cross and the resurrection, and Paul was at
pains to establish that his own preaching was in line with it. 'First and
foremost,'[3] he wrote, 'I handed on to you the facts which had been
imparted to me.' The Greek original is striking. 'You hearers received
the thing, I too received it and I passed it on.' It is as if a relay race is in
mind with the runners in a team handing on the baton. And 'the thing',
or baton, is four facts about Christ. He died, he was buried, he was
raised to life on the third day, he was seen by certain witnesses.[4]

The first fact is not left bare but amplified with a theological interpretation, 'Christ died *for our sins*' and to substantiate this the words
are appended—'according to the scriptures'. Apparently Paul counted
the sin-bearing purpose of the death of Christ as of the essence of
orthodox preaching. We should also note that he wrote, '*Christ* died
for our sins', not Jesus, not the historical man, but Jesus the historical

---

[1] I Cor. 15:14 (R.V. Margin).
[2] I Cor. 2:2 (R.V.).
[3] I Cor. 15:3 (N.E.B.).
[4] The four-fold repetition of the Greek preposition *hoti* gives this passage the
appearance of being an early creed, which if received by Paul must be *very* early. The
preaching of the early Church was then based on the creed of the early Church.

man *seen through the eyes of faith*. This is the One who is proclaimed in the Church.

The second fact, 'that he was buried', is stated as baldly as any fact can be stated. 'Dead and buried', *mortuus sepultus*, as the Latin Apostles' Creed starkly records what is meant to protrude as a hard, historical event. There could be no resurrection unless there were a physical death so final that it was sealed by burial. No one is buried while there is hope of life. That Jesus of Nazareth was buried means that there was no more hope of him on this earth beyond that of a pleasant, perplexing or obnoxious memory. He would soon be 'yesterday's man.' All four gospels provide a circumstantial account of the burial. The primitive *kergyma* proclaimed the end of Jesus by those accounts including participation in our human life up to the very last event, which has to be carried out for us, we cannot bury ourselves. Joseph of Arimathaea had Jesus' body put in a tomb because he saw that he was finished.

The third fact is the resurrection— 'that he was raised to life on the third day.' This, too, like the first fact is substantiated by an appeal to the scriptures— 'according to the scriptures'— possibly Psalm 16:9 and 10, cited in Acts 2:26–28, and 13:35–37, so the meaning is 'according to an interpretation of an Old Testament scripture recognised in the early Church'.[5] The Church's preaching then, and Paul's own preaching, were 'according to the scriptures'. The hint is that all preaching ought to be able to substantiate this claim for itself.

The fourth fact is the appearances of the risen Christ as experienced by six witnesses, the last being himself. First, Cephas (Peter), probably because he was the first of the Twelve whose matter-of-fact approach to life could not be questioned. (Why are the women not mentioned?). Then the Twelve (note the official title), then to 'over five hundred of our brothers at once', most of whom were still alive and presumably available for consultation, then to James (the Lord's brother was an unlikely candidate for being easily convinced of the resurrection), then all the Apostles (does this mean gathered together as in Luke 24:50–53 and Acts 1:6–9?), and 'in the end' (N.E.B.) to Paul himself, described as 'one born out of due time', not as if he were an 'afterthought' and 'a crowning witness', quite the reverse. He was like something aborted, a dead foetus, spiritually worthless. Yet Christ appeared to him also, providing for him a birth which was 'monstrous' (N.E.B.), something not fit to be called an apostle because he had persecuted the Church.

[5] Older commentaries make little of the phrase 'that he was buried'. In recent times it has received much attention because of the controversy about 'the empty tomb'.

The question has to be asked, what does this word 'appear' mean? It is used of all 'the appearances' including that to Paul. Does it refer to a vision? or to a bodily appearance? Can the Greek word be made to mean 'showed himself', or that God 'showed him', so that the reference is not to something always there but to something given to certain people to see? Or, since the word is used of Paul's experience, presumably on the Damascus road, could sudden spiritual awareness be in mind such as anyone might experience in a revivalist or Eucharist gathering today, described afterwards in some such terms as 'I was suddenly converted. I saw the light'?

In his letter to the Corinthians Paul did not overtly answer these questions. After listing the four basic facts of orthodox preaching and addressing witnesses for the fourth to give it strength, he returned to his original concern, 'This is what we all proclaim, and this is what you believed' (v. 11). The preaching then was rooted in the resurrection of Christ which clearly Paul took to be historical. He did not, however, see the resurrection as an event standing by itself able to evoke faith by reason of the verification of those who could bear witness to it. The resurrection was the resurrection of the Christ who 'died for our sins in accordance with the scriptures'. That is to say, the resurrection must stand within some kind of theological framework before it will speak and become the word of the resurrection; the word of the resurrection has to be addressed to existing faith.[6]

Because the resurrection case is of this nature, certain perennial questions about it arise, illustrated perhaps in recent years nowhere more clearly than in the correspondence in *Theology*[7] between C. F. D. Moule, Lady Margaret Professor of Divinity at Cambridge and Don Cupitt, Fellow and Dean of Emmanuel College, Cambridge. The former insisted that the event called the resurrection sparked off the distinctive life and witness of the Church, whereas Cupitt insisted that some prior theological understanding was necessary in order that the resurrection event might be brought to this way of functioning.

It has become fashionable in recent years to by-pass the historical question about the resurrection and to concentrate on the functional; as if to say, 'Never mind whether or not the resurrection was an event in history, concentrate rather on the religious question "Does the Spirit which raised up Jesus dwell in me?" '[8] On the face of it this sounds attractive until the question is asked, 'What does "raised up

[6] In the gospels the risen Christ did not appear to unbelievers.

[7] October 1972.

[8] Romans 8:11. See *Theology*, March 1967, article by Lady Oppenheimer.

Jesus" mean?' The fear behind these questions is that the theologians will be trapped among the historians and archaeologists. So he disengages, a process begun by Schleiermacher.[9]

This disengagement is accomplished in various ways.[10] Christ, it is said, is risen *in the preaching*, that is to say, *the word* of the resurrection is where the rising takes place. Bultmann asserts that the risen Christ is not the historical Jesus but the Christ of experience. He meets us in the word of preaching and nowhere else. Any attempt to prove the resurrection by historical enquiry is an indication of unfaith. The unprovability of the resurrection is essential for faith.

A variant of this view associated with Ebeling and Fuchs and the new hermeneutic is that the word *about* the historical is the effective power of God. The preacher should set himself to discover what the Biblical writer meant when he wrote, let the message challenge the preacher himself and then reformulate it to address contemporary man. Then he will discover Christ *risen* in the preaching.

Both these views work with a theology of the word by means of which the disengagement process from history made dominant by Barth is maintained. Some theologians, however, originally pupils of Barth and Bultmann, do not reject the historicity of the resurrection; what they mean, however, by an historical event is unclear. Bornkamm probably speaks for most New Testament scholars when he says that scholarship can only take us as far as the faith of the early Church. The apostles certainly believed that Christ was risen from the dead,[11] but history cannot establish the resurrection as an historical event. Marxsen holds that the living and permanent presence of Jesus is the essence of the Easter faith, but the concept of the resurrection of Jesus is merely a notion of first-century apocalyptic which we cannot share. Pannenberg is especially significant in these discussions because along with Althaus and Campenhausen he supports the tradition of the empty tomb and the resurrection as history. This represents a break-away from the word of God theology. Instead of asserting like Ebeling and Fuchs that God reveals himself in the word *about* the resurrection, he declares that God reveals himself in the action itself and in the word about it. The same would be true of the Exodus, the Exile, or any other of what are commonly called the saving acts of God recorded in the Bible. Pannenberg therefore, has come back to engage again with

[9] See above p. 72.
[10] See article by Alan Richardson in *Theology*, April 1971.
[11] Michael Ramsey, *The Resurrection of Christ* (Bles, 1945) p. 43. Also Pannenberg, *The Apostles' Creed* (S.C.M. Press, 1976) p. 97.

history. It is a view not unlike that maintained in England by such theologians as Temple and Baillie, who taught that revelation consists in divinely inspired interpretation of divinely controlled events in history.

At this point the bewildered preacher may ask where in all the ebb and flow of this discussion can he find a firm foot-hold. The matter is serious because if in consequence of his bewilderment he has no word of resurrection to preach, his preaching is empty, he might as well forsake the pulpit, as indeed some preachers have done, and given themselves instead to other ministries. Let the preacher, however, be reassured. One thing is certain. The resurrection of Christ, whether as event or word, or both, is exceedingly tough. It does not, it will not, go away. There it stands like a rocky island in the midst of an ocean of swirling unbelief, belief, criticism, re-examination, re-assessment and demythologising, but it is still there to intrigue, challenge, and perhaps, even to exasperate the next generation as it has the generations that have gone before, for almost two millennia. What it does is to stimulate faith in a dimension of life other than the temporal, a faith already aroused by the historical Jesus, and the marks of that life in his contemporary followers.

Let the preacher then preach to the limit of his understanding of the resurrection of Christ. What he must not do is relapse into silence on this subject and still continue to function as a minister of the word of God, because without the resurrection there can be no such ministry.

We turn now to consider how the resurrection of Christ is to be interpreted. First, it must be interpreted in relation to the Cross. It must look back before it looks forward, back to the stripped and forsaken man, the reject from the righteousness of the Torah. God raised him who was labelled by his contemporaries as a blasphemer. The resurrection of *this man* is what produced the new *kerygma* and the new righteousness which is of faith. For if God raised this dishonoured man then the world is shown in the crucified Christ an entirely different gospel from that which asserts that at the end of the day every man will receive his deserts, and this is God's justice. This man, Jesus, was rejected by the righteous in the eyes of the law because he preached the justification of sinners, and not only lived with them but died with them as an outcast— but *God raised him*. So Paul was able to write to the Romans, 'He was delivered to death for our misdeeds, and raised to life to justify us.'[12]

[12] Rom. 4:25 (N.E.B.).

And not only does the resurrection furnish the good news of God's justification of sinful men, it creates a new kind of humanity when seen against the background of the Cross. Moltmann[13] writes of the resurrection of the crucified Christ,

> the executioners will not finally triumph over their victims. It also says the victims will not triumph over their executioners. The one will triumph who first died for the victims and also for the executioners, and in doing so revealed a new righteousness which breaks through the vicious circles of hate and vengeance and which for both victims and executioners creates a new mankind with a new humanity.

So the resurrection of Christ does not evacuate the Cross. It does not erase it or let it fade into the oblivion of past history as an unpleasant episode, *because* this is where God spoke to sinful men and continues for ever to address them. The gospel stems from the Cross. Therefore the resurrection lifts it high and turns the spotlight on it, even placarding it before the world, thus producing *the word* of the resurrection which says, 'Look, here is your deliverance, your forgiveness, your reconciliation with God, your open way to his presence, your hope, your life. Yes, your eternal life, that is, life of such a quality that death has no power over it, in short, your salvation.' The resurrection makes *the Cross* the heart of the gospel, and provides the only gospel for preaching in line with the New Testament.

What else does the resurrection say? It says God's new age has already begun. Outside Jerusalem's walls — that first Easter the life that is to come was anticipated. Christ was raised *from the dead*.[14] That is to say, the resurrection *of the dead* did not take place then but the resurrection of one from among the dead. The resurrection life is therefore present now in our world which is dying. There is life in the midst of death instead of only death in the midst of life. So the old structure of Life-Death is set aside, and in its place a new eschatological understanding of time. The future is within the present. So Romans 13:12 reads, 'It is far on in the night; day is near', and 1 Peter 4:7, 'the end of all things is upon us' (N.E.B.). This, however, is not meant primarily to provide material for philosophical speculation, but for the promise of new life now, and for resurrection-life hereafter. So Paul was able to write to the Romans, 'Moreover, if the Spirit of him who raised

[13] *The Crucified God*, p. 178.
[14] Rom. 6:9.

Jesus from the dead dwells within you, then the God who raised Christ Jesus from the dead will also give new life to your mortal bodies through his indwelling Spirit.'[15]

The word of the resurrection which lights up the Cross, providing the good news of the justification of sinners, does not mean that the sinners continue in sin, but that they receive the power of Christ's resurrection life for a new life now, developing entirely new standards and bringing about what can only be described as new men, 'dead to sin and alive to God, in union with Christ Jesus'.[16] Or as Paul wrote to the Corinthians, 'His purpose in dying for all was that men, while still in life, should cease to live for themselves, and should live for him who for their sake died and was raised to life. With us therefore worldly standards have ceased to count in our estimate of any man; even if once they counted in our understanding of Christ, they do so now no longer. When anyone is united to Christ, there is a new world: the old order has gone, and a new order has already begun. From first to last this has been the work of God.'[17] So the justification of sinners is not the end but the beginning. Were it the end, it would be a dead end, but because of the resurrection, justification develops into sanctification. New life begins on the basis of the new status.

The resurrection looks to the future and the present, and also the past. Because Christ has been raised those who are united with him will be raised from the dead. There is thus a word for the future. There is also a word for the present. The resurrection power is available for us in the risen Christ now. There is also a looking back into the past in the light of the resurrection and especially to Jesus. Who was this Jesus? And to answer the question various titles came to be applied. Jesus was 'the Christ', he was 'the Lord', he was 'the Son of Man' and 'the Son of God',[18] titles not imported from the Judeo-Hellenistic world in which the early Church developed,[19] but evolved from the words and work of Jesus himself.[20]

Not only was there a looking back at the identity of Jesus in the light of the resurrection for an interpretation of his person, but also for an interpretation of his works, though these two should not be too sharply

[15] Rom. 8:11 (N.E.B.). See also Phil. 3:10.

[16] See Rom. 6:1–11 (N.E.B.).

[17] 2 Cor. 5:15–18 (N.E.B.).

[18] See Rom. 1:4.

[19] The view taken by *The Myth of God Incarnate*, edited by John Hick (S.C.M. Press, 1977).

[20] See C. F. D. Moule, *The Origin of Christology* (Cambridge University Press, 1977) pp. 11–46.

separated. This involved taking an account of his sufferings. The resurrection did not solve the problem of suffering, it left it a mystery, and to that extent it left the Cross of Christ a mystery, but it declared that those sufferings were *for us*, they took place *for our sins*,[21] which means more than on account of our sins, and they show supremely the love of God for us. To the Romans Paul wrote, 'Christ died for us while we were yet sinners, and that is God's own proof of his love towards us.'[22] And to the Corinthians, 'God was in Christ reconciling the world to himself, no longer holding men's misdeeds against them, and that he has entrusted us with the message of reconciliation. We come therefore as Christ's ambassadors. It is as if God were appealing to you through us: in Christ's name, we implore you, be reconciled to God!'[23] Such is the word of preachers who preach in the beam of the light which shines from the resurrection on to the Cross of Christ, the rejected man for us.

[21] Ibid. pp. 107–126.
[22] Rom. 5:8 (N.E.B.).
[23] 2 Cor. 5:19,20 (N.E.B.).

8

The incarnate Word

INCARNATION IS NOT A NEW TESTAMENT WORD, BUT IT IS EMBEDDED in the life of the Church through the wording of the Nicene Creed. 'And was incarnate by the Holy Ghost of the Virgin Mary.' The purpose of the creeds was to safeguard the apostolic preaching or more accurately, the Apostles' experience of which their preaching was an expression. It is clear, however, that the doctrine of the Virgin Birth with which the Incarnation is commonly associated, formed no part of the primitive *kerygma*. This is not what the apostles used as one of the essentials in the message which they proclaimed in the mission of the early Church. Paul does not mention it, and only two of the four gospels record it, and that very briefly. The question, therefore, arises, is the Church committed to it? Must the Virgin Birth be proclaimed? Should the Incarnation be proclaimed? Should the Incarnation form part of contemporary preaching?

To attempt to answer these questions on the basis of academic considerations only is a temptation. To fall here however is to fail. Recognition must also be given to the empirical fact that the message of Christmas is able to be heard by mankind in a way which exceeds any other Christian proclamation, not excluding Easter. On any count the recognition given to the birth of the Christ child at the turn of every year across the world is remarkable. Clearly Christmas says something, even if the admission has to be made that exactly what is doubtful. It is not as if the child whose birth is commemorated exhibited what is popularly attractive. He was born in poverty and obscurity, so the record has it. He grew up to conquer no lands like Alexander, nor exhibit philosophical genius like Plato. He built no cities and left no literature for posterity. He ended his life as he began it, outside even the civilised kindness of men, a feeding trough in a cattle cave for a cradle, an instrument of cruel torture for a death bed. Yet something about that child speaks to all races, all classes, all ages, all periods of history, as does the birth of no other. Somehow even though it be laced with sentimentality, this events speaks. Surely what can be heard by so many cannot possibly be irrelevant to them. What is it? To what deep chords in human experience does Christmas appeal? If preaching is to address itself to man's condition this question cries out for an answer.

Perhaps the strength of the Christmas event lies in its power to remind that we are all tossed into a hostile world where we have to struggle for survival, and at the last no one escapes the enemy called death. The child of Bethlehem speaks of the basic solidarity of the human race. All men and women everywhere are together as a strange anomaly in a universe whose vastness and impartiality is frightening. When we pause to reflect on our condition we feel like that baby, precariously cradled, lonely and fragile. Whatever differences there may be among peoples, all are together in this common predicament.

Or could it be that the Christmas event is a stimulus to the idealism that lies buried in human hearts generally? In our better moments we all know 'in our bones' that innocence, humility and gentleness are the lasting qualities, and that life cannot be constructed on a basis of intrigue, vainglory and violence. Somehow Christmas points to the essential nature of existence, proclaiming what is true in a language that speaks even to those whose reactions barely rise above emotion.

The Church is wise when it does not reject these instinctive reactions, but allows itself to be encouraged by them to proclaim the identity of the child whose nativity the world commemorates. Christmas is the birthday of the man who was crucified and rose from the dead. This is who he is. What this means is that we cannot come upon the full significance of the child in the manger at Bethlehem by advancing straight to it, but only after a circuitous route by way of the crucifixion, death, burial and resurrection. The manger is not the place to begin appreciating Jesus, it is the place to which to return, and if we do not, if we stop short at the Cross and resurrection, we have not been starved of the gospel of Christ, on the contrary, we have in those events the iron rations for the pilgrimage of life, but not its riches; this must be said, the riches are only available when we make our way from the wood of the Cross to the wood of the manger, and are inspired by what we see to echo the words of the fourth gospel, 'So the Word became flesh; he came to dwell among us, and we saw his glory, such glory as befits the Father's only Son, full of grace and truth.'[1] In a word, we see there the incarnate Word.

This, however, is a faith concept. We cannot prove that the Christ child is the incarnate Word. We can only believe that he is. And if we

[1] John 1:14 (N.E.B.).

proclaim the nativity of Jesus in incarnational terms, it is a faith that we proclaim. So the birth narratives in the gospels of Matthew and Luke are faith proclamations.[2] What they offer is the good news of the birth of Christ as apprehended by faith. Form-criticism suggests their origin in a preaching situation. Possibly they were compiled in order to answer questions raised by the proclamation of Christ, questions about his origin and the origin of the apostolic mission. Like the passion narratives they appear to have existed at one time as a unity separate from the gospels to which they are now attached. Like them they also relate to preaching. They are *gospels*, not introductions to the biography of Jesus. They are good announcements of the infancy of Christ, using such materials as were available to proclaim Christ. They are *structured* narratives. The author of Matthew's account sets out to answer the two questions who Jesus was (*Quis?*), and where he came from (*Unde?*), seeking throughout to connect the events of Jesus' birth with the divine activity in Israel. The author of Luke's account presents a gallery displaying two sets of complementary and contrasting pictures in order to present the annunciation and the birth and the consequences of these two events. Both authors mould their material with striking literary skill, and both employ *midrash*. This is not to deny the existence of historical facts, but to assert that the facts are embedded in artificial compositions, the aim of which is preaching. Sermons are not to be rejected as devoid of genuine historical material simply because they have been composed *as sermons*. In such a light the birth narratives in the gospels of Matthew and Luke ought to be valued.

Stress cannot be laid too heavily on the necessity for careful study of these narratives before opinions are allowed to harden both on the Incarnation itself and on its mode, namely the Virgin Birth. All too frequently the doctrine is rejected *a priori* as unscientific, and the birth narratives are dismissed as parallels to Hellenistic and other mythologies. Such dismissals are too superficial.[3] And when the outcome is a lack of conviction about what word there is to proclaim at Christmas, the situation is serious, because there is no time when men and women are more willing to hear some word of God.[4]

The points on which the two birth narratives are in agreement are very few. They serve, however, to show what is important. Both give

[2] Ortensio da Spinetoli, *Introduzione ai Vangeli dell' Infanzia* (Paideia-Brescia, 1967) p. 22. This book supplies comprehensive footnotes supporting the text and a valuable bibliography.

[3] Jean Daniélou, *Les Évangiles de l'enfance* (Paris: Éditions du Seuil, 1967) p. 7.

[4] Ortensio de Spinetoli, op. cit., p. 7.

the names of Jesus' parents as Joseph and Mary, both declare that he was born in Bethlehem (though Matthew gives us to understand that the family lived in Bethlehem while Luke explains how the birth only occurred there because of the census). Both assert that no sexual intercourse took place between Joseph and Mary before the birth of Jesus, and both ascribe the conception as due to the Holy Spirit.

Jesus was born in Bethlehem. The place can be found on a map. It can be visited. This together with the identification by name of the parents is primarily seeking to lift the event out of a vague 'once-upon-a-timeness'. This birth actually took place (this is what the narratives are asserting), it did not merely *seem to take place*, and Jesus did not merely seem to be a real human being (docetism), he was a real baby boy and became a thoroughly human man. Christianity is rooted in the historical and the particular.

Jesus was born of a virgin.[5] Neither Matthew nor Luke explain this, justify it or theologise about it, all they do is describe it and in as few words as possible. What key could be lower than Matthew 1:18 (R.V.), 'Now the birth of Jesus Christ was on this wise'? Macquarrie says there is no point in discussing its historicity: 'the conception of a child is not a publicly observable event open to historical investigation.'[6] Maybe, but the writers of these birth narratives present it as a historical fact. So the problem remains. Attempts are made to solve it by asserting that in the Hellenistic environment in which the Church grew up, Christians would naturally attempt to ascribe to their hero (Christ) a supernatural birth such as was accorded other leaders, for example, Hercules or Plato. The weakness of this argument lies in the fact that the birth narratives of Matthew and Luke are thoroughly Jewish, and bear no trace of Hellenistic influence. In any case the parallel does not exist because those mythological births were not virgin births but the outcome of unions between a woman and a divine being, an idea repugnant to Jewry.[7]

Another objection to the Virgin Birth is that it removes the true humanity of Christ. If he was not born as we are born, how can he be one of us, 'in all points tempted like as we are'?[8] Suppose, however,

[5] Matt. 1:18; Luke 1:34.
[6] J. Macquarrie, *Principles of Christian Theology* (S.C.M. Press, 1966) p. 258.
[7] See Gen. 6:1-4. Perhaps the clearest refutation of the idea that the Virgin Birth has its origin in Hellenistic mythological parallel is to be found in C. K. Barrett, *The Holy Spirit and the Gospel Tradition* (S.P.C.K., 1947) pp. 6-10. See also Douglas Edwards, *The Virgin Birth in History & Faith* (Faber, 1943).
[8] Heb. 4:15 (A.V.).

his birth were other than Matthew and Luke state it to be, would not Christ then be trapped in the sinful network which envelops mankind? And if it be argued that he escaped from this trap and became saviour, does he then show us what we can do with God's help? But this is not the gospel. The initiative must be with God.

It is unlikely that progress will be made with the problem of the Virgin Birth if we discuss it at the historical or at the biological level. Examples of parthenogenesis[9] in areas of nature other than the human do not help. Macquarrie is right when he urges consideration at the theological level, and when he commends Barth in maintaining that the doctrine of the Virgin Birth upholds the divine initiative in the Incarnation.[10] The birth narratives in Matthew and Luke do just this. They emphasise the action of the Holy Spirit[11] in this event. It is the fourth point in which the two narratives agree. Here then is the preacher's cue. This is the word of the Incarnation. This is what the catholic creed seeks to safeguard. This is the heart of apostolic preaching.

Recently, however, some distinguished scholars have contended (in *The Myth of God Incarnate*), that the essential proclamation of Christ can be maintained without the Incarnation. Thus Professor Wiles writes:

> I have been arguing that its abandonment as a metaphysical claim about the person of Jesus (for which there seems to me to be a strong case), would not involve the abandonment of all the religious claims normally associated with it. Of course it would make a difference. But the truth of God's self-giving love, and the rôle of Jesus in bringing that vision to life in the world would remain. For myself much even of the traditional incarnation language and imagery would still seem appropriate as a pictorial way of expressing their truths.[12]

And Leslie Houlden asks whether 'the centrality of Jesus for all that concerns man's understanding of God' is an allowable equivalent for, or development of, the relevant Christological statement of the Nicene Creed or the Chalcedonian Definition. And is 'the deep and intimate involvement of God with the world' an allowable interpretation

---

[9] See E. L. Mascall, *Christian Theology & Natural Science* (Longmans Green & Co., 1950) pp. 307–311.
[10] *Church Dogmatics*, p. 177.
[11] Matt. 1:18,20; Luke 1:15,35,41,67; 2:25-27.
[12] *The Myth of God Incarnate*, p. 9.

of what is at stake in the statement that 'the Word was made flesh'? Many, he thinks, will hold that they are not, though he himself apparently would take this view. He is of the opinion that if 'the Christian message is to make its way in the diverse and multiform world of discourse now before it, it must strive harder for clarity and intelligibility',[13] by declaring how we have had the lot and privilege of being brought to God by innumerable routes as a result of Jesus.

In the essays which comprise this book the emphasis is on man's experience of God. This is proper in so far as revelation does not by-pass human experience, *but* even when Jesus is said to be the divinely appointed disclosure point of God for us, the general impression left is that *our experience of Christ*, and not Christ, is the substance of Christian proclamation, and this places man and not God at the centre. Preaching must get beyond this. Christ must be proclaimed as Someone transcending our experience and greater than our experience. It may be that with these interpretations something of the form of the gospel as traditionally proclaimed remains, but the proclamation is seriously weakened and altered. In seeking to make the message more acceptable to modern man it has lost the dimension of God *acting* on our behalf. What can men and women do who know themselves powerless to achieve their own salvation? It looks as if there may be a gospel for the righteous and for the spiritually perceptive, but not for 'the tax-gatherers and sinners'. Testimony to 'the man Jesus through whom some of us in different ways have come to know God', omits the divine initiative and dynamic which alone is able to effect the rescue of men separated from God.

What then is the message of the incarnate Word?

First, that with the birth of Christ we have entered on a new era. It is a proper insight that marks this by dividing time into B.C. and A.D. Not that God was not, is not, and will not, be operative in the world apart from the Incarnation, but he is operating in a new way. Matthew and Luke associate the birth and the new era with the action of the Holy Spirit. There has come about a new creation, a new beginning, a new genesis,[14] embodied in God's new man, the one whom Paul calls the second man or the last Adam.[15] So the birth of Christ is unique. There is nothing like it. There has been nothing like it, and there will be nothing like it. It is an antedated last event, it is eschatological. It has the character of 'once-for-allness'.

[13] Ibid., p. 132.
[14] Matt. 1:1 & 18.
[15] 1 Cor. 15:45–48.

This incarnation of the Word is not to be thought of as God becoming a man—else (to put the point crudely), how could God be upholding the universe while cradled in a manger?—but of the Godhead being extended to include human nature, and thus we see Jesus. Our right reaction to this proclamation of a new era initiated by God through the Holy Spirit is to recognise it and live in the new opportunities it provides.

Secondly the message of the Incarnation is that God has entered our finite world of space and time and lived under the conditions it requires. So the creator of his own free will becomes subject to his own creation. There is a limit on his own almightiness. Nothing provides an insight into the mind and character of God to compare with the Incarnation, and if it took place 'for us men and for our salvation', then God is so different from what, without the Incarnation, we might have thought him to be, that the title, 'Father', which Jesus used, is possible. The author of the fourth gospel having written, 'So the Word became flesh', went on to add, 'No one has ever seen God; but God's only Son, he who is nearest to the Father's heart, he has made him known.'[16]

Thirdly, this entry of God into our world of space and time shows how God is, and always has been, involved in the world's darkness and pain. This is a message to which men and women, in their blackest hours, respond. Few experiences are more hurting than the consciousness of abandonment, and the real hurt of pain is its isolating property. The sick man, the persecuted man, the condemned man, feels cut off from the living, and to be cut off is to foretaste death. But God in Christ entered this kind of world, cancelling the aloneness which presages our death. This is the gospel, the good news of the Incarnation. It is the word of the Incarnation to be preached. And there is more. God did not only enter the realm of darkness, but the areas of light. There he also dwells, which means that all the loveliness, all the utility, all the precision that contributes so fully to the pleasure of man, as well as to his joy in community (which is life indeed), is God indwelt. This is the message of creation for the Creator is manifest in his works, but the plenitude of that message is in the Incarnation. God does not stay outside his living world, but lives in it. Here is the proclamation that makes for wonder, contentment and laughter. Here is the preacher's opportunity at Christmas to speak what men and women are waiting to hear, and if they do not hear it, they will respond as best they can to what they imagine Christmas must mean.

[16] John 1:14 & 18 (N.E.B.).

And fourthly, the entry of God in the Incarnation means that God has not despised our human nature, he has assumed and lived sinlessly in it, that is, in a relationship with God wholly devoid of separating barriers. Human nature is not essentially bad, any more than matter is essentially evil. Such ideas were nonsense to the Greeks who were therefore shocked to read in the gospel, 'So the Word became flesh', but this is the firm word of the Incarnation that God took 'our nature upon him',[17] and in doing this he revealed its potentiality for the closest possible union with God. No longer can we imagine that divine and human are opposites. There is humanity in divinity and divinity in humanity, sin notwithstanding. Such is the optimism of the gospel of the Incarnation. And God with us means redemption. What else could it mean? The divine presence cannot leave that in which it dwells unchanged. Here is an aspect of redemption on which the Eastern Church in particular has fastened. So the Incarnation evokes proclamation calling for the recognition that 'God has turned to his people, saved them and set them free',[18] and that there can be freedom from our enemies because of it.

But is it true? Can the Incarnation be reasonably given the primacy of place it holds in the Christian faith? 'From one point of view Jesus represented simply another human life, the life of a turbulent innovator in the eyes of most who saw him. But to the disciples, this life was the focusing of the presence and action of God. Faith perceived the dimension which is not publicly observable, and could not be. Was this leap of faith just an arbitrary leap, or could it be defended? Certainly, it could neither be proved nor disproved by any observation or argument. But it is confirmed in the community's subsequent life of faith, where the miracle of incarnation interprets the community's existence, lends meaning to it, strengthens its being. And again, the miracle does not remain isolated, but is confirmed in a whole series of "miracles", foci of the divine presence and action. These happen in the life and experience of the community of faith, continually leading it into fuller being, ultimately showing that they have no illusory character. The sacraments, for instance, are such foci. Talk of the "miracle of the Mass" is not just superstitious talk but points to the focusing of the divine presence in the Eucharist. Another example is afforded by the lives of the Saints. Men have attributed "miracles" to them, and this may often have been in the mythological way of ascribing public marvels to them. But this need not obscure the general sense in which sainthood is the focusing

[17] See the Collect for Christmas Day, B.C.P.
[18] Luke 1:68 (N.E.B.).

in a human life of the divine presence. Miracle is not magic, but the focusing of holy Being's presence and actions amid the events, things and persons of the world, and this has the highest reality.' So writes Macquarrie.[19] Nor is this all. As Kenneth Leech[20] has reminded us, both the mystical element in the Christian religion and social action on the part of the Church, two apparently opposite directions of movement, the one contemplative and the other activist, the one in retreat and the other outgoing, both alike, stem from the doctrine of the incarnate Word. This doctrine therefore is not dispensable if the Christian faith and practice are to live. How then can the Incarnation not be proclaimed? How can it be other than basic in the ministry of the Word?

---

[19] *Principles of Christian Theology* (S.C.M. Press, 1966) p. 232.
[20] *Theology*, March 1976, 'Believing in the Incarnation'.

9

The word of judgment

JUDGMENT IS A RARE INGREDIENT IN MODERN PREACHING. TO INCLUDE it in a pulpit ministry would be regarded as hopelessly old-fashioned. Time was, no doubt, when preachers were willing to dangle their hearers over the pit of hell, and congregations were neither shocked, surprised, nor even amused by this kind of preaching,[1] it was certainly part of the stock-in-trade of evangelists, especially those known as the 'hot-gospellers'. Apart, however, from the placards carried by religious fanatics on Epsom Downs on Derby Day, or wherever crowds assemble, placards bearing such words as 'The wicked shall be turned into hell' and 'After death the judgment', no one now expects judgment to figure in preaching, certainly not in Christian preaching which proclaims a God of infinite love. Judgment and love cannot co-exist.

Moreover, has not the notion of God's wrath been exploited for the sake of monetary gain? Has not even the Church manipulated it in order to extort cash for the provision of some of its most famous buildings? Was not the sale of indulgences one of the abuses that prompted the Protestant reformation?

Furthermore, to cause people to be motivated by fear is psychologically unsound, if not ethically suspect. The Churches generally were much impressed by this argument between the wars. They did not know then how widely fear would be employed in the second half of the twentieth century by public secular authorities, in road safety campaigns and the anti-smoking drive. Fear of the consequences of recklessness and over-indulgence has been deliberately employed in the interests of human well-being. In the Church, however, fear is out, along with judgment and condemnation. From all that could be gathered from contemporary preaching there is no word of God on judgment.

[1] For man to believe in God as judge, if he believes in God at all, seems to be part of the history of man. Primitive man, but not only primitive man, is ready to attribute calamities and suffering to a retributive God.

But is there no word? Is there no word in the Bible? Is it possible to read the Old Testament prophets without being made sharply aware of God's judgments, especially on nations?[2] A curious process of selection has however operated in the case of these prophetic pieces. During the last hundred years they have been lauded to the skies for their proclamations of social justice, not least by people of no religious profession, as if their discovery was one of the great advances of our time, but the vast tracts of their messages which tell of judgment on account of *injustice* have been largely disregarded.

But this can be dismissed as Old Testament preaching. What of the New Testament? What of the teaching and preaching of Jesus? Can judgment be said to form no part of his message? But his ministry was seen from the outset to be in the Old Testament prophetic succession. He was actually called 'a prophet'. And his message was supported by the same two pillars as supported those prophetic messages—mercy and judgment. And what is to be made of the following?

'Then he spoke of the towns in which most of his miracles had been performed, and denounced them for their impenitence. "Alas for you, Chorazin!" he said; "alas for you Bethsaida! If the miracles that were performed in you had been performed in Tyre and Sidon, they would have repented long ago in sackcloth and ashes. But it will be more bearable, I tell you, for Tyre and Sidon on the day of judgment than for you. And as for you, Capernaum, will you be exalted to the skies? No, brought down to the depths! For if the miracles had been performed in Sodom which were performed in you, Sodom would be standing to this day. But it will be more bearable, I tell you, for the land of Sodom on the day of judgment than for you." '[3]

Was this said in anger? But to read these words rather more as the sigh of Jesus over the inevitable consequences of man's impenitence is far more in keeping with his lament over an even greater city—Jerusalem.

'When he came in sight of the city, he wept over it and said, "If only you had known, on this great day, the way that leads to peace! But no; it is hidden from your sight. For a time will come upon you, when your enemies will set up siege-works against you; they will

[2] See Amos chapters 1 and 2 for a beginning.
[3] Matt. 11:20–24 (N.E.B.).

encircle you and hem you in at every point; they will bring you to the ground, you and your children within your walls, and not leave you one stone standing on another, because you did not recognise God's moment when it came." '4

Here is no vindictive reaction to opposition and personal rejection, but a clear recognition of what the prophets plainly saw—that a moral principle operates within life generally, set there by God himself, and which cannot be flouted with impunity.

Is this so difficult to understand or so repulsive that it is necessary to expunge from the outset every notion of judgment? But take an illustration of a motor car. On delivery, the purchaser is provided with a handbook which sets out in detail the maker's instructions for operating the car. Servicing is to be undertaken every three thousand miles, the level of distilled water in the battery is to be checked, the tyres are to be kept at a certain pressure. Suppose the owner flouts every one of these instructions. Suppose he neglects to have the car serviced, or to check the battery or the tyre pressure, will the manufacturer descend upon him in wrath to punish him for his negligence? Not so, but the owner will experience judgment on his misdeeds *by the breakdown* of his car. It will not run in defiance of the rules upon which it has been made to operate.

Granted there is a flaw in this illustration if it is meant to cover God's relation to his creation. God has not made his world and washed his hands of it. He is not an absentee machine manufacturer who does not even know his customers; but the illustration serves for one important point if only for this—it is possible for judgment to operate in a form which is *without any kind of vindictiveness*.

As it happens, the illustration can be made more effective by supposing a father to give his son a new car. To his utter dismay, however, he observes the lack of care his son bestows on it. No servicing, no tyre pressure checks, harsh driving of the engine. The father may advise, but he will not punish. His son has come of age. Nevertheless, judgment does fall on the son for his misconduct, the car breaks down and the father is left to grieve at such a prodigal waste of the gift he has made.

Judgment through breakdown is the form in which it is most commonly experienced at a national level. It was so in Jesus' day. His countrymen would not see that the way they were operating their country was bound to precipitate a terrifying catastrophe. 'O

4 Luke 19:41-44 (N.E.B.).

Jerusalem, Jerusalem,' he cried, 'the city that murders the prophets and stones the messengers sent to her! How often have I longed to gather your children, as a hen gathers her brood under her wings; but you would not let me. Look, look! there is your temple, forsaken by God.'[5]

Breakdown of British life, and perhaps of American life, is alarmingly possible if the reckless spendthrift attitude is not reversed. For years Britain has been spending more than it has earned. The pound loses its value dramatically every six months. Unemployment is the highest since the war. Yet the nation refuses to cut its coat according to its cloth, instead it borrows cloth and yet more cloth from overseas creditors who will sooner or later require their accounts to be settled. Selfishness and sectional self-interests are not the principles upon which a country can run. What they produce is dwindling resources, dwindling job opportunities, and a decline in the general standard of life, *and this is the judgment.*

This unwillingness for restraint presages catastrophe in another sphere—the prodigal expropriation of the earth's natural resources. This applies to fossil fuels, to cultivation of the soil, even to fishing. And the reckless use of chemicals to force production coupled with thoughtless disposal of waste promises a poverty of resources which is frightening. Yet this must be the outcome if man will not see himself as the trustee for nature. The poverty will constitute the judgment.[6]

And now the so-called liberation from the long-standing taboos surrounding sexual relations. Like taboos in general, these have been presented by some psychiatrists and progressive social workers as unenlightened and dangerously repressive, freedom from which therefore is an urgent necessity. This has been fastened on in an age when revolt from all forms of authority has become characteristic both by the young for whom sexual adventures mean an ever-present temptation, and by sharp-witted financiers who see new markets for quick profits. So the drift to 'permissiveness', so called, has run on to pornography as an industry, the production and marketing of contraceptives on a vast scale, abortions as a source of income for a few with the 'know-how' when the contraceptives fail, and all the time the systematic procuring of young girls for those willing to pay for their sexual adventures.

[5] Luke 13:34,35 (N.E.B.). This verse also serves as a reminder that in the Bible judgment is not impersonal.

[6] See Barbara Ward, *The Home of Man* (Pelican, 1976). Also H. Montefiore, *Apocalypse. What Does God Say?* (Southwark Cathedral Publications, Provost's Office 9, St Thomas Street, London SE1).

The introduction of the contraceptive pill has been the biggest factor in the overturning of traditional attitudes to sex. Writing in the *Daily Telegraph*,[7] Ian Donald, Professor of Midwifery at Glasgow University, said,

> The introduction of the contraceptive pill has produced a situation without parallel in human social history, compared with which atomic nuclear fission and fusion are almost insignificant. Its very success in enabling couples to control their family size responsibly has brought in train a whole host of new problems when abused. Here admittedly, it is easy to confuse cause and effect . . .
>
> The paradox of today is that, in spite of the Pill effectively segregating sexual activity from responsibility for its designed consequences, namely, pregnancy and motherhood, nevertheless the illegitimate rate is rising as never before, and the abortion rate per number of live-born children continues to rise as even members of the Family Planning Association admit, and in some quarters even extol. It is a sad fact that the more contraception is used the more does the abortion rate increase as a long-stop method in the event of failure or neglect, particularly in the immature.
>
> The sex crime rate was never higher, this in spite of more so-called sex education available today. Perhaps the most distinctive feature of all is that it is the youngest teenager groups who are suffering most, not only numerically, but in terms of venereal disease, pelvic ill-health, attempted suicide, disillusionment and misery, predominantly female . . .

Preachers are shy when it comes to speaking about sex in the pulpit, not on account of the subject *per se*, but because sexual morals can so easily be counted as the one area of morality with which they concern themselves when sins in other departments of life can be more damaging. The awkward fact is however that wrong-doing in what is commonly called an individual's 'love-life', personal, private, and even secret, to all intents and purposes a gentle thing, turns out to have consequences in human misery and even violence, seemingly out of all proportion to the original misdeed, if misdeed it is reckoned by some 'progressives' to be. This being the case, it begins to become clear why civilisation, and certainly not only the Christian, has hedged sexual relations around with regulations. Judgment on transgression in the sexual sphere appears to be an inescapable reality and the proclamation

[7] 10th April, 1978.

of it as the word of God by the Old Testament prophets for whom adultery was a horror, was not out of place for men concerned for the welfare of their nation. It is to be wondered therefore if prophetic preaching on the part of the Church for 'such a time as this' can stand back in silence on this particular word of judgment.

Strange as it may at first sound, the theme of judgment is most prominent in the New Testament in the fourth gospel. It has been called the Gospel of Judgment. The key passage is so important that it needs to be quoted in full:

> God loved the world so much that he gave his only Son, that every one who has faith in him may not die but have eternal life. It was not to judge the world that God sent his Son into the world, but that through him the world might be saved.
>
> The man who puts his faith in him does not come under judgment; but the unbeliever has already been judged in that he has not given his allegiance to God's only Son. Here lies the test: the light has come into the world, but men preferred darkness to light because their deeds were evil. Bad men hate all the light and avoid it, for fear their practices should be shown up. The honest man comes to the light so that it may be clearly seen that God is in all he does.[8]

Here we see divine judgment as a process now. In one sense it is not an action on the part of God, for God's primary intention is not to judge the world, but to save it, and Christ judges no man. In another sense, however, God does judge the world because (to use Johannine language) he sends his Son into the world who becomes the means by which the men judge themselves.[9] It is as if some visitors to London should enter the National Gallery in Trafalgar Square, and on seeing a Rembrandt pronounce it as a 'meaningless daub of paint'. What in fact has taken place is not a judgment of the visitor to the Gallery or Rembrandt, or his work, but a man's judgment on himself. He has set himself apart as an utter *ignoramus*. So Christ operates as the judge of all mankind. Or more accurately, so Christ is the means by which all men judge themselves. And let it not be forgotten that Christ is more than the historical Jesus; as the Word of God he is encountered in ways and means by people who may never have heard of the Incarnate Christ. Nevertheless, whenever and however he is encountered as light shining in darkness he is the means of judgment, men

[8] John 3:16–21 (N.E.B.).
[9] John 5:22; 9:39.

separate themselves out by the way they react. It is a process of separation, and it is this process of judgment that the fourth gospel develops
in the story it has to tell. After the healing of the paralytic at the Sheep
Pool in Jerusalem there were those who set themselves apart to perse-
cute him.[10] After Jesus' sermon on the bread of life in Capernaum
some 'disciples withdrew and no longer went about with him'.[11]
Following on the healing of the blind man some commented, 'This
fellow is no man of God'.[12] This theme of self-separation or self-
judgment continues throughout the gospel.

Does this process of self-judgment mean then that there is no final
judgment? To use two Greek words, is there only a *krisis* and not a
krima? Apparently not. The 'Day of the Lord' which features frequently in the Old Testament on the lips of the prophetic preachers,
and often with a reference to the end of time, is not absent from the
teaching of Jesus in the Synoptic Gospels,[13] nor the presentation of it
which the fourth Evangelist sets out. One passage reads, 'Marvel not
at this: for the hour cometh, in which all that are in the tombs shall
hear his voice, and shall come forth; they that have done good, unto
the resurrection of life; and they that have done ill, unto the resurrection
of judgment.'[14]

The form in which judgment appears in Paul's writing is as 'the
wrath of God'.[15] This was a consistent Old Testament theme and
Paul, as a Christian preacher, did not shed it. The coming of Christ
in his view involved no dismissal of the God of wrath, rather divine
retribution continued to fall 'upon all the godless wickedness of men'.[16]

Because of sin the whole world is 'exposed to the judgment of God'.[17]
It may be tempting to set Paul's emphasis on judgment over against
Jesus' message of love, but the attempt will not succeed. Jesus saw himself as the bearer of divine wrath,[18] and in the New Testament as a
whole the Messiah must inevitably exercise God's judgment.[19] Attempts

[10] John 5:16.
[11] John 6:66 (N.E.B.).
[12] John 9:16 (N.E.B.).
[13] Matt. 5:21f; Mark 9:43–48.
[14] John 5:28,29 (R.V.) (see also 11:24).
[15] The N.E.B. avoids translating *orge* by 'wrath', and substitutes 'retribution',
'judgment', or 'vengeance'. John 3:35 and Rev. 19:15 are exceptions.
[16] Rom. 1:18 (N.E.B.).
[17] 3:19 (N.E.B.).
[18] Mark 11:14,20; Luke 13;34f; 19:41–44.
[19] Matt. 25:31f; Rom. 14:10; 2 Cor. 5:10; 2 Tim. 4:1,8; 1 Pet. 4;5: Rev. 6:10;
19:11.

in some degenerate Protestant theology to set the love of Christ over against the wrath of God and to see the Atonement as operating with respect to this situation are quite wrong.

The distinctive feature of the New Testament is that the wrath of God is most clearly seen at the Cross of Christ. The Cross is the ultimate exhibition of what the sinfulness of sin can do. But it is also the ultimate exhibition of what the love of God can do, it can let the consequences of his wrath against sin fall on himself for the rescue of man.

Ought the modern preacher to proclaim a word of judgment? The first answer to the question is that he cannot avoid doing so if he proclaims Christ, for as soon as Christ is set forth, judgment begins to operate. This applies also to the sacraments, they can be sacraments of judgment.[20] But ought the modern preacher to be explicit in proclaiming a word of judgment? It is difficult to appreciate how he can profess to be a prophetic preacher in the Biblical tradition if he refuses the task. And there is this to remember, no judgments, no punishments, no penalties, no sufferings, are reformative till they are accepted as deserved. To bring hearers of sermons to this state of mind is no small part of the function of the preacher. By calling for repentance he can cause the judgments of God to lead to the renewal of men, for of this the scriptures assure him—the word of judgment is never God's last word, but always the word of mercy. It is for preachers to put their hearers (if they will) in the way of experiencing this.

[20] I Cor. 11:29.

10

The word of hope

PREACHING, IF IT IS TO BE CHRISTIAN PREACHING, MUST BE HOPEFUL. This is not to say that it must be buoyant, cheerful and optimistic in the way it is presented, though these moods properly characterise it in its totality; nor is it to demand that from time to time hope should be selected as a theme for a sermon. What is meant is that Christian preaching should consistently promise a future because it is based on the resurrection of Christ.

Life is insupportable if there is no future for it. If it is true to say, 'While there is life there is hope', it is equally true to say, 'While there is hope there is life'. Christian preaching offers life. This offer is the core of the gospel message, but it will stir only a few hearts unless it is related to hope. Life without a future for it is an empty offer.

The Marxists recognise the necessity for hope. One of the reasons for their success in winning vast numbers of people to their allegiance in different parts of the world is the future they hold out for all who are oppressed, suppressed and depressed. Hope for the future generates action in the present, notwithstanding the trials of endurance involved.

Christian proclamation must offer a future. It has a future to offer because of the resurrection of Christ, but because this is based on an event in the past, it is the past that receives the emphasis. This needs balancing with an emphasis on the future.

One of the difficulties is the vagueness of the future as compared with the past. The future in any case in the Christian understanding lies with God, it is God's gift, and not man's accomplishment, but because God can be trusted, hope for the future is safe and sure, operating like an anchor.[1] It cannot, however, be catalogued or dated. It is not open to investigation and research as is the past. The historical past therefore receives an almost overwhelming attention in Christian studies in comparison with the future, and Christian

[1] Heb. 6:19 (N.E.B.).

proclamation can easily give the impression of being an antiquarian activity; and if not this altogether, then pre-eminently concerned with tradition and guarding the inheritance. That it should be dismissed as unprogressive is not surprising.

None of this is to underrate the importance of *deriving* the Gospel from historical events, even datable events, and events relating to places which can be found on a map. There is no 'once-upon-a-timeness' about the Christian story; nor is the Christian message a speculative philosophy, though it may give rise to such. Christian proclamation says in the first place that the man Jesus of Nazareth during the procuratorship of Pontius Pilate was crucified and rose again from the dead, and this event convinced his followers that he was the Christ, the Saviour, the Son of God, and that in him God was incarnate. These things happened, but because they happened meaning for the present can be derived from them, and a future is assured.

The historical events do not however in themselves produce the future. Evolution or development is not in mind here. It is not as if something can be accomplished which must inevitably produce Utopia. These events only operate to produce hope of a future as they evoke faith in God, whose will it is to liberate his people and bring them into what he promises.

Hope is grounded in faith. Moltmann[2] quotes Calvin as saying that

hope is nothing else than the expectation of those things which faith has believed to have been truly promised by God. Thus, faith believes God to be true, hope awaits the time when this truth shall be manifested; faith believes that he is our Father, hope anticipates that he will even show himself to be a Father towards us; faith believes that eternal life has been given to us, hope anticipates that it will some time be revealed; faith is the foundation on which hope rests, hope nourishes and sustains faith. For as no one except him who already believes his promises can look for anything from God, so again the weakness of our faith must be sustained and nourished by patient hope and expectation, lest it fail and grow faint . . . By unremitting, renewing and restoring, it (hope) invigorates faith again and again with perseverance.[3]

[2] *Theology of Hope* (S.C.M. Press, English Translation, 1967) p. 20.
[3] Calvin, *Institutio* III 2. 42. ET. *Institutes of the Christian Religion* (Library of Christian Classics, Vols. XX and XXI), ed. John McNeill. Trans. Ford, Lewis Battle, 1961, p. 590.

If then hope requires faith to evoke it, faith requires hope to sustain it. Or again, as Moltmann expresses it,

Thus in the Christian life faith has the priority, but hope the primacy. Without faith's knowledge of Christ, hope becomes a Utopia and remains hanging in the air. But without hope faith falls to pieces, becomes a faint-hearted and ultimately a dead faith. It is through faith that a man finds the path of true life, but it is only hope that keeps him on that path. Thus it is that faith in Christ gives hope its assurance. Thus it is that hope gives faith in Christ its breadth and leads it into life.[4]

The consequence for preachers of this interrelation of faith and hope is that no proclamation of the *kerygma* lacking a constant element of hope can expect to build up a congregation. The primitive *kerygma* certainly looked forward, treating the death and resurrection of Jesus as eschatological events, and promising a future in the form of the judgment and second Advent. However the latter is to be interpreted it stands as a reminder that preaching cannot stop at the proclamation of the Christ-event and sins forgiven, it must provide a future, it must proclaim a word of hope, and it must reflect hopefulness in all that it does.

Such preaching will stand out in sharp contrast to the world in which it operates. With the erosion of Christian faith in the countries of the West in the latter half of the twentieth century, there has crept over mankind a feeling of hopelessness. The root trouble is that few people believe in anyone or anything. Faith has not only been removed from God, it has been removed from men, and even from organisations, which for long periods have been highly respected, such as democratic forms of government. As a result, despair is widespread, and with it inertia, resignation and melancholy. Not even profit-making industry has buoyancy. So because there is no faith, there is no hope, and because there is no hope there is lack of drive. The literature of the existentialists has painted grey pictures of the modern hopelessness which derives from the vacuum created by the loss of Christian faith and the non-adoption of Marxism.

The tone for Christian preaching is set by the first Epistle of Peter.[5]

Praise be to the God and Father of our Lord Jesus Christ, who in

[4] Ibid., p. 20.
[5] I Peter 1:3-5 (N.E.B.).

his great mercy gave us new birth into a living hope by the resurrection of Jesus Christ from the dead! The inheritance to which we are born is one that nothing can destroy or spoil or wither. It is kept for you in heaven, and you, because you put your faith in God, are under the protection of his power until salvation comes— the salvation which is even now in readiness and will be revealed at the end of time.

This passage is generally, though not exclusively, referred to the the Second Coming of Christ, the *Parousia*. Some scholars[6] assert that hope in the New Testament always bears reference to the return of Christ at the end of the age and cites the above verses as characteristic. The question can however be asked as to whether the hope is not also a hope for the created universe and for this world as well. Paul writes in the Epistle to the Romans,

> For I reckon that the sufferings we now endure bear no comparison with the splendour, as yet unrevealed, which is in store for us. For the created universe waits with eager expectation for God's sons to be revealed. It was made the victim of frustration, not by its own choice, but because of him who made it so; yet always there is hope, because the universe itself is to be freed from the shackles of mortality and enter upon the liberty and splendour of the children of God.[7]

This reflects a deeper insight than is evident in 1 Peter. There is *hope for this universe*. It has a future, not indeed as it is, but as it will be transformed by the power of God.

All Christian preaching about hope must start from the resurrection of Christ. It must proclaim the identity of the crucified with the Risen One. It will not do to assert that Christ is risen 'in the preaching'. There is no hope for material bodies or for material things, if the material of Christ's body was not involved in his resurrection. But if it was involved, then what Christ assumed in the Incarnation, and what is the creation of God has a future, not as it is, or as it was, but transformed by an act that can only be called resurrection. This means that the material, the life in the material, contribute to the future that shall be. They are not wasted. They have not come into being only

[6] See art. *Hope* by Alan Richardson in *A Theological Word Book of the Bible* (S.C.M. Press, 1950) pp. 108–9.

[7] Rom. 8: 18–22 (N.E.B.). See David L. Edwards, *The Last Things Now* (S.C.M. Press, 1969), p. 82ff; also *A Reason to Hope* (Collins, 1978).

to be rejected. What God has created he will not totally destroy. He will not even allow death to destroy it. He will redeem it even from destruction so that the present heavens and present earth, will become the new heaven and the new earth, and men and women live in newness of life.

In the light of this, preaching must in the first place proclaim man's resurrection in Christ. To restrict preaching to matters of personal piety or even to prophetic insights into the contemporary, social and political situation is to forfeit a dimension which preaching requires, and which gives it an unassailable uniqueness. The resurrection of Christ does indeed make its first impact in creating new men with new life now. And new men are a necessity without which no improved environment can of itself produce a better life. But as Paul wrote to the Corinthians, 'If it is for this life only that Christ has given us hope, we of all men are most to be pitied.'[8] Christian preaching fails if it has nothing to say to people in the waiting room of the crematorium, nothing to say to the man who knows his cancer is incurable. Christian preaching must not only teach people how to live, but also how to die. And this is teaching which must be given in the earlier days before the storms of bereavement break or the sudden awareness of the shortness of life's course throws the sufferer off balance, making faith attitudes to the situation difficult, if not impossible. The future to be proclaimed does not consist in a this-bodily resuscitation, the immortality of the soul, or in reincarnation, but in resurrection. This means that the resurrection body will be different from the body which is destined for dissolution and reincorporation into the material stuff of the universe. Even so, the human body is not like an overcoat put on and taken off without any significant effect on the wearer. We are what we are as persons partly through the way we have respected, pandered to, abused, or ill-treated our bodies. The resurrection body which we shall receive will be appropriate to the persons we have become in these earthly bodies. This is partly what makes responsible living in the here and now important. It has an effect on what we shall be.

Secondly, is it not possible in the light of this and of Paul's words in Romans 8:18–22, to acquire a glimpse, albeit hazy, into the future of the universe? It is God's universe, God's creation, God's stupendous handiwork. There is to be a new heaven and a new earth,[9] but is the present to be cast away as useless? Is there not to be a refashioned universe, a universe remade out of the present universe,

[8] 1 Cor. 15:19 (N.E.B.).
[9] Rev. 21:1.

12

even a redeemed universe, a reconstructed universe? In which case as with our human life in the body where we are contributing to that body which shall be, so will not all the good that we have contributed to this universe, or (to speak with more comprehension) to this world, of which we are the trustees, be taken up and used to make the new? Here is a faith which gives point to our earthly struggles for a better world, struggles which so often turn out to be disappointing. With God, however, nothing that is good is lost. Our (in some ways) better world which we have helped to build, God will give back to us in an even better one, from which death itself will be banished. This is the promised future. This is where our future lies.

There is also a third way in which the preacher should proclaim hope, more practical, more down-to-earth than the foregoing, but not unimportant. This is, through faith, to have hope of situations that might otherwise appear hopeless. There are striking illustrations of this in the gospels, in what are commonly called the miracle stories. Here is a man covered in leprosy, how could he hope for anything in the way of life beyond mere existence? But Christ healed him. Here are five thousand people, hungry in a desert place. How hopeless to expect any kind of satisfaction for such a crowd— but they were fed! Here is a wedding party with no wine left to celebrate the occasion . . . Here is a man crippled for thirty-eight years . . . Here is a man blind from birth . . . Here is a boy incapacitated with epilepsy. These are all hopeless situations and hopeless cases from the human standpoint. And there were worse, a child even dead, or so experienced mourners thought. But Christ changed these situations entirely. This is the word of hope for preaching. No situation is too baffling for God. Not that there is any guarantee that God will reverse every calamity. There were lepers in Israel who were never healed. Wedding parties doubtless, where everything went wrong, nothing was put right, paralysed men, crippled children, bereaved parents whose burdens were never lifted. But if we believe in the Risen Christ, if we believe in the real and royal presence of God which Jesus proclaimed, are we ever wise to write off a situation as hopeless? Nothing is impossible with God. These are the questions the preacher has to ask himself. And when his own hope is built up on faith he should live hopefully and preach in season and out of season the word of hope, hope for people now, hope for that which follows our final breath, and hope for the universe, which God made. The future lies with hopeful preachers because they proclaim a future. They stand out like beacons of light at a time when hope is out.

11

The word of justice

In his first Reith Lecture for 1978, Professor A. H. Halsey imagined a journey across the English countryside during which two constructions caught the attention: a church, old, and with its spire pointing heavenwards, and a motorway, brand new, providing quick access to the commuter suburbs, the seaside or a weekend cottage. The Church represented an expectation of satisfaction beyond this life, and in consequence a patient endurance of hardships now; the motorway promised quick satisfaction of desires at once, and any delay, any deprivation would be greeted with protest, strike, if not violence.

It is the achievements of science and technology that have changed the expectations of people, turning their attention from fulfilment beyond this life to fulfilment within the new possibilities of this life. The question therefore arises, ought preaching to be addressed to these new expectations without an eternal reference? a gospel, shall we say, of efficiency, satisfaction and happiness? But this in turn forces a more profound question, what is a human being? Is he a compound of chemical substances that has somehow produced self-consciousness? Is he a bundle of chemicals? Is he a superior kind of animal? Or could it be that he is *sui generis*, a unique being with an eternal destiny? That is to say, is he to be estimated not only by what he is but what he has the capacity to become?

The Christian proclamation of justice—and there is such a proclamation—is rooted in the Christian doctrine of man. The cardinal fact about man from the Christian viewpoint, is his relation to God, man belongs to God and God is his Creator. This refers not simply to his soul but to his body. Man is in fact one united being, finite and created. His mind is not the source of good and his body the source of evil; nor is his oneness with nature the ground of his goodness and his reasoning the cause of what evil he perpetrates. Body and soul are alike, united to God his creator in a unity of being.

This, however, is not all. Man is not only a body/soul, being created by God, he is made in the 'image of God'. This means far more than that man is a rational creature. He possesses consciousness, that is to say, he has the capacity to stand outside the world, and as a subject, to survey it; even more, he possesses self-consciousness, he has the capacity to stand outside himself and survey himself. This consciousness, this self-consciousness, which transcends both the external world and itself is known as 'spirit', and cannot be explained except from beyond itself. It is this 'homelessness' which is the ground of all religion, for it means that it cannot find the meaning of life, or satisfaction in life, either in itself or in the world. The fact then that man is not only body and soul, but spirit, is the reason why any preaching, any gospel, which addresses itself only to the new expectations which science and technology have fostered for the here and now, without an eternal reference, will not and cannot produce lasting satisfaction. Man requires more.

And yet the very fact that man is God's creature possessed of this unique faculty which we call 'spirit', demands certain requirements for him. He must have freedom, not unlimited freedom (for this is an impossibility, and God is his overlord), but freedom to develop his individualism. Freedom to form his own community relationships, freedom to experiment, freedom to make mistakes and to profit by them, freedom even to rebel and perhaps suffer for it. This means that man must have freedom to worship as he chooses, and that all forms of pressure to enforce conformity are wrong. It means also that man must have physical freedom, he must have the free use of his limbs and certainly not be the slave of any other. He must also be free to own property, for without property of some kind he cannot express his unique individuality; he must also be free to raise a family, free to work and free to be educated. All these are basic rights which belong to man as God's creature made in 'his image'. They belong to God's order of creation. They are part of his will for man, and he cannot be what God intended him to be without them. There is therefore a word of justice to be proclaimed, rooted not in a philosophy or political theory, but in the faith-concept that God has created man in 'his own image'. And man means man, any man, every man, not white man or black man, but man, and of course woman, of every race, colour, class or creed. Not that man has basic rights simply as man—this is not the *distinctive* Christian word of justice to be proclaimed, but that man has certain requirements which must be met because he is God's unique creature with an eternal destiny.

This idea of relationship to God and the consequential relationship of man to man is a development of the Old Testament word *Tsedaqah*, translated, maybe, as 'justice', but which is in fact very different from the Western idea of an ethical norm derived from what is thought of as absolute justice, and therefore equivalent to *'justitia'* or *'Gerechtigkeit'*. The Old Testament knows nothing of an absolute justice which watches with impartiality over conduct, taking care that each man gets his own right (*justitia distributiva*). Justice is loyalty *to a relationship*, and what this loyal relationship involves in a particular situation. As such it extends beyond correctness of conduct or legality into acts of kindness and faithfulness to the poor and needy as circumstances require. It was Israel's conviction that Yahweh himself acted in this way towards his people and so Israel never ceased to proclaim the righteous acts of the Lord which constituted her salvation.[1] Understood in these terms justice (*Tsedaqah*), is a proper subject for preaching, because it leads to the wholesomeness (*Yeshuah*) of the community.

The New Testament has very little to say about distributive or contractual justice. Jesus made it clear that he was not concerned with the justice which is applicable to mundane circumstances. When a a man approached him with the request that he should intervene in a dispute over his inheritance, he bluntly refused—'Man, who made me a judge or a divider over you?'[2] The same point is made in the dispute over the tribute money[3] and in the interview with Pilate.[4] What Jesus proclaimed was the order of the kingdom of God, what may be called *justitia evangelica*, and not *justitia civilis*.

This *justitia evangelica* is what Paul calls 'the righteousness of God'.[5] By it he means an activity of God which is directly opposed to merits and claims. It is the love of God, free and forgiving, revealed in the atoning death of Christ. Only through this reconciling gift can God's will become effective in man and it must be received as a gift, not demanded as a right. This paradoxical view of justice is the chief concern of the New Testament and its paradoxical character is seen nowhere more clearly than in Jesus' parable of the labourers in the vineyard.[6]

---

[1] For an understanding of justice in the Old Testament see G. von Rad, *Old Testament Theology* (Oliver and Boyd, 1962) Vol. I, pp. 370ff.

[2] Luke 12:14 (R.V.).

[3] Matt. 22:15ff.

[4] John 18:36.

[5] Rom. 3:21ff.

[6] Matt. 20:1ff.

We are not to infer, however, that Jesus had no interest in civil justice, nor that Paul had no word for his hearers concerning the problems of their everyday lives. Nevertheless what we are bound to say is that this aspect of justice was not their *first concern*, and what follows from this for preachers at all times is that they are only justified — and indeed, only safe— in proclaiming what is commonly called social justice if they do not neglect what we have called *justitia evangelica*, that is, the kingdom of God of Jesus' teaching, or the righteousness of God of Paul's letters, and also do not fail to recognise man's uniqueness as consisting first of all in his *relation* to God. Social justice is called for because man is related to a God who created him and wills to redeem him, whether he is aware of that relationship or not.

In this area what needs to be guarded against is dichotomy. All too frequently the evangelical gospel and the social gospel have been set over against each other, not least in North America. It is understandable that people who are both Christians and socially conscious should become estranged from that form of evangelical proclamation which exhibits itself as an exclusive pietism and is even proud of the fact. Its self-satisfaction and its personal comfort repel. It seems to exhibit little concern for the less fortunate in this world and a dismal failure to share the sorrows of mankind. Over against this its inner joy, sometimes artificial and forced, is offensive.

Perhaps few Christian leaders were more sensitive to this than Christoph Friedrich Blumhardt[7] (1842–1919) in Germany. The son of a father who became famous for his preaching and healing mission at Moettlingen, he at first followed in the same paths, carrying on the same work, but he broke from it, not from evangelical faith and preaching, but from all forms of traditional piety that had no social reference. He severely chastised any 'salvation only' Christianity, that is, a Christianity so much concerned with its own salvation that it loses sight of the victory God promised for the whole world.

They hop around in raptures, crying 'O what bliss!' One is left completely speechless at the sight of these hopping, blissful people. They are happy, they are saved! Not I. While the world is teeming with sin, and it is next to impossible for us to uphold God's kingdom, while God's name is being blasphemed and even good people no longer have any zeal from God, they are all in raptures! I would

[7] R. Lejeune, *Christoph Blumhardt und seine Botschaft* (Zürich and Leipzig: Rotapfel-Verlag, 1938). Trans. N. Y. Plough Publishing House, 1963.

like very seriously to ask those Christian lazy-bones: what are you seeking? Yourselves or God? Your own cause or the cause of the Lord?[8]

Blumhardt felt that basically the fight for a new social order was supported by a faith in God's kingdom promised us by Christ. The struggle for social justice actually became for him a sign of Jesus Christ.

We must not be silent. The social struggle of millions in our time is not a coincidence. It is related to the struggle of the apostles, and to the struggle which later also was fought by other men in secret, the struggle which we too want to fight. The ferment in the nations, the agitation of the poor, the crying out for the right to live—a crying given into the mouths of even the most miserable of men, which can no longer be silenced—these are the signs of our Lord Jesus Christ . . .

Blumhardt recognised the Messianic meaning of this social hope . . . therefore he agreed with the Social Democrats especially in their complete rejection of the existing social order and in the demand for a fundamentally new world. More than once he applied the parable of the two sons to the Social Democrats. 'They are a tool of God, and are like the son who says, "I will not obey my father" yet afterwards does the father's will.—They do not prattle about God; yet they act religiously.'[9]

With all the 'worldliness' of Democratic Socialism, Blumhardt saw in it a divine truth, but this was incomprehensible and offensive to the pious who did not recognise such an 'incognito'. They would have preferred to limit God and his working to the narrow sphere of their pious world. Large circles of people banished Blumhardt because of his support of Democratic Socialism, turning away in abhorrence, because he had gone to the 'godless people', just as Jesus once kept company with tax-gatherers and sinners.

This story of Blumhardt is important far beyond its historical reference in Germany towards the close of the nineteenth century, which is why it has been thought worth while to relate it in some detail. The conflict between ecclesiastical and personal piety and social action is an ever-present reality so long as Christian faith and practice

[8] P. 51.

[9] Pp. 60 and 61.

is alive. But it is a conflict in which reconciliation must be found if the Christian gospel is not to be distorted, not, be it noted, by the suppression of either side— this is not reconciliation, it is defeat in which neither side is victor at the end of the day— but the holding of the two in creative tension. Out of this balance there can issue balanced preaching.

There is one other point of importance to be extracted from Blumhardt's story. After some years he came to be disappointed in the social movement and criticised it severely. 'The attempt to carry any idea of God into earthly things cannot take root at a time when men are filled with the hope that they and they alone can create a blissful humanity. Now they first have to run aground on the rock of earthly things, in order to grasp the higher things.'[10] So he came to see the doubtful element inherent in all human undertakings and movements. Such movements belong to the world that passes away. And there are aspects of Church organisation that must be seen in the same light. Blumhardt was not the first, or the last, to experience disappointment with social movements that promised well. All of which is a reminder not to expect Utopias, by whatever names we call them, and not to be unrealistic about the nature of man. For although it is true that man is made in God's image, that image in him is a spoiled and defaced one. This fallen state of man, to use a theological phrase, is an empirical fact. There is evidence in plenty that even man's noblest efforts exhibit somewhere in time disappointing features. Failure to be open-eyed to this is too often the inherent weakness of social schemes. They do not take account of the sin of man and too frequently miss the seriousness of the situation by thinking only in terms of people's individual sins.

Here then is the preacher's duty. He has a social gospel to proclaim, and if he does not proclaim it he has no gospel to proclaim at all.[11] Nevertheless, he has to remind all who will hear him, and this includes those beyond the walls of the Church, that even the most perfect environment is powerless to safeguard man. There is something about him which rebels even against those restrictions which are necessary to produce the environment which he enjoys. Such is the subtlety of the human predicament which must temper the enthusiasm of all social gospel preaching. The book of Genesis (chapter 3) presents as glowing a picture as could be imagined to the Middle Eastern mind

[10] P. 73.
[11] So Paul Oestreicher, Vicar of the Church of the Ascension, Blackheath, and Chairman of 'Amnesty International'.

of perfect living conditions provided by God himself and makes the fall of man take place there!

This raises another double question which should be answered with a both-and, and not an either-or. Should the Christian mission concern itself with the environment or the individual? The point at issue is this, What is most influential, the conditions under which people are forced, or perhaps even choose to live, or the character of the people themselves? Clearly living conditions have a substantial bearing on what those who have to suffer them, or enjoy them, become. The effect of drab and decaying slums is obvious, perhaps more obvious than the effect of luxurious surroundings. On the other hand, unless people themselves are changed, the environment will not be changed, and improved conditions are no guarantee of improved people. Crime has not decreased in the Western world with the steadily rising standard of living. This double question then—should the environment claim the Christian's first attention, or the character of the people who inhabit it?—is a variant of the question already asked—should *social conditions* be the concern of the preacher, or the *soul of man*? The answer is *both*. Work on the human predicament should proceed from both ends, from the end of the environment, the community and the social gospel, and also from the end of the gospel of redemption for the individual and the concern with what kind of people we are, an answer which might be broadly external by saying, social action and gospel preaching are both required.

We return to the preaching of justice, the particular ministry of the word with which this chapter is occupied. Here the preacher will be wise to concentrate on proclaiming the principles of justice which follow as a corollary from man's relationship to God. He will call upon educationalists to remember that the pupils in their care are pupils with an eternal destiny. He will call on architects and builders to provide houses where family living is possible and neighbourliness is not frustrated. He will remind industrialists that their manual workers need to be able to take a pride in the finished product. In thus speaking he will need to give concrete illustrations of what he means, but should at the same time be careful not to become trapped in detailed programmes which require technical expertise. His task as a preacher is to leave his hearers in no doubt about the principles of justice in the light of which they will need to do their own planning according to their local situation. A Church preaching in this fashion would operate as the conscience of the nation. If it attempted to operate as the brain of the nation it would immediately fail.

The preacher will also be wise not to ally himself with any political party. This is not to echo the cry of those who say, 'Keep politics out of the pulpit'. In so far as this means, 'Let the Church keep to spiritual matters and not dabble in the world's affairs', it cannot be. What the Christian preacher offers is a gospel which, when accepted, becomes a way of life. It affects the way life is lived at every point. It has a bearing on rates, drains, abortion and schooling; it has a bearing on everything which affects people. And if the preacher does not touch on these matters and others like them, in his preaching, as occasion requires, perhaps in some depth, he is not meeting the needs of people *where they are*, he is not assisting them at their points of human experience. Nevertheless, let the advice be repeated, he will be wise not to ally himself permanently to a party because the time will come when duty will require him to criticise the party, therefore his lips need to be kept free to do so. It is not an unknown or even an uncommon phenomenon that parties with laudable social programmes for the welfare of the community begin well but when they succeed and gather power to themselves, they become aggressors in the name of their party and ought to be resisted, which is why the social gospel preacher must remain free. It is a requirement which, for different reasons, raises sensitive questionings, for those Churches which are called 'established', but does not only impinge on them.

We return where we began to the traveller across the countryside observing two constructions, the old church spire pointing heavenwards, and the brand new motorway providing quick accesss to what is desirable. Let it not be forgotten that the preacher in the Church pointing heavenwards has something also to say concerning the motorway, not least the price it demands in the way of death through accidents, and the exorbitant consumption of energy. And the significant fact is that at the end of their journey the travellers may even listen to the preacher because of the widespread despair deeply ingrained in modern technological society. This is no counsel for preaching to man at his point of weakness, but it is a reminder that man is a creature with an eternal destiny and does not in the end find the satisfaction he needs in amenities.

12

The word of wisdom

WISDOM IS NOT ERUDITION, CLEVERNESS OR TECHNICAL EXPERTISE; wisdom is knowledge and experience combined, together with an ability to employ them rightly. Wisdom has reference to practical living. It implies discernment of what are the conditions of human existence, its possibilities and its limitations, and what is the attitude proper to them. At its lowest level it is equivalent to common sense, and at its highest level it is a recognition and acceptance of man's place in the divine ordering of the world. From this higher level there issues a way of life characterised by restraint, nothing is allowed to run to excess. The good things of life are to be enjoyed, but not too much. The earth is to be subdued, but only under the sovereignty of God. Great hopes are to be fostered, but not without the remembrance of man's finitude and mortality. And nothing will be accomplished without striving and possibly not without pain. Wisdom sees all things from the eternal angle as well as the temporal and this induces a sense of proportion as well as restraint. None of this, however, develops automatically, but is the outcome of living by principle, which, if not self-provided, is certainly self-chosen. A man is not born wise but he may become wise. Clearly this is a subject for preaching.

All the great civilisations honour wisdom, they have their wise men and their collections of wise sayings. It is true of the Chinese as well as of the Greeks. The Hebrews were no exception, indeed, the Wisdom literature in the Hebrew scriptures is not the least arresting part of the Old Testament and of the Apocrypha, notably the books of Proverbs, Ecclesiastes and the Wisdom of Solomon. It is true that Wisdom in these books in some places is understood in terms far more lofty than of practical insight into everyday living.

Proverbs 8:22,23 (N.E.B.).
　　　'The Lord created me the beginning of his works,

before all else that he made, long ago.
Alone, I was fashioned in times long past,
at the beginning, long before earth itself.'

And the Wisdom of Solomon chapters 10 and 11 spell out the
guiding hand of wisdom in Hebrew history. 'Wisdom it was who
kept guard over the first father of the human race, when he alone had
yet been made; she saved him after his fall, and gave him the strength
to master all things' (10:1,2, N.E.B.).

This speculative theology of wisdom attributing to it some kind of
personal pre-existence was not however what the wise men preached
to the people, nor is it the main constituent of the wisdom literature.
The book of Proverbs is full instead of wise advice providing more
than one collection of wise sayings which bear on all aspects of every-
day living. Like the author of Proverbs,[1] the author of Ecclesiastes[2]
contrasts wisdom and folly, but is more pessimistic about attainment
of the satisfactions of wisdom; nevertheless the imparting of wisdom
is the Preacher's duty as he sees it. 'So the Speaker,[3] in his wisdom,
continued to teach the people what he knew. He turned over many
maxims in his mind and sought how best to set them out. He chose
his words to give pleasure, but what he wrote was the honest truth.
The sayings of the wise are sharp as goads, like nails driven home;
they lead the assembled people, for they come from one shepherd'
(Chapter 12:9–11 N.E.B.).

Jesus was recognised as a prophet, both on account of his words
and of his deeds, but he was also a teacher of wisdom in the Hebrew
tradition. That one from Nazareth appeared as a sage was no less
remarkable than that he was a prophet. When he preached in the
synagogue the hearers 'were amazed and said, "Where does he get it
from?" and, "What wisdom is this that has been given him?" '[4] It
was an attribute which characterised him from his early years.[5] His
style of speaking also bore resemblances to the wisdom literature, for
example, 'No one sews a patch of unshrunk cloth on to an old coat;
if he does, the patch tears away from it, the new from the old, and
leaves a bigger hole. No one puts new wine into old wine-skins; if

---

[1] Chapters 8 and 9.
[2] 7:1–11:6.
[3] R.V. 'Preacher'.
[4] Mark 6:2 (N.E.B.) cf Matt. 13:54.
[5] Luke 2:40,52.

he does, the wine will burst the skins, and then wine and skins are both lost. Fresh skins for new wine!'[6]

This is an appeal to wisdom understood as common sense. Similarly, 'When a lamp is lit, it is not put under the meal-tub, but on the lamp-stand, where it gives light to everyone in the house.'[7] Elsewhere, with more subtlety, indicating a keen discernment of people in general— 'The man who can be trusted in little things can be trusted also in great; and the man who is dishonest in little things is dishonest also in great things.'[8]

At the close of the Sermon on the Mount there is the same contrast of wisdom with folly as occurs in the book of Proverbs and the book of Ecclesiastes. The wise life is the one that is built on the words of Jesus, and the foolish life is the one that does not use them as a foundation. The conclusion to be drawn is that Jesus' teaching is practical wisdom for all who will hear it, crying aloud the message that life must be lived according to principles, or ruin will result, and Jesus' words, like those of a wisdom teacher, set out the principles of the kingdom of God. This was a form of teaching native to the Jewish mind, and not surprisingly, the Sermon on the Mount is found echoed in the Epistle of James. Moreover, James specifically mentions wisdom, 'If any of you falls short in wisdom, he should ask God for it',[9] and again, 'Who among you is wise or clever? Let his right con-duct give practical proof of it, with the modesty that comes of wisdom.'[10]

Wise advice then on how to live, cast in the form of maxims, proverbs and memorable sayings, formed a part of the Hebrew tradition of teaching which Jesus also incorporated into his own ministry of the word, and which apparently found a place among the Jewish Christians of the early Church. Actually, it would be surprising if wisdom in the form of moral advice did *not* form a constituent part of the general run of preaching because the common assessment of what preaching is consists in precisely this—*Preaching is advising*. But the New Testament as a whole does not agree. Preaching is proclaiming what God in Christ has done for man. This is the word of wisdom which the Spirit gives.[11] This is the wisdom of God as

[6] Mark 2:21,23 (N.E.B.).
[7] Matt. 5:15 (N.E.B.).
[8] Luke 16:10 (N.E.B.).
[9] James 1:5 (N.E.B.).
[10] James 3:13 (N.E.B.). See also Heb. 13:1–6.
[11] 1 Cor. 12:8, cf 1 Cor. 2:5–8.

opposed to the wisdom of the world. Have we then to choose between preaching as proclamation and preaching as moralism? If choice there has to be, it would be better to select the former, for the latter runs to lifelessness. The right reaction, however, is to relate them to each other and not oppose them as alternatives. How to live is man's basic problem and no preaching which does not meet him at this point, however theologically correct, will be given a hearing. Let ten men be questioned on any commuter train about the subjects they would wish to be handled in sermons, and if one of the subjects turns out to be doctrinal it will be surprising. The majority of the requests will be along the following lines; 'How do I face life when my wife deserts me?' 'How can I stop worrying about the possibility of redundancy?' 'Ought I to forgive that car dealer who has swindled me?' 'Tell me how to cut down on the bottle?'—and perhaps, 'Is there a life to come?' Ethical questions are what the preacher will have to face, and he must answer with words of wisdom as a wise man, *but* if he is a true Christian preacher he will have a proclamation to make which will be good news to his hearers because it will be capable, as his own wise words are incapable, of lifting his hearers to that divine resource of power which alone is sufficient for their needs.

The Christian preacher then must be a wise man as well as a prophet. He must possess the practical wisdom of discernment in order to sense the real predicament of his hearers. He must minister to them according to *their actual needs*, and not the needs he would find easier to treat. And he must choose the time to speak, the way to speak, and the depth at which to speak. There is a profound lesson to be learnt from the fact that for the most part the teaching of Jesus was occasional. He did not teach according to a syllabus, always it was the occasion that evoked the teaching; it could be guests at a feast, seeking chief positions for themselves which produced a lesson on humility;[12] or a discontented man asking for an inheritance to be divided which brought out his teaching on covetousness.[13] Like the wisdom teacher of the book of Ecclesiastes, Jesus had a sense of timing.

For everything its season, and for every activity under heaven its time:
    a time to be born and a time to die;
    a time to plant and a time to uproot;
    a time to kill and a time to heal;

[12] Luke 14:7-11.
[13] Luke 12:13.

a time to pull down and a time to build up;
a time to weep and a time to laugh;
a time for mourning and a time for dancing;
a time to scatter stones and a time to gather them;
a time to embrace and a time to refrain from embracing;
a time to seek and a time to lose;
a time to keep and a time to throw away;
a time to tear and a time to mend;
a time for silence and a time for speech;
a time to love and a time to hate;
a time for war and a time for peace.[14]

An examination of Jesus' teaching method as recorded in the gospels makes it difficult to believe that he was unaware of this excerpt from his people's wisdom literature and did not shape his work accordingly. There is a clear understanding of time in the New Testament presented, not in the Hebrew extended concrete and picture form but in the use of the abstract word *kairos*. In classical Greek it meant 'due measure', 'fitness', or 'proportion', but when applied to time, as in the New Testament, it has the meaning of an *opportune or seasonable time*. St Mark records the opening of Jesus' ministry with the words, 'The time has come; the kingdom of God is upon you; repent, and believe the Gospel',[15] and Matthew, reporting Jesus' judgment on the unrepentant cities, says, 'At that time Jesus spoke these words, "I thank thee, Father, Lord of heaven and earth, for hiding these things from the learned and wise, and revealing them to the simple. Yes, Father, such was thy choice." '[16]

The preacher, as a wise man, always has a sense of the fit or opportune time for the appropriate word in his ministry. Without this, what might be an effective ministry will become an ineffective one. And not only is time important but so also is content. Writing to the Corinthians Paul confessed, 'For my part, my brothers, I could not speak to you as I should speak to people who have the Spirit. I had to deal with you on the merely natural plane, as infants in Christ. And so I gave you milk to drink, instead of solid food, for which you were not yet ready.'[17] In so doing, Paul was acting as a steward of God's secrets,[18]

[14] Eccles. 3:1-8 (N.E.B.).
[15] Mark 1:14 (N.E.B.).
[16] Matt. 11:25,26 (N.E.B.).
[17] 1 Cor. 3:1,2 (N.E.B.), cf Heb. 5:12-14; 1 Pet. 2:2.
[18] 1 Cor. 4:2.

answering to the description set out in the question Jesus asked, '... Who is the trusty and sensible (A.V. 'wise') man whom his master will appoint as his steward, to manage his servants and issue their rations at the proper time (*kairos*)?'[19] Every preacher is called to be a wise steward, sensible enough to provide the right word at the right time. This then is the word of wisdom.

In practice the word of wisdom may demand simple subjects for preaching. The Proverbs will provide a score of themes and more, with no proclamation in them, but they could be the right word for the right time.

'Do not flatter yourself about tomorrow
for you never know what a day will bring forth'[20]
or,
'a neighbour at hand is better than a brother far away'[21]
or,
'He who guards the fig-tree will eat its fruit,
and he who watches his master's interests will come to honour.'[22]

This is elementary material scarcely within shouting distance of the Christian proclamation, but it could be exactly right if calculated to evoke an interest on the part of hearers unequipped as yet to hear the word of the gospel. Dr Clement Welsh writes,

In conversations with Japanese non-Christians, Nebreda found any presentation of the gospel produced incomprehension. The difference between the cognitive systems of the Japanese and of the Christians was simply too great. Greek and Hebrew concepts could no longer be presupposed. Nebreda devised, therefore, a communication strategy for his missionary work which he called '*pre-kerygmatic*'. Before the *kerygma* can be presented, the way must be prepared for it. *Pre-kerygmatic* work activates the basic human questions about man and his world, and strives to find a common ground, an initial agreement on the great question of life. For Nebreda, raised in the Thomastic tradition, the *pre-kerygmatic* task was a matter of applied natural theology.[23]

[19] Luke 12:42 (N.E.B.).
[20] Prov. 27:1 (N.E.B.).
[21] Ibid. v. 10 (N.E.B.).
[22] Ibid. v. 18 (N.E.B.).
[23] *Preaching in a New Key* (Philadelphia United Church Press, 1974) p. 106.

Dr Welsh's contention is that the first task of the preacher is to enable his hearers to make sense of the universe in which they feel themselves cast as strangers.

If the preacher is bound as a wise steward to provide simple and basic theories, he is also bound to offer rich fare suitable for special occasions and for mature Christian believers. The Church will not be sustained by *pre-kerygmatic* preaching, nor by *kerygmatic* preaching alone, it must advance towards a Christian interpretation of life in depth with a proclamation of Christ as the one in whom 'the universe, all in heaven and on earth, might be brought into a unity',[24] and in whom 'the complete being of God, by God's own choice, came to dwell.'[25] This also is the word of wisdom.

Jesus said, 'And yet God's wisdom is proved right by all who are her children'. So the intellectual preachers of the seventeenth century in England and perhaps even 'the witty preachers' could have been right for their age as was John Wesley's unadorned style for the eighteenth century, and C. G. Finney right for America as well as Henry Ward Beecher, but not if the *kerygma* is never reached in the preaching or is so overlaid with learning that it cannot be heard, or has ceased to be counted as that which has power through the work of the Spirit to make the hearing of it possible. If any of these happen 'the wisdom of the world' has taken over the Christian pulpit.

We have said the preacher must be a wise man. He must be known as a wise man. He must be the kind of man to whom his fellow-men would naturally turn with their problems and expect answers. He must possess sufficient strength of character not to succumb to the temptation of simply providing only those answers which his enquirers are willing to hear. At the same time he must be kindly, especially with the ignorant and foolish, and must never employ his wisdom to make his enquirers appear foolish. A wise man is patient, not given to hasty words and always in control of his temper. He must enjoy life, and be seen to enjoy life, but there will be no excess in his behaviour, nor even in his labours and certainly not in his pleasures. If he has the gift of humour he should employ it, but not be so light-hearted that he cannot issue a rebuke, if necessary with scorn. From such a man's lips, sure of the gospel of Christ, will come words of wisdom, suitable in content presented in the mood the occasion requires.

This skill of the wise man suggests a pattern for a Christian counsellor. Be that as it may, the work of preaching and counselling

[24] Eph. 1:10 (N.E.B.).
[25] Col. 1:19; 2:9 (N.E.B.).

must not be confused. A preacher is not a counsellor *in the pulpit*, however necessary it may be for both of them to be men of wisdom. A counsellor deals with individuals, and his advice is given *ad rem* and *ad hoc*. A preacher deals with a congregation comprised of an aggregation of individuals, not one of whom is in exactly the identical situation with his neighbour. Ethical advice given from the pulpit might be salutary for one and disastrous for another. The task of the preacher is to proclaim those principles of conduct which derive from the *kerygma* but to refrain from directions which all his hearers are to follow. Perhaps this may be summarised neatly by saying that the preacher is to provide a sense of direction, but not directions. And the reason—let it be repeated—is because each individual situation has an element of uniqueness about it. This does not mean the ethical teaching is to be left vague, there is nothing vague about the Sermon on the Mount, or the practical teaching given in St Paul's letters, nor does it debar examples of how the general ethical principles that flow from the gospel apply in particular circumstances, but they are to be given as *illustrations* and not as patterns of conduct to be followed by all. What the preacher who is a wise man must do is to provide in addition to his preaching opportunities for meeting individuals with their problems, and also, as circumstances afford, opportunities for people to meet in groups to work out together the answers to their own problems *in the light of the Christian proclamation*. What is more, in his preaching, the preacher should from time to time announce the facilities that he has provided. Wherever preaching is understood as part of the pastoral office and not as an independent professional activity (which is dangerous), proclamation works hand in hand with counselling. It is in both spheres that the wise man ministering words of wisdom, comes into his own.

III
Practical

1

The preparation of a preacher

'HOW LONG DID IT TAKE YOU TO PREPARE THAT SERMON? WAS THE genuinely appreciative question asked of the preacher at the West End of the church after the service. 'About fifty years!' came the reply. This is a well-worn anecdote and it may be apocryphal, but it serves to introduce the idea of the remote preparation that is necessary to make a preacher and therefore the kind of sermon he preaches. All that the preacher is, all that his life's experiences have taught him, have some responsibility for the kind of ministry of the word which he exercises.

Perhaps a preacher at the farthest remove cannot prepare himself at all for preaching. Preachers are not made, even by the preachers themselves, they are born. 'Before I formed you in the womb I knew you for my own; before you were born I consecrated you, I appointed you a prophet to the nations.'[1] This was the word of the Lord that came to Jeremiah. And to the servant in Isaiah, 'from birth the Lord called me, he named me from my mother's womb. He made my tongue his sharp sword and concealed me under cover of his hand.'[2] It is unlikely perhaps that any modern preacher would care to make this claim to divine election to be a preacher, modesty forbids it, but the verse stands in scripture as a reminder that the preparation for a sermon does not begin when there is a preaching assignment to be filled,[3] but way back somewhere in the counsels of God. It could be that the general absence of this kind of awareness is one reason for the

[1] Jer. 1:4,5 (N.E.B.).
[2] Isa. 49:1,2 (N.E.B.).
[3] 'From a preacher's point of view a sermon is no mere ten minutes' offering. It is the top of an iceberg compounded of prayer, reading, thinking and writing. Conversations and experiences, hopes and indeed fears, the whole lot come together and are there for ten minutes. The iceberg either melts and is gone, or its sharing by the congregation can more than double its size.' Norman Ingram-Smith, *St Martin's Review*, May 1978.

lack of awe with which the ministry of the word is too often approached.

It is a curious fact of history that those people in whose life a sense of election, or predestination, is most operative, have shown themselves to be the most energetic. It might have been imagined that the reaction might have been— 'God has chosen me, why need I trouble?' But the reverse is the case. 'God has chosen me, I will live up to my calling.' In general we rise to the privilege of selection. Perhaps one of the first encouragements preachers need is the reminder that God may well have called them to his work, their natural gifts and their faith constitute the evidence.

If 'destined to be a preacher', or 'made for a preacher' is one aspect of the remote preparation for a preacher, a *second* is the actual call to this ministry. Moses, Amos, Isaiah and Jeremiah prefix their preaching with an account of their call, so also does Paul in the New Testament. It is presented as a justification for their activity in this field, and this very fact suggests that on human grounds they saw themselves as *un*qualified for this task, so unqualified that justification was necessary, and they sought it in the experience of the call which came to them and this is why they set it out.

There are modern parallels to this. One outstanding case is C. H. Spurgeon, the great Baptist preacher of the nineteenth century at The Tabernacle in South London. Neither his background nor his physical appearance would seem to qualify him for the mighty ministry he experienced. Clearly the call which came to him was the secret.

Is this possible for every preacher? It is certainly expected by the Ordinal in the Anglican Church and not only in that Church. Maybe as with conversion, date and place are most frequently unable to be supplied, nor is it important that they should, but the reminder that the ministry is based on a call is salutary because it moves the mind of the preacher away from himself, and if this does not take place, pride can quickly make his work ineffective. All this, of course, takes for granted a personal experience of Christ expressed in regular public worship, private prayer, witness and Christian service; there cannot be a call to the ministry of the word in default of these, however fondly it may be imagined that such a call exists. The call to preach comes in the congregation, not outside it.

There is a *third* element of remote preparation in the making of a preacher, namely the experience of life. This again is not something which the preacher chooses but which comes to him. Before a preacher becomes a preacher and also after he becomes a preacher and distinct from his professional life as a preacher, he is a man whom life hits in various ways as in varying fashion it hits everyone else. Perhaps he comes to sample the taste of pain. Perhaps he knows the drag that accompanies some physical deformity or incurable illness. Perhaps he knows the horrible blackness that faces a man who has looked for the last time on the face of someone he has loved almost more than life itself, doubting how he himself can go on living. Perhaps he has taken his turn at nights watching by the bedside of an ailing child, his child, and all in vain. And there are other experiences. A woman's love he does not really deserve, an honour, a success, good things he never expected. And boredom and frustration and temporary loss of faith, on occasions successfully surmounted, at other times hopelessly defeated.

What makes a man the preacher that he is? Why is one man listened to avidly? Why is it said of this preacher and not of that, 'Somehow, when he speaks he gets in your shoes'? It is because when this particular preacher touches on sorrow, exhilarating joy, boredom or pain, though he never displays his own soul, for that would be vulgar, he speaks from the experience of what it *feels like* to be broken, elated, bored, or full of dragging pain. This preacher is never glib, never superficial, never clumsy, never insensitive. He is the man to whom the hearers feel they could go and he would understand. This preacher is in fact the priest who 'is able to bear patiently with the ignorant and erring, since he too is beset by weakness'.[4] Preaching of this quality comes by way of experience of life which is why a man does not reach his prime as a preacher till he has reached his prime as a man. Not that there is not a distinctive and valuable ministry for the young preacher, but that *he* preaches will probably be more effective than what he preaches. But when a preacher can still feel what it is to be young and can also begin to feel in the opposite direction what it is to be restricted by physical limitations, even if only that he must begin to wear spectacles, then is the time when he will reach the widest circle of hearers for his experience will span life. All this and more is part of the unplanned and remote preparation that goes to make the preacher the kind of preacher he is.

And now the less remote, one might almost say, the more immediate preparation. *First* there is Bible Reading or Bible Hearing. This precedes Bible Study and it occurs automatically for those preachers whose clerical life is disciplined by the reading of the Daily Office or its

[4] Heb. 5:2 (N.E.B.).

equivalent. Exceedingly fortunate are those who at least at times, hear the various lections well read to them. What is happening is that unwittingly the raw material of preaching is being stored in the preacher's subconscious ready to make itself available when the occasion is right. Then it rises to the surface. A full preaching ministry cannot be sustained without this kind of regular exposure to scripture reading (as distinct from study). A corollary of this is that those who hear preaching will only be able to be fed by it in so far as they too have some familiarity with the text of scripture. Where the Bible is unknown, preaching will largely fall on deaf ears. The public reading of the scriptures therefore as well as the private reading of them by preachers is necessary if preaching is to be an effective ministry.[5]

But there is also private *study* of the Bible, all that is represented by the preacher as a life-long Bible student. For the modern preacher however, unlike his predecessors of more than a century ago, there is a pressing problem. The likelihood is that he will have been trained in Biblical criticism only to discover as soon as he begins his preaching ministry, how useless is a great deal of this learning in the pulpit he is called to occupy, and how unhelpful are the majority of the Bible commentaries that embody it. The enormous sale of William Barclay's commentaries is partly accounted for by the avidity with which preachers have seized upon them to assist them in their work. To criticise the preachers and even to condemn them for laziness is easy, but their problem is a real one, not lightly to be dismissed.

At bottom the dilemma of the contemporary preacher derives from our modern awareness of history. We are aware today, as not before, that the men and women of the past were very unlike ourselves. It is difficult, if not impossible, for instance, to think ourselves into the minds of medieval man who was not wholly embarrassed to burn heretics. The Biblical writers wrote long before the Middle Ages and in an entirely different cultural, economic and geographical milieu. The more thoroughly, therefore, we elucidate with our academic tools the meaning of the Biblical texts as they were understood by those who wrote them and those to whom they were written, the further away we remove them from usefulness for our generation which seems to be (in general) constitutionally unable to respond to anything which is not modern.

[5] On the importance of systematic Bible reading, preaching at Great St Mary's Cambridge on February 6th, 1977, Professor G. R. Dunstan said, 'In isolation from the scriptural tradition in Morning and Evening Prayer, the sacrament becomes a mere celebration of human fellowship.'

It is possible that the 'New Hermeneutic',[6] as it is called, can help us at this point, although there are difficulties in this approach as in all existential systems. Instead of concentrating on history in Biblical interpretation the New Hermeneutic concentrates on language. This is of obvious interest to the preacher. The Biblical text is understood as encapsulated speech. It is speech that makes things happen, bringing about what is called by the German theologians responsible for the method, an *Ereignis-sprache*, a speech event. Language is not an extra to man's life, by which he is able to describe his existences, it actually *contributes* to his existence and is one of the chief keys to it. Man is a linguistic animal. Language is therefore able to free what was living and effective in the past and make it free and effective in the present.

When this method is applied to the Bible it is applied to texts, many of which are not descriptive but proclamatory. They proclaim what God is and does and says. When therefore these are encountered again and heard again they create again through the medium of language. What Biblical preaching does is to continue the intention of the Biblical text and this is not primarily to provide information but to introduce to the living God.

It is the preacher's duty then to study the Bible using all the aids of scholarship in order to ascertain what it was the writer was intending to say about God in the situation in which he was writing, and then to let that message be addressed to himself. Having heard it the preacher must then set it out in words which his contemporaries can hear and respond to, *because they are able to hear them*, perhaps using the Biblical story where the message originally was set as an illustration. It is important that the labour of scholarly exegesis as a first step be not skipped by the preacher in his study, otherwise the interpretation of the text is likely to become fanciful and certainly be unattached to the original purpose of the writer of the scriptural passage under review. The material with which the preacher operates is not a collection of 'telling' texts extracted from the Bible, but the word of God *in context*, the context as always contributing to the meaning of the message. Two rough and ready questions, in practice could initiate the preacher's approach to a passage of scripture in the work of preparing a sermon— What did this scripture say about God to him who wrote it? What does it say to me now about God? It is surprising what even so apparently unproductive a scripture as Genesis 1 for a modern congregation can yield if these, and not some other, are the questions which are put to it.

[6] See C. F. Evans, *Explorations in Theology*, pp. 69–83.

The modern preacher will complain that he has no time for Bible study of this nature or any other. He needs however to be guided by modern work studies and to shape his programme by *limited objectives*. Of course the Bible is a daunting book for any priest or minister in an understaffed pastoral situation, but he could determine to study one book of the Bible a year, and he could be a little more ambitious than to fasten on III John! It is surprising how a preaching ministry can be enriched by a determined mastery of one book of the Bible per year, say Genesis, or St Mark's gospel, not forgetting to address to the books the two rough and ready questions already indicated.[7]

A second more immediate preparation for preaching is the study of theology. Untheological preaching is a contradiction in terms. One might as well speak of an unmechanical mechanism or an unmedical physician. To preach is to proclaim Christ, but who is Christ, and why proclaim him? Is the proclamation able to have any bearing on people? If so, why? In a matter of two sentences then we are already plunged into the realms of Christology, man, sin and grace, not to mention the idea of creation. Every preacher must have his own Christology, his own doctrine of man, sin and grace, his own doctrines of creation, and *he does not possess them* until he is able to proclaim them to a congregation composed of both men and women who are *not* theologians, so that they can follow him. No one possessed this skill more than the late Professor D. M. Baillie of Edinburgh, indeed his exposition of the doctrine of grace, a notoriously difficult subject, under the image of a young woman given charge of a little boy, is a masterpiece, a model to be emulated by all who would preach. This is the question the preacher has to ask himself— what is my doctrine of Christ? Not what is Barth's doctrine, or Tillich's, or Bultmann's, or even what is Paul's doctrine of Christ? The preacher will be wise if he takes into account the views of all these masters, not least the latter, but at the end he must be able to answer his own question. This is *my* doctrine of Christ, even if he does feel compelled to append three tiny extra words, 'at the moment'. If the preacher approaches the theological aspect of his preaching this way, he will discover how educative of himself his own preaching has been. The way to learn is to teach.

Is this all? No, the preparation of the preacher has not covered the basic necessities for a preacher till a *third* lesson has been mastered. How to be an observer. Jesus was a keen observer of the nature of

[7] On the subject of Biblical preaching see John Bright, *The Authority of the Old Testament* (S.C.M. Press, 1967) especially pp. 168–182.

men. The trees, the birds, the flowers, a woman making bread, the tactics of an unscrupulous bailiff, the sordid behaviour of a servant when his master was absent—all this and far more was open to the eyes of Jesus, and he used what he saw in his preaching. A preacher must first of all be a *seer*, using the word in its simplest sense. He must observe the world around him *as it is today*—a man who walks in the public park every day from nine till five because he dare not break the news to his wife that he has been declared redundant. The way people sit in an aircraft when the engines are 'revving-up' just before take-off, how seedlings 'damp-off' unless treated with 'cheshunt compound'. The sights are legion, but they make up our world and the preacher must be heard to be at home in it. All of which may add up for the preacher to build up a natural theology, and for preaching to encourage this discipline which has fallen into an unfortunate oblivion. Preaching needs a natural theology.

And now *fourthly*, the collection of illustrative material.[8] Most young preachers 'make heavy weather' of this, and some who are not so young. To avoid the labour the claim is sometimes made that illustrations in sermons are unnecessary, which is indefensible. It might as well be argued that a house has no need of windows. Admittedly, sermon illustrations can be so inappropriate, so forced or so startling that the sermon would be enriched by their omission, but this is not normally the case when their function is understood.

Sermon illustrations are employed in order to illustrate, which implies that there must be something to illustrate and something that needs illustrating. Their function is to provide light on what would otherwise be dark. They operate like windows. They are strictly functional, which does not mean they are unattractive or of poor workmanship or design in themselves, nor are they to be set in a building without regard to the overall appearance. The placing of windows is important, both for light and for structural harmony.

Sermon illustrations are not for entertainment. There is a temptation on the part of preachers, laudably anxious to hold the attention of their hearers, to be on the look-out for, and to prize highly stories or anecdotes which are startling in themselves, and to build sermons round them. This is like constructing a building around a window. Anyway, the method fails. In such cases the hearers remember the startling illustration and that is all. They are found to be in complete

[8] Parish churches with stained glass windows, murals, carvings, paintings and interesting architectural features provide not only illustrations, but visual aids for preaching. It is astonishing how few preachers ever refer to them in their sermons.

ignorance as to what the story was meant to illustrate. Such stories are too arresting to be serviceable.[9]

Sermon illustrations, for the most part, need to be taken from the lives and surroundings of the hearers. Admittedly, to quote from Dante, Dumas, Dostoievsky and Dickens is impressive, but for most hearers sermon illustrations taken from 'Coronation Street' or 'The Archers' would be more telling. What a congregation will most readily hear is references by the preacher to objects, events, and people's comments which he has seen and heard himself *in the recent past in the locality*. An illustration drawn from a derelict house in the next street, the aftermath of a recent storm, a local flower show, a current play at the theatre, is the kind that is most serviceable. What the preacher needs is to go about his ordinary life seeing and hearing with the eyes and ears of a preacher, perhaps with a notebook readily available for note-taking.

Perhaps this whole craft of sermon illustration has been dealt with by no one more thoroughly than Dr W. E. Sangster.[10] From his book the reader will learn how to cull illustrations from newspapers and books, and what is equally important, how to file them for subsequent use so that they can be found. It is probably true to say, however, that the average run of preacher will not be able to live up to such a demanding organisation, nor to that of Dr Leonard Griffith, successor to Dr Leslie Weatherhead of the City Temple. His method was to set up one hundred and four files during his annual summer holiday, representing the two sermons he would have to preach on each of the fifty-two Sundays of the coming year. Each file would be allocated a subject, great festivals would be easy, the other Sundays not so easy. Then, as he lived through the year reading widely—history, science, poetry, novels, together with periodicals and the newspapers—he would extract appropriate illustrations and other material bearing on those one hundred and four subjects and insert it in the appropriate file. Then when the time came for a particular sermon to be preached, the file for that day would yield a crop of good things waiting to be processed.

Most preachers would faint at the prospect of such a daunting system,

[9] The present writer having enjoyed some of the stories of L. Pirandello in Italian was delighted when the Oxford University Press produced in 1965 a volume of these stories in English. He thought they would solve the problem of his sermon illustrations for some time. They were a complete failure. They were too startling for this particular use.

[10] See his book *The Craft of Sermon Illustration* (Epworth Press, 1946).

nor would it be justifiable for them. It does, however, serve to show the concentrated and systematic labour that has been bestowed on some of the big preaching ministries. We recommend a much more modest programme. We advise simply the open eyes and ears of the parish priest or minister as he lives his life and goes about his pastoral duties. What we ask is that he shall see and hear *as a preacher*. And this is the surprising experience. If a preacher knows on Monday what he will be preaching about on the following Sunday, between Monday and Saturday suitable illustrations will present themselves to his mind, but he must know early in the week what his subject is to be. This is essential. Perhaps there is nothing remarkable in the way this works out. If someone is a collector of sea-shore shells and has a cabinet at home with various drawers where the different kinds will be housed, he is far more likely to pick up specimens when wandering along the shore than is the man who has no classified collecting system into which they may be inserted. Half the battle with picking up sermon illustrations from life consists in knowing what it is you wish to illustrate *next Sunday*, or that special occasion on which you have to preach in a month's time.

We have said that the purpose of sermon illustration is to illustrate what needs to be illustrated. There is one possible exception and this has to do with placing. A sermon may 'sag' two-thirds of the way through, not because the material is dull or solid, but because the hearers' attention has been held taut for as long as is possible without relief. Unless at this point something lighter is introduced, the remainder of the sermon, however brilliant, will probably be wasted. An effective sermon has its moments of relaxation as well as of effort, and to place an illustration in order to relieve strain on the hearers' part is a proper use of it, but it must of course be related to the sermon as a whole, and not operate as something extraneous. It ought also to be said that an anecdote or story at the beginning of a sermon must not operate as a device merely to catch the attention, but should embody the main theme of the sermon in illustrative form. Failure to observe this rule will result in loss of attention as soon as the opening of the sermon is concluded, attention which will probably not subsequently be recovered.

We turn now to consider, in the fifth place, the voice of the preacher. A preacher cannot preach without a voice, but how little attention is given to it by preachers is surprising. Not that there is any necessity or even value in his possessing detailed knowledge of its mechanism, though an understanding of a few elementary facts might be helpful.

Essentially the vocal mechanism consists of lungs, vocal cords and pharynx (throat), together with the mouth. The lungs, like bellows, supply the stream of air which passes up the windpipe (trachea), impinges on the vocal chords, making them vibrate like a double reed. (These vocal cords are not really cords or strings as in a stringed musical instrument, but folds of contractile living tissue.) Vibrating columns of air then pass through the pharynx and the mouth which act as resonators. Vowel sounds are produced when the air stream is continuous, consonants when it is more or less interrupted by the tongue, teeth and lips. Speech in contrast to singing emphasises consonants.[11]

The timbre or quality of the voice is more or less one of the 'given' things about a person.[12] Voice is a birthday present or liability as the case may be. Little can be done about it, but all is not lost, even with an ugly voice. The natural quality of Sir Winston Churchill's voice could scarcely be described as beautiful, but what he achieved with a relatively poor instrument was remarkable. The secret of effective voice production is to use the mechanism. This is what poor voice production fails to do. If the timbre of the voice is to some extent fixed by the physical shape of the voice-producing organs, this is not the case with the lungs, the mouth and the lips. With care and practice the lungs can be filled with air and controlled with the diaphragm (without raising the shoulders) so as to sustain speech with power. The mouth can be opened far wider than it often is to give volume, the lips can be moved to give precision, and the consonants making for clear articulation. The speaker can also learn to throw his voice forward, perhaps even giving it a hint of a nasal quality (words like king, ring and sing are useful for this exercise) and certainly keeping the voice away from the throat where it can be ruined through constant and improper use.

If laziness is the enemy of clear speech, it is also the enemy of colourful speech (the reference is to the sound and not to vocabulary). Too few speakers use the whole range of their voices. They operate like an organist who uses only one stop on his instrument. But there are

---

[11] For an introduction to a study of this aspect of the subject see N. Punt, *The Singer's and Actor's Throat*, Laryngological Adviser to the National Theatre (Heinemann, 1952, 2nd Edition, 1967), 99 pages. There is a comprehensive bibliography on pages 92–95.

[12] There are no two voices exactly alike just as there are no two persons exactly alike, and voice is an index of personality. Because of this we are able to identify people on the telephone.

high notes in the range of the human speaking voice, and low notes. If this is doubted, then try the experiment of kicking a man's shins and compare the notes he emits then with those which constitute his groaning with the pain afterwards. Emotion alters the pitch at which voices are used. Voices are *raised* in anger and *lowered* in kindly advice. Speech without tone-range may indicate a speaker lacking in feeling, and a speaker lacking in feeling is likely to be boring. And not only should voices employ change of tone but change of speed. Words dripping out at regular intervals from the speaker's mouth like the rhythmic sound of the wheels of a railway coach passing over the joins in the rails is soporific. Speech needs its *andante* as well as its *lento* if it is to hold the attention. If variety is the spice of life, it is certainly the spice of speech, in tone, volume (*piano* and *forte*), and speed, not forgetting the importance of the pause as a means of emphasis.

Emphasis ought only very rarely to be made by means of shouting, and even more rarely still by means of thumping on the reading desk. Emphasis is properly obtained by means of a pause before the word to be emphasised and a pause after the word emphasised. What is isolated stands out. To cover a wall with pictures is not the way to draw attention to them, but if there is one picture in glorious isolation on a wall it is almost certain to be noticed, perhaps even studied with care.

To sum up this fifth piece of preparation for the preacher—he has been given a voice, he must use it to the full, recognising the archenemy here as laziness.

The *sixth* more immediate preparatory work is the use of the personality. This is dangerous, but it is a risk that has to be run. The danger is self-display which is repelling in the pulpit, but if the risk is not run the preaching will be tedious.

Nature has provided all speakers with visual aids, and aids assist. The aids are the speaker's body, face, hands and eyes. No one speaks entirely with his lips. Meaning is conveyed by the flexibility or rigidity of the body, the shoulders, the look in the eye and the movement of the hands. Some nationalities (the French and the Italians) employ these aids more than others (the British), but all speech is less effective to the degree that it is impersonal, that is, without engaging the personality. What in practice is required in the case of preachers and speakers is not that they should be taught to use their eyes or gesticulate, but that they should be released from rigidity. One of the first needs in training preachers is to set them free to be themselves *in public*. Time and time again the present writer has had to complain to a preacher that his main trouble is plain dullness in the pulpit, only to discover what he suspected, that when the man is provoked in private conversation, perhaps even brutally goaded, he responds with vigour and animation, even gesticulating with his hands in self-defence. All that was required at this point was to say quietly, 'Please be alive like that when you are preaching', and when the remark was added, 'I like you as a person but I can't stand you in the pulpit', all would be forgiven and the lesson learnt. Perhaps there was truth after all in Luther's remark, 'I preach at my best when I am angry.' Committal of the whole personality (not long since a heresy in homiletical instruction) is essential, not least in the Television Age where viewers are accustomed to speakers projecting themselves.

It is important to remember that a speaker speaks before he opens his mouth. His bearing, the light or darkness in his eye, his purposeful or sluggish movements, his happy demeanour or his appearance as one who is carrying the world on his shoulders (instead of leaving this impossible task to God), all convey their message before any sound is uttered and conditions what is said. Appearances count, and if it be said that no one can help what he looks like, this must be countered with the remark that by the time a man reaches middle life, he is responsible for his face. Such then is the remote, and less remote preparation of a preacher, and if some of it, even much of it, is outside his control, it is not outside the control of the God he is called to proclaim, which is why he ought to commit himself to the one who is able to fashion his servant according to his will.

2

The preparation of a sermon

THE FIRST DECISION TO BE MADE IN PREPARING A SERMON CONCERNS *the subject*. 'What shall I preach about?' On some occasions there will be little choice, even for those preachers who do not closely follow 'the Christian Year'. On Christmas Day the theme will have to be the Incarnation, and on Easter Day the Resurrection, though a decision will still need to be made concerning the way in which these basic themes are to be handled. Moreover, most preachers who have been 'long in the saddle' will actually find the great Festivals a cause of greater anxiety than the lesser occasions, owing to the difficulty of finding a fresh approach. But leaving aside Christmas, Easter, Whitsunday, Harvest Festival and Remembrance Sunday (Americans will have a slightly different list), what is to be the preacher's subject for his next sermon, and how will he choose it?

The Anglican preacher will be wise, if preparing for the ministry of the word at the Eucharist, to consult the (Old Testament reading), Epistle and Gospel first. He may not be able to draw his sermon from any one of these lections, either because somehow they do not 'speak to him' on this occasion, or because some local or national situation cries out for a totally different subject to be handled, and he would be an irresponsible pastor who did not do so.[1] To consult the Lectionary first (whatever Lectionary is used), should be the first step in seeking to choose a subject for other acts of worship as well as the Eucharist. Lectionaries as guides to a choice of sermon subjects should be taken seriously. A Lectionary is comprehensive. It covers the whole range of Christian experience. The preacher who is loyal to it (though not slavishly, for 'the letter killeth but the Spirit giveth life'), will be released from partiality in his preaching. Furthermore, the

---

[1] One such occasion was when the late President Kennedy was assassinated. For a preacher not to have discarded the sermon he was going to preach the following Sunday in favour of a word about that event would have been an affront to the many people who, shocked and numbed, attended Church expectantly, even in London.

long-suffering congregation will not be subjected to an exposition of
the doctrine of the Spirit *every Sunday*, because the preacher happens
to be a Pentecostalist, or the needs of the Third World *every Sunday*,
because the preacher happens also to be Chairman of the local
Christian Aid Committee. And who would preach on the Trinity
if there were not a Lectionary providing for Trinity Sunday?[2]
Lectionaries then can contribute to comprehension and to variety in
the subjects handled in the pulpit. They can also assist in that most
important task of binding in the theme of the sermon to the theme
of the act of worship in which it is set, so that worship and sermon
constitute one intelligible whole.

The preacher is advised, therefore, to count the Lectionary as his
ally but not as his master. A preacher is not a teacher working to a
syllabus, the other name of which is the Lectionary. A preacher is
primarily a pastor. He is there to shepherd people according *to their
needs* at the time he preaches to them. He is not in the pulpit to deliver
lesson five or thirty-five, regardless of his hearers' requirements simply
because the book makes that provision. As well might a physician
prescribe ointment for eczema on the neck when the patient has corns
on his toes. Must all preachers then become topical preachers? Fosdick[3]
thought so, but the great majority of preachers in pastoral situations
will find this an impossible burden to be borne; and burdensomeness
is not the only risk, the urge to popularise may get out of hand and a
wrong kind of cheapening of preaching result. Evidence of this is not
hard to find if only a casual glance be devoted to some of the 'sermon
titles' that are advertised. Better no advertisement of sermon subjects
at all than that the ministry of the word be construed as entertainment.

The real skill of the experienced preacher lies in his ability to choose
his sermon subject with an eye on the Lectionary and/or the Christian
Year, *and to relate* the material to the current needs of his hearers in
so far as he knows them, not overlooking the general political and
social background against which his own life and theirs has to be
lived. By so doing he will not only be presenting a rounded message,
taking the year as a whole, but he will be demonstrating that the
word of God at all points makes sense of day-to-day experience. So
the Bible and Christian doctrine can come alive, and if the preacher

[2] What silent thanksgiving there must have been among preachers (and congregations) in those Churches when Trinity Sunday became the day for appealing for
ordination candidates!

[3] Henry Emerson Fosdick (1878–1969) Minister of Riverside Church, New York
1931–51.

is conscious of a reaction of mild astonishment on the part of his hearers, coupled with satisfaction, he may be assured that he is accomplishing his task as a minister of the word.

So far the local pastoral situation has been in mind and the regular diet of preaching for which the parish priest or minister is normally responsible. But what about the special occasion[4] when the preacher is called upon to give 'an address', at (say), the annual service of a large girls' school, or some Trades Union Conference, or the Festival of St Cecilia? What is the use of the Lectionary or the Christian Year in this situation? And if the preacher is somewhat daunted by these occasions, as well he might be, for to bore the assembly then makes preaching more harmful than beneficial, let it not be forgotten that those responsible for the special services are also daunted at the prospect of trying to discover a preacher who will 'not let them down'. The stories of City men at formal dinners in London swapping names of possible preachers are not all apocryphal. But what shall the preacher preach? And if the proper, short answer is 'the gospel' then let the question be rephrased—'How shall he preach?' And the answer is—along the lines of the particular congregation's interest (which he must take pains to discover). If the audience is young, then with plenty of lively illustrations, all contemporary, even up-to-the-minute.[5] For boys, appreciative references to science and technology, for girls, relations with, and attitudes to people, and in the case of schoolgirls, as they affect teachers and parents. Old people need illustrations drawn from the past, even the fairly remote past, it makes them feel at home with the preacher, and therefore more ready to receive what he has to say. Middle-aged congregations respond to the problems that come with middle age, the generation gap, illness and death of parents, 'making ends meet', mortgages, and the rat-race. A mixed audience presents special problems, but this is a situation that obtains in parochial settings rather more than on the special occasions when the audience is a selective one, even a select one. Suffice it to say, however, that Jesus ministered to mixed audiences by means of the parabolic method. Superficially what he offered was something like a story interesting in itself especially against the background, where and when it was told, but there were deeper levels of meaning to be derived from it by those possessing the capacity to do so. The parable is the model for addressing mixed audiences.

[4] See my Preaching on Special Occasions (Mowbray, 1975).
[5] The present writer learned this skill (in so far as he has learned it) from Horace King, a former Speaker of the House of Commons, and at one time a schoolmaster.

There is one other word of advice to be given to the preacher on the special occasions when he is a visitor and probably unknown to a large section of the assembled congregation, except by name. Early on in his sermon he must disclose something about himself. We receive from people we know and trust, rather than from strangers. If the visiting preacher therefore wishes his message to be received, he must hasten to cease being a stranger to his hearers. A sentence or two as an aside will suffice. 'I live in Lowestoft, Luton or Lancaster', 'My mother died when I was quite young', 'In my present job I meet a large number of students', 'My wife said when I left home this morning, "Don't forget to bring back a present for each of the girls."' (This last sentence will tell the discerning a great deal.) I repeat, these personal betrayals of himself on the part of the preacher must be cursory, wholly uncoloured and more like 'throw-aways', but they make all the difference as to whether or not a strange congregation will 'come to' the preacher, and if they do not, communication is unlikely to be established. This is the point—communication requires a bridge. There can be no traffic between two opposite river-banks without it. When therefore a visiting preacher faces his largely unknown congregation, he himself must be the bridge.

Suppose however the preacher, be he the local minister among his own people, or the visiting preacher, cannot find a subject for his sermon. This can happen. It may not be his fault. Spiritual dryness is not unknown, nor is such mental fatigue that no inspiration comes. Moreover, weeks do occur in any pastor's life when everything gets thrown into a turmoil by the demands of unexpected events or calamities. What then? Does the preacher appear in the pulpit with the confession, 'I have no word for you today. I have been overwhelmed with the cares and problems of this week.' It could sound honest. It could also provoke the retort 'from the floor'—'What about us? We have come partly because we wish to know how to rise above the cares and problems of the week.' The wise preacher in these circumstances, if he is not too proud, will take down from his bookshelves a volume of someone else's sermons and start to read. When he discovers that he is actually paying attention, he should replace the book on its shelf and begin to prepare his sermon. He has his subject. What has he done? Stolen someone else's work? Plagiarism in the pulpit? No, he has merely primed his own pump in the dry season. A little water poured in first will cause his own supply to flow. Such is the function of other men's sermons.

We assume now that in general terms the subject of the sermon has been chosen. Let us say, by way of example, that it is based on the epistle set for reading at the Eucharist, or the Old Testament lesson appointed for Sunday evening in the Church where the preacher is to minister. It is a mistake in preparing the sermon to consult the Bible commentaries too soon. The preacher must settle on his own interpretation of the passage of scripture. It will not be entirely individual because presumably he will have received some kind of academic training in the past which will have shaped, to some extent, the patterns of his approach to Scripture. He will however bring his own experience to the particular Bible passage and read it in the light of his congregation's pastoral needs. So he will receive from it the word of God *given him for them*, and this will form the substance of his sermon. Before, however, he shapes it up, he ought to consult the commentaries to make sure that his exposition is not hopelessly at variance with reputable scholarly exegesis. Failure to understand this function of Bible commentaries causes too many preachers to write off their value for sermon preparation on the grounds that they do not provide sermon material suitable for use in the average parish or congregation.

At this stage of sermon preparation the preacher must decide what his *aim or target* is going to be.[6] This is of paramount importance. He cannot tell himself that he is going to expound (shall we say) the story of the turning of the water into wine (John 2:1–11), because it is the gospel for the day. The question he has to resolve is, which, of the many lessons able to be drawn from this scripture passage, and that legitimately, is he going to develop? Will it be a sermon about miracles? about glory? about obedience? about prayer?—any one would be defensible.[7] The aim of the sermon therefore must be clearly specified. There is wisdom in writing it out at the head of the paper on which the rough notes of the sermon are being prepared. Failure to be clear and definite at this point is a frequent source of failure in communication in preaching. Here are some examples referring to the story of the water turned into wine.

---

[6] For all the care the preacher exercises to determine his target or aim, and rightly so, the Holy Spirit may *apply* the message, or some part of the message, in unexpected ways, conditioned, no doubt, by the precise needs of some of the hearers.

[7] The Archdeacon of York (the Venerable L. C. Stanbridge) once gave a lecture in which he listed twenty-two different lessons from this scripture passage, every one of them taken from a sermon of a famous preacher.

The aim of this sermon is:—
To encourage the hearers to look for disclosure points of God's presence and power in their every-day lives (Miracles are such disclosure points, they are signs).

or to show that when the servants of Christ obey their Lord's commands, however demanding, surprising benefits follow.

or to teach the lesson that intercessory prayer is simply stating our needs in Christ's presence and leaving him to answer how he will.

Let the point be made that only one of these aims is to be pursued in one sermon, not more than one. A marksman at Bisley does not fire at two targets. Two, three, four or more shots at one target, perhaps, but that is proper. Similarly, a sermon can relate two, three, four or even more points (pity the congregation) to one aim, but one aim, one target only there must be. Some preachers (alas) appear to fire into the air, left, right and centre, with no target at all. This is wildfire. If anything is hit, lucky chance is the operative force and not the Holy Spirit who calls for dedicated effort on the part of preachers and will not prosper laziness.

The subject being settled, and the aim (or target) settled, what follows? Surely the *substance* or *content of the sermon.* The possibility exists, it is no more than a possibility, that with the aim settled, orderly content will flow into the preacher's mind as he prepares his sermon, like water into a cistern. If so, let him be thankful, but let him not expect a repeat performance with any frequency. For most preachers, and for most of their efforts in sermon preparation, the process of assembling content will resemble the laborious task of filling a tank with a bucket rather more than having it fill up spontaneously through a feed pipe. Here is the point at which a large sheet of paper is required. On it will be scribbled ideas that bear on the subject and aim of the sermon. They may be higgledy-piggledy, it does not matter. They provide the raw material heaped up for shaping into the streamlined sermon.

Shaping is the next step. This involves arranging the material under two or more headings, developing the main theme in steps, each with an eye on the conclusion which is to be reached. Jettisoning some of the material assembled will almost certainly be required in the interests of simplicity and streamlining. Something like an outline or skeleton of a sermon should be the outcome of this stage of work. What it will lack is a top and a tail, in other words, an introduction and a conclusion.

The *conclusion* of a sermon should be short, strong and crystal clear. To end with a few lines of poetry is a mistake, unless it be taken from a well-known hymn, perhaps one to be sung in the accompanying act of worship. The purpose of the conclusion is to gather up the content and aim of the sermon in a memorable form, so constructed as to evoke a response in the hearts and minds of the hearers, not forgetting that a *practical* outcome of the sermon is desirable. Let the conclusion to the sermon, therefore, be so presented as to expect this. When the communicants come forward to receive the Sacrament of the body and blood of Christ *after* the sermon at the Eucharist, their active response is an indication of what hearers of all Christian preaching should wish to do. The sermon could appropriately end with a short passage of scripture, perhaps a text, summing up or illustrating all that he has said. The whole sermon could lead up to this. It is even possible for the very first mention of a text or a passage of scripture to be at the conclusion. It would be right in some circumstances especially with a congregation unfamiliar with scripture. Or the sermon could close with a question — 'What do you think about this? "What do you suppose your action should be if these things are true?' An ending with a question certainly has dominical precedent.

And now *the introduction of the sermon*. This is of overwhelming importance. If the preacher does not capture and hold the attention in the first two minutes, he is unlikely to recapture it. With children and young people generally, the interval is even shorter. Television has taught us that unless a speaker establishes two points about himself in the first minute, namely, that he is going to be interesting, and that he is authoritative, viewers will switch to another channel. The wrong way to begin a sermon, except one addressed to theological students, is by means of an analysis of a Biblical text. 'St Paul said these words at Thessalonica . . .' is a sure recipe for sending the hearers' thoughts chasing after every extraneous thought imaginable. Most moderns have very little interest in St Paul, and could not care less about what happened at Thessalonica. Harsh observations, no doubt, but corresponding to reality. Textual analysis as an opening to a sermon could only be paralleled for ineptness by the announcement of ecclesiastical hooks on which to hang what is going to be said, 'This is Septuagesima

Sunday', 'This is Pentecost Eight', 'On this Sunday the Church teaches . . .' Very likely, and with good reason, but that is not why anyone is going to listen.

Sermon introductions are of two kinds in the main. The first is a strong and arresting comment or a text already announced, and which is to serve as the theme of the sermon— 'John, chapter 4 verse 9, "Give me a drink" You've heard that request before. You've heard it many times. Perhaps you have made it yourself. "Give me a drink". But when the request was made in the circumstances I am going to describe to you, the hearer was astonished. It did not seem proper. Truth to tell she was a little shocked, for the request was not only made by a man to a woman, a strange man, but (by the look of him) a good man, and she had had at least five men in her life, and as if that were not enough, a strong racial bar separated them. But there was no mistaking what he had said— "Give me a drink!" And all the while in the fierce glare of the midday sun he looked at her steadily. Then she answered, pouring all her surprise and all her scorn into the words she uttered, "What! You, a Jew, ask a drink of me, a Samaritan woman?" Who was this Jew? Who was the Samaritan woman . . .?' — This is one way of beginning a sermon, actually in this case a sermon on the 'Divine Initiative', a distinctly theological subject preached to schoolgirls and leading to a practical conclusion about the duty for those who profess to follow Christ to take the first step in crossing barriers that divide people, yes, between one girl and another in that school.

Another method of introducing a sermon is by means of an illustration, story or anecdote after the fashion of the medieval 'exemplum'. This calls for careful handling, but it can be effective. A preliminary warning needs to be given. This kind of introduction is not designed to be a mere device for gaining attention. There is no point in the preacher telling his congregation how he fell off a bus last week and nearly broke his neck, if the sermon that follows is not closely and consistently connected with this incident. The drop when he passes from this lurid tale to the meat of his sermon will be so great that the preliminary attention will make the subsequent inattention even more profound than if he had never begun his sermon in this fashion at all. No, the opening must contain in picture, concrete or dramatic form what the whole sermon is to be about, then its usefulness will be considerable. Take an example, 'Some time ago a friend of mine, a professor in Science and Technology, took me into his laboratory to show me an experiment on which he was working. He took a bar of metal 12″ × 3″ × 1½″ and inserted the two ends into the jaws of a machine. He pressed a button and the two jaws drew slowly apart tearing the metal bar as if it were a piece of plasticine. I was astonished at the strength of the machine and said so, but I had missed the point. What interested the professor was the measurement of the tension required to fracture that particular metal. He was in fact working on what is called "metal fatigue", with a view to making possible the flights of aircraft at supersonic speed. And in due course this problem was *mastered*. Concorde became possible, and flights to the moon . . . Now all life proceeds by way of mastery, first mastery over the environment . . .'

This was the way a sermon preached to a thousand schoolboys was introduced. The theme was mastery over the environment, mastery over situations, and mastery over self—for which we are insufficient in ourselves but need the power of God, available in Christ. The sermon began without a text but led up to one at the very end. The text was Philippians 4:13, 'I have strength for anything through him who gives me power' (N.E.B.).[8]

Sermon introductions take time to prepare and are usually thought out last in the process of sermon construction (like the introduction to a book), but they repay the labour by the attention they arouse. They do however necessitate buoyancy in the rest of the sermon, and for this the employment and careful placing of the illustrations throughout the sermon are important. If these illustrations are compared with windows in a building, a simile suggested in a previous chapter, then none of the major points or sections of the sermon will be without its window, any more than a living room would be windowless in a house. The point in sermon preparation therefore is reached when the fenestration needs checking. Are there any windows at all? Are they set in the proper places?

And now *the writing or non-writing* of the sermon, using the outline or skeleton that has been prepared. Many words have been written on these alternatives, and not much would be gained by adding to them. Suffice it to say that some preachers ought to write out their sermons, and some ought not. For the first few years of their ministries preachers ought perhaps to place themselves in the first category— they ought to write out their sermons. It will deliver them from the peril of being long-winded. It will also develop their style, excise

[8] I have used this introduction on two different occasions. See my *Preaching on Special Occasions*, p. 45.

shoddy jargon, and build up a reserve of preaching material.[9] Those who have engaged in broadcasting will know the necessity to be able to deliver a complete sermon 'on the air' in exactly eight minutes, ten minutes, twenty minutes, or whatever is required. Only the acquired discipline of writing out a sermon can accomplish this successfully. And this is very important for preaching at the Parish Communion where the time for preaching is severely limited. To prepare a short sermon that says something worth while requires more skill than one of average length. The development of almost a new art form is required in this situation if perfection is to be sought and this requires writing.

But will the working out of a sermon result in a literary production rather like an essay instead of a spoken message which is of the essence of preaching? This is possible, and some preachers are so prone to it they must abandon the practice. Writing, however, can be accomplished with the end-point of speaking in view, otherwise plays could not be written. It is however a skill that needs to be learnt and certain principles must be borne in mind.

Sentences must be short with a plentiful supply of subject-verb-object structures. Not every sentence must be constructed in this fashion, or monotony will result, indeed, some sentences may be lengthy on purpose in order that the short sentences following shall produce a stabbing effect compelling attention. Subordinate clauses should be used sparingly and never an inverted negative subordinate clause. 'He always spoke in abstractions than which none more complicated could scarcely ever be imagined.' This will not do. The words used need to possess a cutting edge if they are to be effective in preaching as spoken words. Words like coins can become defaced through constant use till they are almost valueless. The verb 'to get' is an example. 'I have got to get a book' expresses little except a lazy speaker. Avoid the word. In general transitive verbs possess more force than intransitive verbs, they strike their object. Anglo-Saxon words possess a certain strength lacking in words with a Latin origin. Technical jargon, 'in-words' and slang should be avoided. They date the preacher. 'Churchy' words should not be used. To announce that some one has been 'laid aside' suggests that he is an outworn tool or a pair of discarded mittens. To say that so-and-so 'is ill' is all that is required. 'Holy Bible' and 'Holy Church' sound sanctimonious. Care should be taken not to use two words where one will suffice, and

[9] Most of this will be outgrown every five years, but the possession of it may be an advantage in an emergency.

adjectives can weaken the nouns they qualify and should be used sparingly if strong speech is being sought. If these points carry weight they constitute a forcible argument for the written manuscript, since it is unlikely that an extempore preacher can incorporate them unless and until he has so developed his own style that they have become part of his normal diction.

There are of course skills in public speaking beyond the straightforward and elementary (though effective) level in mind in giving the above pieces of advice. Rhythmic sentences can be constructed competent to charm the hearer into gratified acceptance of the pleasantness he is experiencing through the beauty of language, only to be abruptly dragged out of his reverie by a sudden alteration of style, sharp, staccato and alerting with its dissonance. Phrases can be repeated and expanded by degrees till they worm their way into the hearer's consciousness. 'I know that this is true, I have known ever since I became a preacher that this is true. I have known even from the day when I felt called to the sacred ministry and went forward to be examined and tested . . . *that this is true.*' Preachers who can manipulate language are able to hold their hearers in the hollow of their hands. If few possess this gift, it may be as well, for it wields dangerous power, not least for the preacher himself, for he and the congregation can be mesmerised with language, a state of affairs not after the mind of Christ.

Apart from the language in which the ideas that make up the sermon are to be clothed, the form in which the ideas are presented must be given attention. The general rule for preaching is that concrete, rather than abstract forms are to be employed. That the Bible thinks in Hebraic fashion is fortuitous, not to comment on the fact more strongly. The Hebrews did not expatiate (in general) on justice in business, they forbade, in particular terms, the using of false weights on the scales. And Jesus, in true succession did not produce a homily on importunity in prayer, he told a story about a man seeking his friend at midnight and knocking him up because he was suddenly short of bread owing to the arrival of an unexpected guest. The story is concrete. The man asks for three loaves. It is so vivid that it is almost possible to see the petitioner peeping through the keyhole to make sure his friend really had gone to bed! Jesus understood how people think in pictures and not in abstract forms. It may be right for the university lecturer or even the school-teacher with the senior classes to propound a theory and then proceed to illustrate it with particular examples, but the preacher's rôle is different. He must argue from the particular to the general and not from the general to the particular, indeed, it may be proper for him to leave his hearers with the particular, that is, with the picture only, and to trust them to learn from it what they can. Such was Jesus' way. This is not an easy discipline for those preachers with a philosophical turn of mind or training, but it must be learned if success is to be obtained with the general run of congregations, not forgetting that women do not, as a general rule, think in the abstract, and they form a high proportion of many congregations.

And now, *testing the sermon for sound*. The preacher who does not write out his sermons in full has no need of this, he has finished the preparatory work. He has an outline in note form on paper, of what he is going to say, perhaps with certain parts, such as quotations, or the ending of the sermon, written out more fully. The preacher, on the other hand, who has his sermon written out in full, or in type-script, has, however, not finished. He (we hope) has written his sermon *for speaking* it. He must therefore make as sure as he can in the artificial surroundings of his study that it does speak well. He must speak it out loud, and, as a result of his assessment *how it sounds*, he must correct his manuscript. The result will probably involve some crossing out and substitution of other words and phrases. Strips from 'economy labels' stuck over impossible sentences and used for the rewriting on top is one way of dealing with this emendation process. The resulting manuscript will appear a somewhat patched and even untidy production, but there are grounds for distrusting a too neat and uncorrected manuscript taken into the pulpit. It probably means that it has never been *tested for its sound*. This final correction is too often omitted by too many preachers with the result that the sermon, when it comes to delivery, lacks the life it might otherwise possess. Obviously as the preacher learns the skill of *writing for speaking*, his corrections will be fewer than in the early years of his ministry, but he ought never to omit testing his written manuscript for sound before he preaches it.

The foregoing are not hard and fast rules for every preacher preparing his sermon, but they are guide lines which have proved their worth for many. Moreover, if some such careful attention as this be given to the preparatory work on a sermon, any need for learning the manuscript by heart will be rendered unnecessary. And this is important because learning by heart can prevent those spontaneous and often most telling interjections in a sermon made *when it is being delivered*, which may carry the immediate inspiration of the Spirit. At least the maker of the sermon will, as a result of his work, know it sufficiently well to be able to preach it with freedom when the time for delivery comes—the subject which will occupy our attention in the next chapter. He may indeed feel that he knows it so well that he can reduce the sermon to a few headings, leave the manuscript at home and go into his pulpit ready to preach, unbound to any written work before him at all, except perhaps a few headings, and maybe not even those. This is preaching in the Alpha class and few will wish, or be able to aspire to it. In an age, however, when television viewers are accustomed to face-to-face speech (even though it is contrived), preaching 'without a note' is even more arresting than ever.

It ought to be possible to omit all reference to the style of the sermon which the preacher will adopt in any particular place as being obvious, but perhaps it ought to be included at the end of the chapter. Clearly a conversational style appropriate for a small village church would be ineffective in St Paul's Cathedral, and the measured diction for St Paul's Cathedral ludicrous in a village church. Elementary sensitivity to situations would surely determine for each preacher and each sermon what his style is to be. The age, education and experience of the congregation are the determining factors as well as the intimacy of the building.

3

The delivery of a sermon

THE DELIVERY OF A SERMON WILL NOT TAKE CARE OF ITSELF ANY MORE
than the *preparation* of a sermon will take care of itself. Nor is enthusiasm sufficient, nor dedication, nor even a thoroughly prepared
manuscript. Indeed it is possible for a week's effort on sermon preparation to be wasted by fifteen minutes' poor delivery. The situation
would not be unlike that of a cook spending hours on the preparation
of a meal in a kitchen up to 'cordon bleu' standard, and then tossing
it through the dining-room hatch in the direction of the table.
Attention to serving is as important as attention to preparation. It is
even the crowning point of the preparation. Similarly, the work in
the pulpit is related to the work in the study.

Resistance to work on sermon delivery may be put up on the
grounds that it involves artificiality. If so then it had better be left
alone. The truth, however, is that artificiality indicates that the work
on the delivery has been unthorough. An actor who does not
appear so natural that he does not seem to be acting is a poor actor.
A preacher who is not himself in the pulpit has a great deal to
learn.

Resistance has also been put up on the grounds that working at
delivery makes for insincerity. It involves 'playing to the gallery'.
There certainly is this risk but it is a risk which runs through the whole
of the preaching ministry. Work *in the study* preparing the sermon may
be carried out with an eye on personal popularity in place of delivering
the counsels of God which are not always popular. Is therefore sermon
preparation to be omitted in order to avoid this danger? And if the
preacher is to believe that his study work begun and ended in prayer
is to receive the enabling power of the Divine Spirit, why must he
refuse his delivery work in the pulpit that same possibility? God
blesses man's labours, not his laziness. All of which means that the
preacher must take care of his sermon delivery, it will not take care
of itself. Not a few sermons which might have been impressive have

failed for lack of attention to this important fact, sometimes through ignorance, sometimes deliberately.[1]

A competent preacher has three hooks which he throws out and which fasten on to the congregation, holding them from the beginning to the ending of his sermon. The first is the *content*, that is, what he is saying, which, if not new, is fresh and so well lit up with illustrations that it is arresting in itself. Then secondly, there is the *form* in which the content is cast. This means the way the preacher says what he says, his turn of expression, and the unusual language he employs. Thirdly, there is his skill in *delivery*, the use of his voice, his hands and his eyes, in short, his complete mastery of the instruments of communication which belong to his own embodied personality.

Mastery of the art of delivering a sermon is able to be learnt first at the lectern. Generally speaking, poor public reading means poor public preaching. A man who cannot read well will not be able to preach well. Unless therefore he first masters the lectern he will not master the pulpit.

An initial lesson for him to learn is the level of personal involvement. In the leadership of public worship personal involvement is at its lowest in the prayers and the reading of the liturgy, which does not mean that it is read without feeling, but that the tone range, volume and variety of speech is strictly limited. In reading the lessons there is more personal involvement. This is because the reader is there not simply to give out information like the announcer on a railway station, but to interpret the passage of scripture for the hearers *by the way he reads it*. But he must remember that he did not write the Bible himself, which fact behoves him to read with modesty and reserve. When however the reader comes to preach, his personal involvement will be at its highest. This does not necessitate an excitable display which can be either comic or pathetic, and certainly repelling to the Englishman, but that he will speak from his heart as well as his head. He is committed to his utterance though he stands quite still and like the servant in the first of the Servant Songs, 'he will not call out or lift his voice high.'[2]

The reader must learn to concentrate on his reading. This is obvious, but his concentration must be directed to the right ends. To some

---

[1] The present writer has, on more than one occasion, in working with 'sermon classes', taken a sermon which a group has reckoned as indescribably dull, and caused a competent preacher to preach it. The reaction was a revelation. The group would not believe it was exactly the same sermon.

[2] Isa. 42:2 (N.E.B.).

extent he must concentrate on himself—his breathing, his articulation, and the speed at which he speaks, bearing in mind that a large building does not only require more volume of sound, but a slower pace. The reader will need to concentrate rather more on his hearers than on himself. He wishes them not only to hear but to understand and appreciate. He will therefore bear in mind their intelligence and age. Younger people appreciate faster, older people slower, speech. His chief concentration, however, will be on the scripture he is reading. When he is reading about David and Goliath he will see them both in his mind's eye. When Jesus bids his disciples 'consider the flowers of the field' it is flowers that he will see. And if the reader sees neither David, Goliath nor flowers, it is certain his hearers will not see them either. There will be very little communication between reader and hearer without this kind of imaginative perception.[3]

When the lectern has been mastered, and the reader understands how meaning is conveyed largely by inflection,[4] he is well on the road to success in the delivery of sermons. He will need confidence of course but this is more likely to come if he has thoroughly prepared himself and his sermon. Nervous he may be before he enters the pulpit. This is not unusual, even with some of the most famous platform artists. Caruso wrote, 'Of course I am nervous. Each time I sing I feel there is someone waiting to destroy me, and I must fight like a bull to hold my own. The artist who boasts he is never nervous is not an artist—he is a liar or a fool.'[5] This nervousness is the product of sensitivity, not of fear, and no one can be a great artist without sensitivity. A conscious attempt to relax before the performance is salutary. Preachers need to remember this. Therefore a service so arranged that the preacher may be set free from active participation for a few moments before actually preaching is not only kind to him personally, but beneficial for his work. If he cannot sit he could breathe deeply six or seven times and make sure that his shoulders are relaxed. In an attitude of prayer he can commit his work already done, and to be done, to God, in whose service he operates. A trustful approach is of great practical

---

[3] Perhaps one of the most severe tests is the reading of 2 Sam. 18:19–33. Anyone who can read this scripture aloud with the changes of mood and inflection called for has achieved the mastery.

[4] For example, 'Bach's organ works' can mean two entirely different things depending on whether the accent is placed on the last or the last but one word, cf 'He has a French mistress.'

[5] Quoted in N. Punt, *The Singer's and Actor's Throat*, p. 4.

assistance. It is doubtful if the man to whom none of this makes sense will ever become a significant preacher.

A new question to be faced in the 1970s about preaching is, where shall the preacher go in his church to preach? Twenty years ago the question did not normally arise. The pulpit was taken for granted as the proper location. Now, however, a visiting preacher will be wise to raise the question in the vestry before the service begins. He may find that he is expected to speak from the chancel, from the altar steps, or from the lectern. In the first two situations he may be embarrassed by having no desk on which to place his notes or manuscript.

A pulpit, it must be admitted, has come into being for preaching in order to meet the necessities of certain situations. In a small group of worshippers it is more fitting for the preacher to stand among his fellows without any furniture between himself and them. Preacher and worshippers are together in making the word of God possible in their midst. No *thing* comes between them—if possible not even a manuscript—nothing but the Holy Spirit—'the go-between God' to use John Taylor's striking phrase. But as soon as the assembly grows in numbers the preacher has to be elevated in order that he may be seen; and because he is elevated he needs a fence around him to safeguard him from falling. Then, maybe, a door for entry through the fence and a stairway for mounting, then a balustrade, and before long ornamentation, perhaps even statues. Still the situation is capable of development. A desk for the notes or manuscript adjustable by the operating of a thumb screw. Then a lighting device often in the form of a piece of tubular lighting housed in a kind of horizontal elongated cocoa tin, that may once have been brass. It was designed to illuminate the preacher's notes, and does this most effectively, also illuminating his stomach which, if it is arrayed in a white surplice, succeeds in radiating a deathly paleness on the preacher's face half hidden in the darkness. If this preacher happens to be preaching on life, it must be confessed that he looks like death. Still the complex of furniture for preaching is not completed. Modern technology requires a public address system, causing either a microphone to be fixed to the desk in the pulpit or hung around the preacher's neck like some ecclesiastical decoration. And let no preacher be too supercilious about these electronic speaking aids. The younger generation are unlikely to be impressed unless the speaker is seen to have wires trailing from him across the floor. Finally, or is it finally, the pulpit may be roofed over with a canopy, originally designed for the purpose of keeping the preacher's voice down from the rafters in the roof

15

where it could be lost, but now in the days of public address systems retained only for decoration.

Well may it be asked, is all this paraphernalia necessary? It may be, and before it is abandoned as a dusty relic in the corner of the church, let the furniture be simplified a little. Is that tin illuminating device dispensable? Could there not be a simple lamp above the preacher's head invisible to the congregation but lighting up the whole preacher, and his notes if necessary? And is that ugly adjustable wooden desk with its uncertain elevating and lowering device desirable? Why not a cushion? And does not the pulpit 'fall' draw attention to the notes, or manuscript, the very thing that needs to be avoided? Is there not too an over-eagerness to install microphones and loudspeakers where they are not really required? All this adds up to a plea for simplification. It is noticeable that second-rate artists seem to need the support of more 'effects' around them than do the first-rate who can manage with the minimum. In general it can be said that if the congregation can see only the head and shoulders of their preacher then there is something drastically wrong with that particular pulpit and its critical examination is long overdue.

And now the time has come for the preacher to enter the pulpit,[6] be it cluttered with furniture or decently simplified. How shall he begin? With the formula, 'In the name of the Father, and of the Son and of the Holy Spirit' or with a short prayer according to the tradition of the Church, but whichever it is, let it be said deliberately and not mumbled or gabbled. At this point time must be allowed for the congregation to sit and become settled. It is well then if momentarily the preacher lets his eye sweep over the whole congregation. Next, if he has a text from scripture, he will announce it deliberately, not twice, but once only, otherwise he will be training his hearers not to bother to listen the first time, and an element of lazy hearing creeps in. What the preacher needs is attention from the very beginning.

A pause should follow the announcement of the text (if any), and then the sermon begins— *modestly*. For the opening words to be too strong, loud and energetic is a mistake. There is a true story of a visiting preacher in what can only be described as a select West End Church in London opening his sermon after the announcement of his text with three shouted hurrahs! Maybe the hearers ought to have perceived from his text about the ascension of Christ into heaven that he was joining in with the disciples who, we are told, returned to Jerusalem

[6] The manner in which the preacher accomplishes this simple and apparently automatic procedure is important, It could suggest eagerness or utter boredom.

with great joy.[7] The preacher was, in fact, setting a tone of praise and thanksgiving, a thoroughly justifiable key in which to pitch what he had to say, but he said it too soon and with too much gusto. The congregation was not only bewildered but stunned. They were not ready for this outburst, and what was more of a pity, they never recovered their balance sufficiently to appreciate the good things he had to say later on. The medieval preacher who wrote:—

> Begin low, speak slow,
> Rise higher, catch fire,
> Wax warm, sit down in a storm.

was a wise man and a more subtle preacher. A congregation has to be eased into a sermon and their attention wooed. What this calls for is a modest start so far as voice production is concerned.

What about the written manuscript? Obviously it is placed on the desk or cushion in the pulpit, which, as already indicated, must not be too high so that only the preacher's neck and face are visible. It ought to be not less than two feet away from the preacher's chin. And the preacher should stand well back from it, otherwise when glancing down at his manuscript from time to time, he will appear to those in the congregation with a comical turn of mind to be more like a chicken picking up grains of corn in the hen-run. It is easier to look at the congregation *and* at the manuscript more or less simultaneously, or at least with only a slight movement of the head if the body is not close up to the desk. And whether the pages of the manuscript are turned or slipped one under the other, at that point of turning or slipping the preacher should have his eyes, not on his hands, but on the congregation, otherwise they will be directing their attention at that point to the mechanics of the operation, to turning or slipping of paper, which is undesirable.

When the preacher is well launched upon his sermon, he should give attention to the variety of speed, tone and volume of his diction. In the same way that it is a mistake to begin a sermon with too much volume and energy, so it is a mistake to imagine that clarity will only be achieved if a deliberate, unvarying steady pace is sustained throughout, with as much volume as can comfortably be produced.

> Out it streams, this panting diction,
> Carries all things save conviction.

[7] Luke 24:52.

The monotony of this kind of preaching is insufferable, moreover, it is artificial because no one speaks in this fashion in ordinary discourse. There is perhaps even a worse fault. This is when the voice is dropped in an exactly similar fashion at the end of every sentence. It adds depression to boredom almost unable to be endured by any sensitive hearer. What is required is variety. Sometimes the speaker scampers along, at other times so deliberate that listening is guaranteed. Some sentences, those that raise questions, end on a higher note than they began. Other sentences are given a sharp, staccato cutting sound. And occasionally, when some word requires special emphasis, there is a deliberate pause, and the word comes out of the silence with astonishing effect. It is possible also to produce a rare and very occasional whisper, not inaudible, but spoken loudly in such a way that it sounds like a whisper. The reader could be forgiven for wondering if a sermon containing all these 'effects' listed together in this fashion would sound anything like a sermon he has heard outside a comedy show in a music hall. No great art however is ever vulgar, loud or excessive. Every device is used with delicacy and reserve, but the result is to lend colour and therefore interest to the diction. What is more important, the hearing of what is being said is not in doubt.

And now gestures. Harold Macmillan, in two broadcast lectures entitled, 'The Past Masters', about predecessors of his in the office of Prime Minister of Great Britain, had this to say about gestures, 'Lloyd George told me how to make a speech, but Hugh Cecil told me about gestures. "Well," he said, "the English don't like gestures . . . There should be few but they should be powerful. Never make a gesture from the elbow, that is a very weak gesture. Hugh Gaitskell always did it. If you make one at all, it must come from the shoulder. And the other great thing, the gesture must precede the phrase. I don't say to you, "there's a man who has betrayed England" and then point. I say (throwing his whole arm at Robert McKenzie first), "*there* is the man who's betrayed England." '

This is good advice. Perhaps a little more is needed. The gestures must say in actions (first) what the lips also say in words (afterwards). The point is they must say the same thing. The gestures are carried out in order to reinforce the words, or to be more accurate, the words are said in order to reinforce the gestures. The most common error is for gestures to be undisciplined. The speaker has an unconscious impulse to strengthen his words with actions, and so he moves his hands this way and that. Perhaps he presses them together. Perhaps he punches his left-hand palm with the fist of his right hand; perhaps he uses them when hoping to be concise, as if he were patting and shaping up a half pound of butter. He may perform any one of these actions with his hands, even when (let us say) he is hoping to drive home the point that Christians should get out into the world with their gospel. But his gestures do not suggest any form of outward movement. If anything, they suggest compression, indeed if a judgment had to be made on gestures alone, moving inwards would seem to be a chief element in what was being proclaimed. Appropriate gestures do exist, and they may be employed by speakers capable of doing so. Pointing heavenwards, or outwards, or downwards, could all belong to occasions that were entirely proper. To roll the hands over and over could indicate the turning wheels of human experience or the sheer 'on-and-on-ness' of routine. The pressures of life can be illustrated by pressing the hands together, including even the arms and shoulders in a kind of shrugging movement.

Let the preacher however who is unaccustomed to gestures proceed with caution or he can make himself look ridiculous and ruin his message. The golden rule is for gestures to be infrequent, disciplined and in harmony with the words that follow them.

Mannerisms belong to another category. They are personal idiosyncrasies. Do not try to rub them all out. They are part and parcel of individuality, and individuality is important in preaching. Mannerisms must however be curtailed when they are absurd. Fiddling with spectacles or even cleaning them while preaching. All forms of scratching. Smoothing down the clothing that is being worn. Examining the finger nails as if the idea has just impinged on the preacher's mind that he ought to set about manicuring them. Stroking the hair or the nose . . .

What to do with the hands seems to constitute a problem for some preachers. They should never be thrust in the pockets. They should not clasp the scarf, stole or lapel of the coat, reminding of Mr Gladstone; neither should they hold on to the sides of the pulpit as if there was an overwhelming need to steady it, a posture incidentally which, from the angle of the congregation's vision, can look as if the preacher has his hands on the handle-bars of a motor-cycle. The hands can be at rest lightly on the desk, though not as if they are glued to it, or they can be kept behind the back. The overriding necessity is to be natural and to take care not to fall into stupid mannerisms *unwittingly*.

The eyes need some attention. They should be focused in the direction of the congregation. Note the point—not into the eyes of the members. This is impossible with a large congregation, and embarrassing with a small one. There is such a thing as a 'communal face' wherever people are assembled together. This is what the preacher must look at. Attention to this will prevent him from fixing his eyes permanently on his notes or manuscript, though he will need to glance at them from time to time. It will also eradicate that other advertisement of nervousness, gazing up at the top left-hand corner of the building where the back wall meets the roof as if an angel were about to appear. Why the left is a mystery, but this idiosyncrasy usually appears in this form. There needs to be a discipline of the eyes as well as of the hands. The soul is seen through the eyes.[8]

The general appearance of the preacher cannot be neglected. Fortunately in most Church traditions ceremonial robes are worn, and these present a dignity in themselves. But they must be clean and worn properly. Hands, too, must be clean and hair brushed. 'Dolling up' as if for the stage is not required, but inattention to general appearance can be a means of some hearers being too 'put off' by slovenliness to be able to hear at all.

And now the sermon is about to end. Let it end swiftly, neatly and tidily. There should be no false endings, no suggestion that it is about to end when in fact it meanders on. The possibility will not arise if the sermon is written out, or at least the ending is in full manuscript, but for those who preach extempore the danger is real.

When the sermon is finished, there is the traditional way of closing with the ascription to the Blessed Trinity of might, majesty, dominion and power, or the bidding to prayer, 'Let us pray' and prayer follows, or 'the subject of our thoughts is taken up in the hymn which now follows, number . . .' or, in the case of the Eucharist the recitation of the Nicene Creed expressing the faith which (we hope) has been expounded in one of its aspects in the sermon. ·

When the preacher reaches home, his ministry ended, he may feel depressed or elated, as he thinks back over his sermon. It is possible that more people will thank him for the sermon he estimated as a poor performance than for one he reckoned a masterpiece, the moral of which is that the preacher should do his work and leave the results to God, paying little attention to his feelings which may have little more substance than reaction after strenuous labour. If he is wise however he will annotate his notes or manuscript about

[8] The present writer was impressed by the way in which students for the American Roman Catholic ministry being trained at their college in Louvain (Belgium) lifted their eyes perhaps once, or possibly twice when reading the gospel at Mass to reinforce what they thought was the point of the passage being read.

ways in which, judging from actual delivery, the sermon might possibly be improved, because he may need that sermon again some day and the notes will be useful for a revised and possibly better version.

Perhaps no better way to end this chapter could be than to quote from *The Country Parson* by George Herbert, Vicar of Bemerton, Salisbury in 1630. The quotation is from chapter 7, entitled 'The Parson Preaching' of the 1834 Edition, pages 15f. It will at least show that the needs of the present day are not all that different from those of more than three centuries ago. The length of the sermon has changed. Few modern congregations would survive an hour's sermon; twenty minutes, perhaps, from a first-class preacher, twelve to fifteen minutes from an average, seven minutes on occasions, and for these short sermons very special skill will be required.

When he preacheth, he procures attention by all possible art, both by earnestness of speech—it being natural to man to think, that where there is much earnestness, there is something worth hearing—and by a diligent and busy cast of his eyes on his auditors, with letting them know that he marks who·observes and who not; and with particularising of his speech now to the younger sort, then to the elder, now to the poor and now to the rich—'This is for you and this for you'—for particulars ever touch and awake, more than generals, therein also he serves himself of the judgments of God; as of those of ancient times, so especially of the late ones: and those most which are nearest to his parish; for people are very attentive at such discourse, and think it behoves them to be so, when God is so near them, and even over their heads. Sometimes he tells them stories and sayings of others, according as his text invites him; for them also men heed, and remember better than exhortations; which, though earnest, yet often die with the sermon, especially with country people, which are thick and heavy, and hard to raise to a point, zeal and fervency, and need a mountain of fire to kindle them, but stories and sayings they will remember. He often tells them that sermons are dangerous things; that none go out of church as he came in, but either better or worse; that none is careless before his judge; and that the word of God shall judge us.

By these and other means the Parson procures attention; but the character of his sermon is holiness. He is not witty, nor learned, nor eloquent, but HOLY, . . . a character that Hermogenes never dreamed of, and therefore he could give no precepts thereof. But it is gained first by choosing texts of devotion not controversy; moving and ravishing texts, whereof the Scriptures are full. Secondly, by dipping and seasoning all our words and sentences in our hearts before they come into our mouths, truly affecting and cordially expressing all that we say, so that our auditors may plainly perceive that every word is heart-deep. Thirdly, by turning often, and making many apostrophes to God; as 'O Lord, bless my people, and teach them this point' or 'O my master, on whose errand I come, let me hold my place, and do thou speak thyself; for thou art love; and when thou teachest all are scholars.' Such irradiations scatteringly in the sermon, carry great holiness in them. The prophets are admirable in this. So Isaiah 64, 'O that thou wouldest rend the heavens, that thou wouldest come down' etc. And Jeremy 10, after he had complained of the desolation of Israel, turns to God suddenly, 'O Lord, I know that the way of man is not in himself' etc. Fourthly, by frequent wishes of the peoples' good and joying therein . . . Lastly, by often urging of the presence and majesty of God.

The parson exceeds not an hour in preaching because all ages have thought that a competency; and he that profits not in that time will less afterwards; the same affliction which made him not profit before, making him thus weary; and so he grows from not relishing to loathing.

Epilogue

THIS BOOK IS BEING PUBLISHED AT A TIME WHEN THE ADMISSION MUST be made that to a large extent the general public, and this includes the Christian public, even the Church-going minority, has lost the appetite for hearing sermons. It is probably true that the pulpit has less power now than at any time since the Reformation. This failure is a fairly recent phenomenon. At the beginning of the century, even as late as the 1930s, it was possible in London to sample a number of 'great preachers'. That time has gone. Various reasons could be offered as explanations among which sound broadcasting and television would have to figure, but whatever the reasons, the fact remains that the great majority of people below the age of fifty have never experienced preaching as a powerful instrument for communicating the gospel, not only have they never heard it, they have never seen it, certainly not in the regular ministries of almost all the churches, Billy Graham excepted, but he is a *travelling evangelist*.

The time has therefore come for a case to be made out for preaching, if preaching is to be retained in the churches with any degree of conviction and therefore with any degree of power. Some people will have to say why they believe in preaching. The result will not be an immediate supply of convincing preachers, but unless more people believe in it than they do at present, and have good reason to believe in it, the slot provided for 'the sermon' in the various orders of worship will not rescue it from the doldrums.

I believe in preaching. I believe in it as so necessary for the health of the Church, that it could almost be said to be necessary for the life of the Church. The existence of the Church does not depend on preaching but on election, nor is the essence of the gospel safeguarded by preaching as it is by the sacraments of the gospel, but unless preaching takes place first in the Church, and from the Church, the Church will not reflect in its private and public life the gospel of Christ as it is proclaimed in the New Testament.

Preaching does not end in the Church. The Church's preaching ministry has not been completed when it has included sermons in the course of its public worship. Ordained ministers are not the only members of the Church to have committed to them the ministry of the word. Every Church-man, every Christian, is required to be at least a witness to what he believes, certainly if asked, and witness is a form of Christian proclamation. And between the ordained ministry and the personal witness of individual Christians there is a whole variety of ministries in industry, the armed forces, education, the stage, the care of the sick, and in other spheres, where varieties and variations of preaching are exercised. But—and this is the point— unless the ministry of the word is strong *first of all* in the course of ordered public worship, it will not be strong in those other places where laymen exercise it, and where it is increasingly important that it shall be strong. The Church or Chapel pulpit is still vital for the outreach beyond the church or chapel, for Christian proclamation.

Biblical preaching is what is required. This is not to say preaching should be restricted to expository preaching, though its revival would be welcomed, but the Biblical revelation is what should be preached and this reaches its peak in Christ. Preaching is the proclamation of Christ and any overall pulpit ministry which does not proclaim him is not preaching. The living Christ as the living Lord is the heart of the message, a message which must be related to the whole of life and not merely to the inner and religious, but to the outer and secular.

More than ever, preaching must be carried out in context. Churches as 'preaching shops' never were justified, now they are even impracticable. Sermons, like words themselves, derive their meaning from the context in which they are employed. He or she then who concentrates on preaching alone is doomed to disappointment. Attention must be given (almost as a prerequisite) to worship and pre-eminently the sacraments, to fellowship, to social work of all kinds, to counselling, to education, to discussion groups, to lectures and involvement in the life of the locality, and *then* to preaching. Only in context will preaching penetrate the hard hearing of contemporary man, but if all these activities are continued without preaching, his deafness will continue, and if as Paul says, faith comes by hearing and hearing by the word of God, then that impressive activity will end in failure.

The question will be asked, what is the preacher's authority? No discussion on preaching fails to raise this question. This is not surprising in an age when imposed authority is almost universally rejected. No preacher in the second half of the twentieth century can expect to be heard because he is ordained. This may be shocking, but it represents the truth. Not that authority does not pertain to ordination nor to the Bible which the ordained person ministers, but authorisation by an authority does not, in a fiercely democratic age convey the kind of authority which is recognised. This belongs almost wholly to the authority of expertise, and is an authority which is accorded because it is seen to work. But is this an altogether different situation from that which obtained for Jesus? When however people saw what he could do, what his words could do, they recognised and acclaimed his authority. This is all the contemporary pulpit should look for, but it will require work, never-ending work to acquire the expertise which is self-authenticating, and the grace and power of God to sustain it. What is involved in the way of work, this book has made an attempt to describe.

What is the preacher's authority? We have not answered the question. Authority does not lie in authorisation. It is more likely to be accorded on grounds of expertise. But this is not the final answer. A preacher in the last resort only has authority if he is a *man of God*, and is known to be a man of God. The category is rare and is more likely to be sensed than classified. Yet somehow with such a man you become aware of an indefinable presence so different that only a term like 'holy' will suffice. When such a man of God speaks there is nothing you can say or do except listen, and even if you disobey, the disobedience will itself stand as a witness to the fact that a preacher with authority has spoken. All who hear him know it, they know it 'in their bones'.

Bibliography

Allmen von, J. J., *Preaching and Congregation* (1962).
Angus, S., *The Early History of Christianity* (1914).
Baillie, D. M., *God Was in Christ* (1947).
—— *To whom shall we go?* (1955).
—— *The Theology of the Sacraments* (1957).
—— *Out of Nazareth* (1958).
Baker, J. A., *The Foolishness of God* (1970).
Barrett, C. K., *The Holy Spirit and the Gospel Tradition* (1966).
Barth, K., *Church Dogmatics* Vol. I, Part I (E.T. 1975).
Beeson, T., *Britain Today and Tomorrow* (1978).
Black, M., *An Aramaic Approach to the Gospels and the Acts* (1946).
Black, Max, *The Labyrinth of Language* (1968).
Blench, J. W., *Preaching in the late 15th and 16th Centuries* (1964).
Bornkamm, G., *Jesus of Nazareth* (1960).
Box, G. H., *Religion and Worship of the Synagogue* (1911).
Braaten, C. E., *History and Hermeneutics* (1968).
Bright, J., *A History of Israel* (1960).
Brooks, Phillips, *Eight Lectures on Preaching* (1879 & 1959).
Brown, J., *Puritan Preaching in England* (1900).
Browne, R. E., *The Ministry of the Word* (1958 & 1977).
Bruce, A. B., *The Parabolic Teaching of Christ* (1882).
Bultmann, R., *Marburger Predigten* (1956).
—— E.T. *This World and Beyond* (1960).
Burney, C. F., *The Poetry of Our Lord* (1925).
Coggan, F. D., *The Ministry of the Word* (1945 & 1964).
Crichton, J. D., *Christian Celebration. The Mass* (1971).
Dalman, G. H., *The Words of Jesus* (E.T. 1902).
Daniélou, J., *Les Évangiles de l'Enfance* (1967).
Davies, H., *Varieties of English Preaching 1900–60* (1963).
Dibelius, M., *From Tradition to Gospel* (E.T. 1934).
Dodd, C. H., *The Apostolic Preaching and its Development* (1936).

Dodd, C. H., *The Founder of Christianity* (1971).

Duhm, B., *Israel's Profeten* (1916, 2nd Edition 1922).

Dunn, D. G., *Unity and Diversity in the New Testament* (1977).

Ebeling, G., *Introduction to the Theology of Language* (1973).

—— *Theology and Proclamation* (1966).

Edersheim, A., *The Life and Times of Jesus* (1900).

Edwards, Douglas, *The Virgin Birth in History and Faith* (1943).

Edwards, D. L., *The Last Things Now* (1969).

—— *A Reason to Hope* (1978).

Eichrodt, W., *Theology of the Old Testament* Vols. I & II (1961).

Evans, C. F., *Explorations in Theology 2* (1977).

Farmer, H. H., *The Servant of the Word* (1941).

Farrer, A., *Said or Sung* (1960).

—— *The End of Man* (1973).

—— *Interpretation and Belief* (1976).

—— *The Brink of Mystery* (1976).

Fendt, L., *Homiletik* (1948 Revised by B. Klaus 1970).

Fleming, J., *The Art of Reading and Speaking*.

Flemington, W. F., *The New Testament Doctrine of Baptism* (1948).

Flender, H., *Bibeltext und Gegenswartsbezug in der Predigt* (1971).

Forsyth, P. T., *Positive Preaching and the Modern Mind* (1907: 4th Impression 1953).

—— *The Cruciality of the Cross* (1909).

Fuller, R. H., *What is Liturgical Preaching?* (1957).

Garvie, A. E., *The Christian Preacher* (1920).

George, F. H., *Semantics* (1964).

Griffith, L., *The Need to Preach* (1971).

Heidland, H. W., *Das Verkündigungsgespräch* (1963).

Hick, J., *The Myth of God Incarnate* (1977).

—— *Evil and the God of Love* (1966).

Holland de Witte, *Preaching in American History* (1969).

Hopkins, H. E., *Charles Simeon of Cambridge* (1977).

Hordern, W., *New Directions in Theology Today*, Vol. I (1968).

Hunter, A. M., *Interpreting the Parables* (1960).

Ireson, G., *How Shall they Hear?* (1958).

Jeremias, J., *New Testament Theology* (1971).

Jones, G. V., *The Art and Truth of the Parables* (1964).

Keir, T. H., *The Word in Worship* (1962).

Ker, J., *Lectures on the History of Preaching* (1888).

King, Martin Luther, *Strength to Love* (1964).

Knox, J., *The Integrity of Preaching* (1957).

Küng, Hans, *On Being a Christian* (E.T. 1978).

Lampe, G. W., *God as Spirit* (1977).

Lejeune, L., *Christoph Blumhardt und seine Botschaft* (1963).

Lightfoot, J. B., *The Apostolic Fathers* (1869).

Lloyd-Jones, D. Martyn, *Preaching and Preachers* (1971).

Macgregor, G. H. C. & Purdy, A. C., *Jew and Greek: Tutors unto Christ* (1936).

Macquarrie, J., *Principles of Christian Theology* (1966).

Manson, T. W., *The Sayings of Jesus* (1949).

Marshall, H., *I Believe in the Historical Jesus* (1977).

Mascall, E. L., *Christian Theology and Natural Science* (1956).

Mezger, M., *Verkündigung heute* (1966).

Milner, P., *The Ministry of the Word* (1976).

Mitchell, H., *Black Preaching* (1974).

—— *The Recovery of Preaching* (1977).

Mitchell, W. F., *English Pulpit Oratory* (1932).

Moltmann, J., *The Theology of Hope* (1967).

—— *The Crucified God* (1974).

Montefiore, H., *Apocalypse. What Does God Say?* (1976).

Moule, C. F. D., *The Origin of Christianity* (1977).

Mueller, W. R., *John Donne, Preacher* (1962).

Neill, S., *Jesus Through Many Eyes* (1976).

Nicholson, E. W., *Preaching to the Exiles* (1970).

Nye, R., *The English Sermon* Vol. III (1976).

O'Connor, J. M., *Paul on Preaching* (1964).

Oesterley, W. O. E., *The Jews and Judaism During the Greek Period* (1941).

—— *Religion and Worship of the Synagogue* (1911).

Ong, W. J., *The Presence of the Word* (1967).

Pannenburg, W., *The Apostles' Creed* (1976).

Pears, D., *Wittgenstein* (1971).

Punt, N., *The Singer's and Actor's Throat* (1952 & 1967).

Quick, O., *The Christian Sacraments* (1944).

Rad, von, G., *Old Testament Theology*, Vols. I & II (1962).

Rahner, K., *Theological Investigations*, Vol. IV (1966).

Ramsey, I. T., *Religious Language* (1957).

Ramsey, M., *The Resurrection of Christ* (1945).

Read, D. H. C., *The Communicating of the Gospel* (1952).

—— *Sent From God* (1974).

Richardson, A., *A Theological Word Book of the Bible* (1950).

Robinson, I., *The Survival of English* (1973).

Robinson, J. M. & Cobb, J. B., *The New Hermeneutic* (1964).

Sangster, W. E., *The Craft of Sermon Illustration* (1946).

—— *The Craft of Sermon Construction* (1949).

Schaff, P., *History of the Christian Church* (1884).

Scherer, P., *The Word God Sent* (1966).

Schurer, E., *A History of the Jewish People in the age of Jesus Christ* (1910, Revised Edition 1973).

Seymour-Smith, M., *The English Sermon*, Vols. I & II.

Sharp, J. C., *Studies in Poetry and Philosophy* (1872).

Smart, N., *The Concept of Worship* (1972).

Smith, C. W. F., *Biblical Authority for Modern Preaching* (1959).

Smith, P., *Donne's Sermons. Selected Passages* (1919).

Smyth, G., *The Art of Preaching* (1953).

da Spinetoli, O., *Introduzione ai Vangeli dell' Infanzia* (1967).

Stanton, G. N., *Jesus of Nazareth in New Testament Preaching* (1974).

Stewart, James, *The Gates of the New Life* (1937).

—— *The Strong Name* (1940).

—— *Heralds of God* (1946).

—— *A Faith to proclaim* (1953).

—— *The Word of the Spirit* (1968).

—— *King for Ever* (1974).

Taylor, J., *The Go-Between God* (1972).

Thielicke, H., *The Waiting Father* (1960).

—— *The Prayer That Spans the World* (1960).

—— *Encounter with Spurgeon* (1964).

—— *The Trouble with the Church* (1965).

—— *Christ and the Meaning of Life* (1965).

—— *I Believe* (1968).

Tillich, P., *The Shaking of the Foundations* (1954).

—— *The New Being* (1956).

—— *Systematic Theology* (1968).

Underhill, E., *Worship* (1936).

Wand, J. W. C., *Letters on Preaching* (1974).

Ward, B., *The Home of Man* (1976).

Ware, T., *The Orthodox Church* (1963).

Welsh, C., *Preaching in a New Key* (1974).

Welsby, P., *Sermons and Society* (1970).

Whyte, A., *Bible Characters* (reprinted 1952).

Williams, C. S. C., *Acts of the Apostles* (1957).

Williams, R. R. (Editor), *Word and Sacrament* (S.P.C.K. Theological Collections No. 10, 1968).

Wingren, G., *The Living Word* (E.T. 1960).

For a Bibliography covering 446 books, 1,081 articles and 610 master's and doctoral dissertations during the years 1935–65 see *Recent Homiletical Thoughts* (Tooley & Thompson, New York, Abingdon Press, 1967).

Biblical References

Index of Proper Names

Index of Subjects

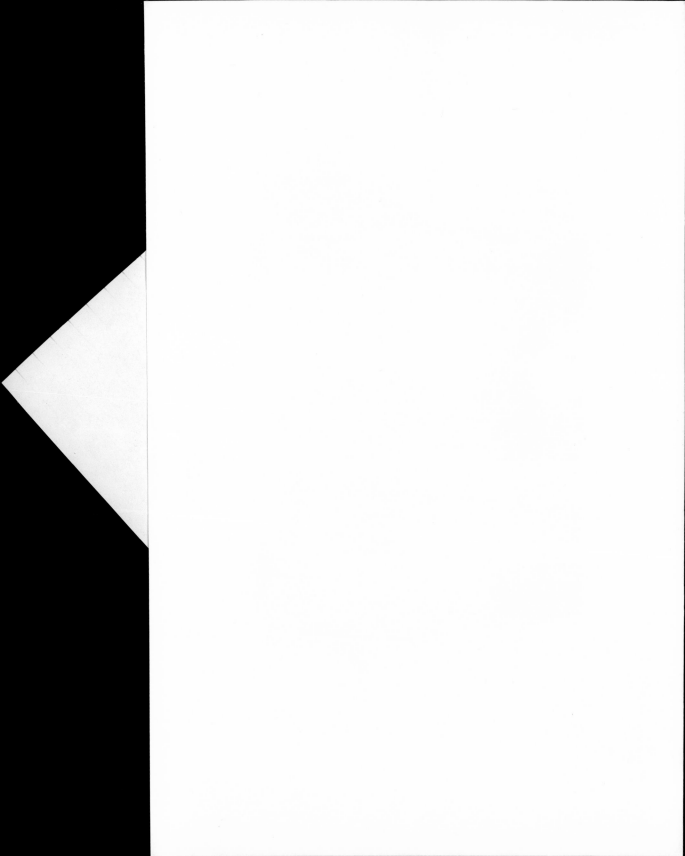

251
F69m

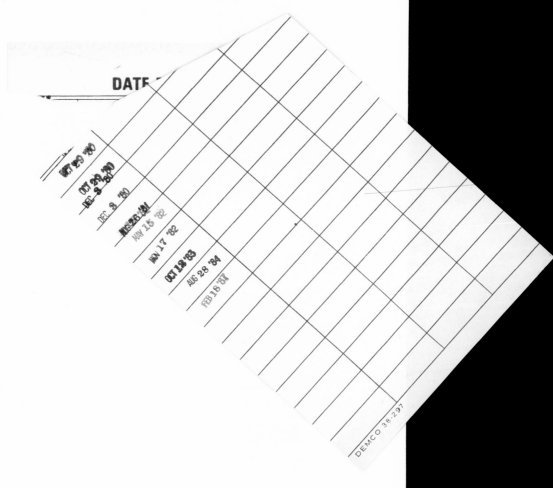